# Successful Investing *with* Fidelity Funds

Revised & Expanded
3rd Edition

## Jack Bowers
Editor, *Fidelity Monitor*

**PRIMA PUBLISHING**

*To my family, whose love and support*
*made this project possible.*

PRIMA PUBLISHING and colophon are registered trademarks of Prima Communications Inc.

FINANCIAL DISCLAIMER
Investment decisions have certain inherent risks. Prima therefore disclaims any warranties or representations, whether express or implied, concerning the accuracy or completeness of the information or advice contained in this book. Any investment a reader may make based on such information is at the reader's sole risk. You should carefully research or consult a qualified financial advisor before making any particular investment.

### Library of Congress Cataloging-in-Publication Data

Bowers, Jack.
   Successful Investing with Fidelity Funds / Jack Bowers.—Rev. & expanded, 3rd ed.
     p.  cm.
   Includes index.
   ISBN 0-7615-2100-3
  1. Mutual funds—United States.  2. Fidelity Funds (Firm)
   HG4930.B69   1999
   332.63'27—dc21                    99-27983
                                        CIP

99 00 01 02 HH 10 9 8 7 6 5 4 3 2 1
Printed in the United States of America

### How to Order
Single copies may be ordered from Prima Publishing, P.O. Box 1260BK, Rocklin, CA 95677; telephone (916) 632-4400. Quantity discounts are also available. On your letterhead, include information concerning the intended use of the books and the number of books you wish to purchase.

**Visit us online at www.primalifestyles.com**

# CONTENTS

# 8

# 9

# 10

# 11

# FOREWORD

Back in the late 1980s and early 1990s Jack Bowers was my competitor. As the writer and editor of *Weber's Fund Advisor*, I was working hard to build my own subscriber base, so I had little use for other newsletters. Yet I could not help but notice that this young fellow out in the suburbs of Sacramento had been quietly compiling a track record in his *Fidelity Monitor* that had begun to outshine my own fund choices, and those of almost everyone else.

When I decided to restructure the money management firm I was running, I invited Jack to become our Chief Investment Strategist. Happily for me—and my clients—he accepted, and so Jack became a partner in my business, and a good friend as well.

What Jack offers in the pages of this book is a large serving of useful information. Whether you are a novice or a seasoned veteran of fund investing, you can be absolutely certain of finding clear, unbiased counsel in these pages. Jack wrote the book, in part, to filter out the noise about fund investing. Starting with the basics about funds, Jack moves on to explain the many reasons why Fidelity has grown to become the world's favorite mutual fund complex. But rest assured—Jack Bowers is no shill for Fidelity. In his *Fidelity Monitor* newsletter and in this book, Jack considers himself beholden only to you, his reader. He has no connection to Fidelity. He vigilantly monitors the comings and goings within Fidelity, the changes in personnel running the various funds, and he especially focuses on the underlying holdings of the funds. And it's all done for one purpose—so that you can put together a portfolio of the right Fidelity funds at the right time.

Jack abhors "hype." Being a former electrical engineer, he focuses on real world results, not the feel-good promises so casually tossed about by so many in the financial advice industry. And I can tell you that Jack offers his advice as though he were talking to a dear friend or family member. He truly wants you to succeed.

If you've ever had the opportunity to talk to Jack personally you know that he is always patient. No question is too naïve—Jack understands that everyone comes to investing with a different level of experience and sophistication.

Mutual funds make sense for almost every investor, and Fidelity, the world's largest fund family, has by far the most choices. But too many choices can lead to confusion, and this book will help you clarify some key issues:

- How many funds should I own?
- Are bond funds appropriate for me?
- What do I need to know about international funds?
- What are the real differences in money market funds?
- Some people do well with sector funds. How do I participate?

And if you are already a Fidelity investor, you will particularly appreciate the section "How and When to Avoid Load Fees." This chapter alone could offset your investment in this book many, many times over!

Jack Bowers is a man of personal integrity who would rather do what's right for his money management clients and newsletter subscribers than turn a profit for himself. That, in the financial services business, is not a common trait.

Nothing any investment expert says should be counted on to be the gospel truth now and forever into the future. But Jack Bowers has established a long, publicly verified record of profitable fund choices, and I can tell you, if you were a cousin of his, he would give you the same advice he offers in his newsletter and here in *Successful Investing with Fidelity Funds*.

Follow his advice. In a few years, investment success will be yours.

*Ken Weber*
*president*
*Weber Asset Management*

# INTRODUCTION

This book summarizes my philosophy on mutual fund investing in general and on Fidelity funds specifically. It shows how a long-term approach with Fidelity funds can help you reach your financial goals.

What I hope to establish is a framework for investing with Fidelity, one that takes away some of the uncertainty and confusion that can accompany making investment decisions on your own.

The opinions presented here represent an independent viewpoint. I have no financial ties with Fidelity, nor do I have any friends or relatives who work at Fidelity (other than the helpful contacts who have provided me with information). Still, I do admit to being a longtime fan of Fidelity mutual funds, an affliction that developed in the mid-1980s when I was doing independent research on mutual fund performance.

In this updated version, I have made an effort to present a balanced view of Fidelity, one that keeps long-term performance in perspective. Too many financial journalists saw Fidelity through rose-colored glasses in 1993, and too many had an overly pessimistic view in 1996. The truth is somewhere between those extremes. One thing is certain: Fidelity didn't get where it is today without working hard and focusing on customers. In the long run, the company is likely to do what it takes to remain a leader in the industry.

*Note:* Jack Bowers is editor of *Fidelity Monitor,* an independent advisory service that makes Fidelity fund recommendations. For information, visit www.fidelitymonitor.com; call 800-397-3094; or write to *Fidelity Monitor,* P.O. Box 1270, Rocklin, CA 95677. Bowers is also chief investment strategist at Weber Asset Management, an independent money management firm that invests in Fidelity Funds for clients with large accounts. For information, call 800-438-3863.

# 1

# *About Mutual Funds*

The Investment Company Act of 1940 defined the structure of present-day mutual funds. This relatively strict act, designed to prevent abuses, requires mutual funds to maintain a separate custodian (usually a bank holding company) as the holder of a fund's assets. It also sets rules governing conflict of interest and requires funds to disclose many different aspects of their operation. It even requires shareholders to vote on any changes to a fund's strategy, a practice that doesn't even exist with regular corporations.

No doubt there was a bit of grumbling among mutual fund industry leaders at the time. Little did anyone know in 1940 that this legislation, which survives today with only minor modifications, would set the stage for the industry's financial dominance in the 1990s. After an era of insider trading, defaulted limited partnerships, corruption among savings and loan executives, overleveraged insurance companies, and a nearly insolvent FDIC, the public has readily embraced the relatively clean record that mutual funds have maintained.

In a country where almost every business leader shuns regulation of any kind, several key players in the mutual fund industry (including Fidelity's Ned Johnson III) met on Capitol Hill in 1993 to deliver a message to a congressional subcommittee. The message: "Please spend more money to regulate our industry!" Over the years the Securities and Exchange Commission (SEC) had assigned several thousand regulators to banks, brokerages, savings and loans (S&Ls), and other investment companies. Only a few hundred had been allocated to the mutual fund industry. The industry's leaders, who play by the rules, wanted to be sure that all mutual funds comply with SEC regulations. The industry's high level of public trust rests on such compliance.

Some benefits of mutual funds are almost taken for granted. Among the most important is how easy it is to follow a fund's performance. Imagine trying to obtain the average five-year return for a stockbroker's clients. Because mutual funds disclose their performance to the public, they have no choice but to act in the interest of their shareholders. Maximizing returns and keeping expenses reasonable is good for both the investor and the fund. In contrast, having a stockbroker make your investment decisions is like having a real estate salesperson decide where you should live and how often you should move! Brokerage companies make their living from commissions and stock underwriting. Other factors being equal, a brokerage portfolio will usually exhibit higher turnover, higher fees, and mediocre security selection. All of these factors reduce long-term returns. Granted, there are many brokers who ignore the inappropriate incentives and act in the interest of their clients, but in many cases these folks are constantly at odds with their employers.

Other benefits of mutual funds are more obvious. If you've ever tried to build a portfolio by picking your own securities, you know it can be a lot of work. Doing the proper research takes time—lots of it. Even if poring over quarterly reports doesn't keep you up late at night, you can still lose sleep worrying about whether or not you've bought the right stocks and bonds. Many investors tend to be either too conservative or too aggressive when picking their own securities. Some keep everything in certificates of deposit (CDs) or government bonds. Others, seeking aggressive growth, dive into the latest technology stock; sooner or later it becomes evident that the stock can go down as fast as it goes up. Eventually, most investors realize that mutual funds offer a well-balanced approach to building wealth without tying up all of their free time.

## ADVANTAGES OF MUTUAL FUNDS

The main advantages of mutual funds lie in diversification, professional management, liquidity and convenience, shareholder disclosure, economy of scale, easy access to foreign markets, protection from insolvency, and services.

### Diversification

Suppose you put $5,000 into a stock fund such as Magellan. You have automatically purchased a small position in several hundred different stocks. Let's say Magellan has 1 percent of its portfolio in Megachips, a semiconductor company with a promising future in computer memory chips. Suppose Megachips now announces that it has fallen behind on shipments because of a quality problem, and the stock price falls 50 percent. If you had put $5,000 into Megachips, it would now be worth $2,500. But in Magellan, where Megachips is only 1 percent of your $5,000 investment, the impact of this event is only $25. Additionally, it's possible that the decline would be offset by some upside surprises in Magellan's other stock holdings.

Although diversification protects against surprise events affecting a single security, it does not protect against events that affect the entire market. In a stock fund, diversification spreads equity risk but does not protect against a market sell-off. In a bond fund, diversification spreads credit risk but does not protect against the impact of an upturn in interest rates.

Diversification does not provide any significant benefit to investors buying government bonds or insured municipals, both of which have near-zero credit risk (although both can have substantial interest-rate risk). A mutual fund offers other advantages for those who wish to invest in these securities, but diversification isn't really an issue.

## Professional Management

When you buy a mutual fund, you are, in effect, hiring a full-time manager to look after your money. The objectives and limitations of the fund provide a framework, but within that framework your manager will try to maximize performance for you and thousands of others who own shares in the fund.

## Liquidity and Convenience

Mutual fund companies agree to buy back your shares if you decide to sell (the exception being closed-end funds that are traded on the exchanges like individual stocks); this agreement creates a liquid market by definition. Although the law allows funds to extend their settlement dates or even repay shareholders "in kind" with actual securities, these measures are rarely invoked unless liquidity dries up in the financial markets. (Fidelity and many other fund companies extended settlement dates by five days in the wake of the 1987 crash.)

Fund families like Fidelity offer many conveniences. If you open a money market fund and set up checkwriting, that fund can be used as the basic account from which other funds are bought and sold. Suppose you've got $40,000 in Equity-Income II and you need $5,000 for your daughter's tuition. Just call Fidelity's 24-hour 800 number and give instructions for moving $5,000 from Equity-Income II to Cash Reserves. Wait until the trade is executed at the close of the next trading day, then verify your account balance and write the check.

## Shareholder Disclosure

Making mutual fund performance a matter of public record creates healthy competition. Providing an attractive return for shareholders becomes a major priority for any fund that wants to survive and prosper. Because a mutual fund's track record includes the impact of expenses, fund companies know that if their expenditures are too high, their long-term performance will suffer. (Management, administrative, trading, and 12b-1 marketing costs are deducted before calculating performance.) Funds with high expense ratios also attract negative attention in the media.

## Economy of Scale

Because mutual funds serve thousands of shareholders, they trade securities in large blocks. Not only does this reduce transaction costs for their shareholders, but it can also reduce the price spread between buyers and sellers in the over-the-counter markets. Transaction costs are further reduced because, on a daily basis, mutual funds are able to match up investors wanting to buy fund shares with those wanting to redeem shares. Fund families such as Fidelity also realize some benefit when one fund sells or buys securities from another fund in the family.

## Easy Access to Foreign Markets

It used to be that investors faced insurmountable obstacles when trying to buy securities through a foreign exchange, but investing globally is now inexpensive and convenient—thanks to mutual funds. Fund companies, acting on the behalf of thousands of shareholders, can afford to deal with the complexities of international research, exchange rates, hedging, and administrative requirements imposed by foreign exchanges. Even as ADRs (American Depository Receipts—foreign stock equivalents) become more common in the United States, mutual funds still offer the best approach for international investing.

## Protection from Insolvency

Because a mutual fund is an independent financial entity owned by the shareholders, the collapse of a management company such as Fidelity would not wipe out any shareholders. Instead, each fund's assets would remain intact and safe from creditors in the hands of the fund's custodian (typically a bank holding company). The fund's board of directors would have to hire a new manager and probably deal with heavy redemptions, but the shareholders—unlike customers of a failed bank or insurance company—would not have to stand in line behind other creditors. In essence, a mutual fund is as sound as the assets in which it invests.

## Services

The law allows mutual funds to engage in a broad range of services. Checkwriting is commonly available on money market funds, and many investors use this feature to avoid the delay of redeeming shares by mail. Direct deposit of a paycheck, making wire transfers, and automatic savings plans are all commonly available features. Fund families like Fidelity provide direct exchanges between funds, and in most cases investors can call an 800 number to make trades.

## THE MECHANICS OF MUTUAL FUNDS

Simply put, a mutual fund is an investment pool. In an open-end fund, shareholders purchase shares from the fund company, and the purchase goes into the fund's asset base. The manager of the fund purchases securities that are consistent with the fund's objectives and limitations, and the fund company obligates itself to buy back (redeem) shares for shareholders who decide to sell.

Every mutual fund has a share price that is determined by dividing the fund's total assets by the number of shares held by shareholders. The share price is often referred to as the net asset value, or NAV. Most funds calculate their share price once a day after the markets close. The value of an individual's investment in a fund can be determined simply by multiplying the number of shares owned by the NAV. A mutual fund's share price does not imply anything about the securities in its portfolio, so it should not be a factor in selecting a fund. (A mutual fund with a low share price could own high-priced stocks, or vice versa.)

A fund's prospectus is a legal document that defines how the fund will be managed and operated. The prospectus spells out fees, investment objectives and limitations, account features, and historical performance. It is required reading, and a mutual fund company is not allowed to let you buy shares until you acknowledge that you have read the prospectus (this doesn't apply to brokerage accounts).

A fund's prospectus may seem overwhelming at first glance, but the important information covering the fund's objectives and limitations will usually be only a few pages long. (In the future the SEC may allow a profile prospectus that lists only key information.) Consider the prospectus for Fidelity Equity-Income II. It states that the fund's objective is to seek income by investing primarily in income-producing equity securities (dividend stocks), considering the potential for capital appreciation. It also notes that the fund seeks a yield exceeding the S&P 500, although it is not required to meet this goal.

Like other funds, Equity-Income II has a set of fundamental and nonfundamental restrictions. The fundamental limitations, which can be changed only by a vote of the shareholders, include restrictions on how much the fund can borrow or lend against its asset base (in Equity-Income II's case, 33.3 percent), along with more complex restrictions to prevent too much of the portfolio from being concentrated in any one company or industry group. There is also a fundamental limit for illiquid or restricted securities (10 percent for Equity-Income II). Nonfundamental fund restrictions are less formal and can be changed by the fund's board of directors. These can usually be found in the prospectus, but sometimes they are not included. One of Equity-Income II's nonfundamental policies is the requirement that the fund invest at least 65 percent of assets in income-producing securities.

Once you purchase shares in a fund, you are considered a shareholder of the fund as long as you own shares. Shareholders have certain rights, which include attending shareholder meetings, electing board members, and voting on changes to the fund's prospectus. Few shareholders ever travel to shareholder meetings, but it is a good idea to vote when you receive a proxy in the mail. Without enough votes, the fund might incur additional expenses in order to obtain the required number of votes. (Fidelity actually calls larger shareholders and reminds them to vote if it looks as if a fund will come up short on proxy votes.)

A mutual fund hires a management company (or advisor) to make the investment decisions for its pool of assets. For example, Fidelity funds hire and pay their management fees to Fidelity Management & Research Company, or FMR. FMR, in turn, is responsible for managing the portfolios for all of the Fidelity funds. In this book I am usually referring to FMR whenever I mention Fidelity.

A fund's custodian (a bank holding company in most instances) accounts for a fund's assets and shields them from creditors. In this regard, mutual funds offer better protection than other types of investments. At a bank or insurance company, your investment is exposed to the tiny but significant risk of being allocated to creditors if the firm becomes insolvent. In a mutual fund, the risk to principal is defined by the securities in the fund and not by the financial health of the management company.

A mutual fund is considered an investment company, and as such it is required by the IRS to distribute essentially all of its income and capital gains realized in the course of buying and selling securities. These payouts can take two basic forms: regular income and scheduled distributions.

### Regular Income

Money market funds and bond funds accumulate interest on their holdings, which is calculated daily and usually paid out monthly. (A fund's yield can give you an idea of the rate at which the monthly income will be paid out.) Unlike a CD, which has a "locked-in" rate, the income stream in a mutual fund fluctuates according to market conditions. A fund's payout of regular income can go toward purchasing additional shares (reinvested dividends) or can be returned to you through such options as getting a check in the mail or having the proceeds deposited to a money market account. In either case, taxes are due on these dividends, unless they come from a tax-free municipal fund or if the fund is held in a retirement account.

### Scheduled Distributions

Mutual funds are required to disburse accumulated dividends and capital gains. Stock funds usually make these payouts in December, but they can occur in other months as well, depending on how the fund is set up. Growth and income funds usually distribute capital gains in December, but most schedule dividend payouts on a quarterly basis. Unlike regular income, a scheduled distribution lowers the share price by an amount equal to the payout. For example, suppose Equity-Income II pays out a 10 cent dividend on its Ex-date (the date of record for distributing assets from the fund) and closes at $20. The share price is then 10 cents lower than it would have been without the payout. Distributions like this do not change the value of an investment, but they do lower the share price.

Many investors set up their accounts so that the distributions are automatically reinvested in additional shares. Suppose you own 500 shares of Equity-Income II in an account that is set up for automatic reinvestment. In the example just given, your total payout would be $50 ($0.10 per share times 500 shares), which would be reinvested at $20 per share. That means an additional 2.5 shares would be purchased, raising your position to 502.5 shares. In the end, the value of your Equity-Income II holdings is unchanged by a distribution. You simply own more shares at a lower share price.

Now the bad news. Unless your shares are in a retirement account such as an IRA, Keogh, 401(k), or 403(b), the IRS requires you to report and pay taxes on the distribution—regardless of how long you have owned the fund.

For that reason, it's usually a good idea to delay the purchase of a fund that is nearing its distribution date. Consider what happens if you invest $10,000 in a stock fund in early December, only to get a 5 percent distribution a few days later. You now have to pay taxes on $500 without any investment gains to show for it.

Scheduled distributions can have three components: dividends, short-term capital gains, and long-term capital gains. You are responsible for the taxes on each of these when filing your 1040, no matter how long you have owned the fund. Dividend payouts come from the fund's accumulated stock dividends, and they usually occur only on stock funds or on funds that mix stocks and bonds. Short-term capital gain payouts represent the fund's profits on securities sold less than a year after purchase, and the long-term capital gain component is from profits on securities sold after being held for more than a year. Capital gain payouts can occur on both stock funds and bond funds. Even municipal bond funds can generate small capital gain distributions (although their regular income is tax-free).

## MUTUAL FUND EXPENSES

Compared to other investment vehicles, the advantages of mutual fund investing come at relatively modest expense—particularly if you are dealing with a no-load or low-load fund (typical low-load funds charge a fee of 3 percent or less). Funds are very cost-efficient when compared with the alternative of building a diversified portfolio on your own. The cost of owning a fund breaks down into two basic components: internal expenses (which are already reflected in the NAV) and external costs (such as loads, transaction fees, and annual account fees). I'll start with the internal expenses because they are common to all funds (including no-load funds).

### Internal Expenses

A typical domestic stock fund will incur expenses and brokerage fees ranging between 0.5 and 1.5 percent. In other words, the fund's assets will be reduced by such a percentage each year. The costs that make up this figure occur continuously and are usually deducted before calculating the share price each day—resulting in performance that takes into account all internal expenses. A breakdown of a mutual fund's internal expenses follows.

*Management Fee*    Sometimes called the advisor fee, this fee is charged by the fund's management company for the job of security selection, and it is often the largest piece of the expense pie. The management fee is the primary source of profits for the management company. Among other things, it pays for the salaries of the fund managers and the analysts who support them. Large firms like Fidelity pool the advisor fees from many different funds and use the money to pay for an entire staff of managers and analysts. Management fees usually range from 0.3 to 1.0 percent for a stock fund (although foreign funds can be higher), from 0.3 to 0.8

percent for a bond fund, and from 0.3 to 0.6 percent for a money market fund.

*Administrative and Overhead Expenses*    The cost of 800 numbers, shareholder reports, statements, quote services, proxy mailings, legal filings, and even the daily cost of calculating a fund's share price fall under this category. Fund families will sometimes combine all of their administrative costs and then allocate them to each fund they serve, based on assets under management. Typically these costs run 0.1 to 0.3 percent of assets.

*12b-1 Fees*    The SEC allows funds to take a small percentage of fund assets each year to pay for advertising, marketing, or even commissions for brokers selling the fund. Often called the hidden load fee, the 12b-1 category is by far the most controversial because there is no direct benefit to existing shareholders. Fund companies that have 12b-1 fees claim they must expand their asset base to remain competitive, but this category is often used just to increase management company profits. Some fund companies avoid the stigma of a 12b-1 charge by inflating their management fee, but either approach has a negative impact on performance. If a fund company is taking too much for itself, the fund's long-term performance will be less competitive.

In Fidelity's case, retail funds have the option of charging a 12b-1 fee but are not currently doing so.

*Trading Costs*    Whenever a stock fund buys or sells assets, it must pay brokerage commissions. Funds that do a lot of trading (high turnover, as it is called) incur more brokerage expenses, whereas the more stable portfolios spend less. International funds come with a higher burden in this area because of the greater cost of carrying out foreign transactions. Most domestic funds have costs of 0.1 to 0.5 percent for trading expenses, whereas international funds typically range from 0.5 to 1.5 percent. A fund's brokerage expenses are relatively hidden because they are reported only in an obscure document called the statement of additional information. For many funds, trading expenses include more than just commissions on the purchase of securities. Through the use of "soft dollars," many fund companies have their brokerage companies provide computers and quote systems. The cost of the equipment is buried in the brokerage commissions. This is a sneaky but legal practice, and it is used widely in the industry.

*Determining Expense Burden*   In most cases, a fund's expense ratio is the best gauge for determining a fund's overall expense burden. If you want to be thorough, request a copy of the fund's statement of additional information and find the total cost of brokerage commissions. Then divide the figure by the fund's total assets to come up with an estimate for the annual brokerage cost percentage. Finally, take the expense ratio percentage and add the annual brokerage cost percentage to get overall expenses. (Trading costs are not included in the expense ratio.) Keep in mind that some fund companies don't accurately report commissions, in which case there's really no way to get a precise number. For example, the cost of brokerage commissions and soft-dollar purchases are sometimes buried in the security price spreads.

In any case, the total for internal expenses should provide a reasonably clear view of the fund's "internal drag." International stock funds' internal drag typically ranges from 1.5 to 2.5 percent. Domestic stock funds are usually between 0.6 and 2.0 percent, and bond funds (which do not break out brokerage expenses) run from 0.4 to 1.0 percent. Money market ratios are usually between 0.3 and 0.8 percent. Fund companies are particularly motivated to hold down internal expenses on bond funds and money markets because of the direct impact on a fund's yield. Consider a money market fund holding a portfolio of 4.5 percent notes. A 0.4 percent expense ratio will produce a yield of

4.1 percent for the fund, but if the expense ratio is 0.8 percent, the resulting yield will fall to 3.7 percent.

Sometimes a fund company will waive or cap fund expenses on a new fund to encourage new money to flow in. This practice is popular on bond funds and money markets because it allows the fund to state a higher yield as long as the waiver is in place. These funds often provide above-average returns, but the benefit can be short-lived. Once the waiver is removed (often without any formal notice), the fund's income stream will edge lower. Although the decline is usually not large, it can sometimes make the difference between an outperforming fund and one that's subpar.

## External Expenses

All expenses discussed so far are internal to the operation of the fund and are fully reflected in a fund's total return figures. External expenses are the fees you can incur when buying or selling a fund and include the front-end load (or sales charge), redemption fees, exchange fees, brokerage commissions, and account fees.

*Front-End Load (Sales Charge)*    This fee comes off the top of your investment before the money ever goes to work. For example, if you invest $10,000 in a fund with a 3 percent front-end load, $300 will go straight to the management company and $9,700 will be invested in the fund. Load funds collect this fee by charging a higher share price (usually called the offering price), which includes the sales charge. Front-end loads can be as high as 8.5 percent, but a broker is probably getting a commission on the sale at that rate. Some fund families (Fidelity included) do not charge a front-end load if you have previously paid a load. Suppose you buy into Contafund II and pay 3 percent on the purchase. As long as you keep that money in a Fidelity fund, you won't have to pay a second time around. This rule applies even if you move into a no-load fund and later move back to a 3 percent fund (see Chapter 12 for more information).

*Redemption Fees*   Also known as back-end loads, these fees are deducted from your balance when you sell shares. Some fund companies, including Fidelity, use a 0.5 to 3 percent charge to discourage investors from frequently switching in and out of a particular fund. Some broker-sold funds in the industry are now being structured with no front-end load but with a 4 to 5 percent load on the back side. Many of these redemption loads are dropped if you stay in the fund for a specified period of time, which can be as short as 30 days or as long as five years.

*Exchange Fees*   Most fund families allow you to switch between funds without cost, although limits are imposed to prevent abuse of the privilege. Other funds charge for redemptions or exchanges. In Fidelity's Select family, there is a $7.50 fee for exchanges (which is currently being waived for automated trades) and a redemption fee of $7.50 if you've been in the fund for at least 30 days (otherwise you pay 0.75 percent of assets).

*Brokerage Commissions*   If you buy a mutual fund through a brokerage account instead of purchasing it directly from the fund company, you'll pay a commission on the transaction unless you are part of a network program where transaction fees are waived on participating funds. (Schwab, Fidelity, and Jack White are the major players offering a wide selection of industry funds.)

*Account Fees*   Some accounts are charged a fixed annual fee. Fidelity, for example, charges $12 per year on balances of less than $2,500 (more on this in Chapter 12). It pays to be aware of these charges if you have a small account. A $800 balance in an IRA account that is charged $12 annually will forfeit 1.5 percentage points in performance on an annual basis.

Fund companies like Fidelity commonly waive external or internal expenses for competitive reasons or to encourage growth in a given fund. Temporary waivers are popular because they retain the flexibility to return the fund to load status when the fund company decides it's appropriate. (Fidelity has some "temporary waivers" that have been in place for years.) Exchange fees are sometimes waived on automated exchanges. Account fees are often waived if the balance in the fund (or the total of all accounts) is greater than a certain amount.

## MUTUAL FUND PERFORMANCE

The percentage that a fund gains or loses in value over time is called total return. In the industry, total return figures are computed with the following assumptions:

- All distributions and regular income payouts are reinvested in additional shares of the fund.
- The impact of income taxes is not included. (This would be difficult to determine because every investor's situation is unique.)
- The impact of front-end loads, redemption fees, exchange fees, and account charges is not included. (Because investors buy and sell at different times it would be hard to include the effect of external expenses.)

Total return figures are usually expressed as a cumulative percentage (total gain or loss) or in annualized form (average compound growth rate). Say that you invest your $10,000 IRA account in Fidelity's Blue Chip Growth fund and three years later your balance is $15,000 with reinvested distributions. In this example, Blue Chip Growth had a cumulative total return of 50 percent, or an annualized total return of 14.5 percent.

In this example, the effect of compounding explains why three years of 14.5 percent growth "adds up" to a 50 percent total return. As the investment grows over time, gains in later years are realized not only on the original investment but also on the gains achieved in earlier years. Over the long run, realizing gains on gains has a dramatic effect. Over 20 years, a 14.5 percent growth rate translates into a 1,400 percent cumulative total return. That original $10,000 IRA balance would grow to $150,000 under such a scenario.

The mathematically inclined can convert between annualized and cumulative total return with a calculator that can raise a number to a power. First, convert the percent-age increase (or decrease) to a *gain factor* by dividing it by 100 and adding 1. Taking the previous example, 14.5 percent becomes 1.145. Next, raise the gain factor to the number of years in the period (for 20 years, raise 1.145 to the 20 power), and you will get a cumulative gain factor (15.000638 for this example). Finally, convert back to a percentage by subtracting 1 and multiplying by 100. You should get 1,400 percent. (Normally it's not a round number.) You can also use this approach to convert from cumulative return to annual return; just follow the same steps but raise the gain factor to the power of 1 divided by the number of years (in this case, 1 divided by 20, or 0.05). If you do the steps correctly you should be able to convert a 1,400 percent cumulative return to a 20-year annualized rate of 14.5 percent.

Total return figures are usually available from the mutual fund companies themselves and are also tracked by industry service firms like Morningstar and Lipper. (Most newspaper and magazine reports on mutual funds will cite one of these two sources.)

When dealing with stock funds, you can calculate total return directly from the share price if the fund has not made any distributions over the period being measured.

(Just divide the current share price by the starting share price for a gain factor, then subtract 1 and multiply by 100 for a percentage figure.) Beware, however, that you could be fooling yourself. If a midyear distribution has occurred without your knowledge, your calculations will be meaningless. It's better to figure from the dollar value of your account—provided that your distributions are being reinvested and you haven't redeemed shares or added new money.

Distributions are sometimes omitted in charting services and in newspapers that report year-to-date gain/loss figures, although in recent years many publishers have started relying on firms like Lipper and Morningstar to supply total return figures. Here's how the tracking services correctly adjust for distributions and regular income:

- When a fund makes a distribution, all share prices prior to that date are divided by an adjustment factor to create what is called an adjusted share price (or adjusted NAV). The adjusted share prices are lower than the original prices, and any previously adjusted share prices are further reduced. The adjustment factor is computed by dividing the distribution amount by the reinvestment price and adding 1. As an alternative, it is possible to approximate the effect of the adjustment by subtracting the distribution from prior share prices, but this approach is highly inaccurate when used over longer time periods.

- For bond and money market funds, prior share prices are also divided by an adjustment factor that includes the regular income. This factor is computed by taking the fund's monthly mil rate figure (a figure that's available from the fund company), dividing by the Ex-price (the share price on the date the income payout is computed), and adding 1. The 30-day yield figure is not used because it does not represent a fund's actual monthly income; rather it is an approximation based on the SEC's yield-to-maturity guidelines.

- Once an up-to-date database of adjusted share prices is established, total return figures can be determined. This is done by taking the most recent monthly closing price and dividing by the adjusted share price at some point in the past. For example, if a fund's current price is $12 and its adjusted share price was $10 one year ago, the division will result in a factor of 1.2, which yields a one-year total return of 20 percent after you subtract 1 and multiply by 100.

## UNDERSTANDING YIELD

Investors who are new to mutual funds can be misled by the yield figures that are quoted for money market and bond funds. In the world of savings accounts and CDs, yield and total return are essentially the same thing. This is not the case for mutual funds.

For a money market fund, the yield that is quoted is based on annualizing the fund's last seven days of income. However, this figure changes with time and market forces. If interest rates were to stay frozen, the total return of a money market fund would be pretty close to its quoted yield at the time you bought in. In the real world, however, stable interest rates are the exception rather than the rule. Over a one-year period, the total return you obtain in a money market fund is likely to be different from the original quoted yield. It may end up a bit higher or lower (due to changing interest rates) than the yield at the time of purchase. In either case, however, the total return will be equal to the monthly income that is reinvested in the fund.

For a bond fund, the total return includes not only the regular income but also the fluctuation of principal that occurs as the fund's holdings rise and fall with the bond market. If rates were frozen and the market's perception of credit risk did not change, most bond funds would have a total return similar to their 30-day yield over a one-year period. However, if rates move up or if credit risk increases, the value of a bond fund will decline (although the income stream would probably go up). Fluctuations in principal usually dominate a bond fund's total return in the short run, because higher interest rates can reduce principal by an amount equal to many months of income. Of course, market forces can also work in the investor's favor if rates decline or if the perception of credit quality improves.

## EVALUATING FUND PERFORMANCE

When comparing performance figures between different funds, it's best to examine funds with similar objectives. Comparing one growth fund to another is a logical comparison, but judging a growth fund against a bond fund is not. (The two invest in completely different markets that have different characteristics.)

Most funds aim to outperform a specific index of securities. For example, many domestic stock funds try to exceed the Standard & Poor's Composite Index of Stocks (or S&P 500), a broad-based stock index made up from 500 of the largest public companies in the United States. When examining fund performance, it's a good idea to examine periods of at least a year. On a daily or monthly basis, the short-term "noise" of the market's random movements tends to mask the underlying trends. Consider a growth fund with an outstanding manager who is outperforming similar funds by ten percentage points per year. Day by day, this fund's advantage amounts to only about 1 cent per share. Over a week or even a month this manager's advantage is virtually invisible because it is buried in daily price fluctuations of 10 or 20 cents. If, however, you measure this fund over a year or more it will become more obvious that something good is going on.

In recent years many studies have focused on risk-adjusted performance. Most have found significant correlation between historical risk-adjusted performance and future performance.

In other words, a fund that performs well on a risk-adjusted basis has a good chance of outperforming its peers in the future. In contrast, the correlation between historical total return and future performance is relatively weak. A fund manager who has simply delivered high total returns is only slightly more likely than others to continue the good record.

Most techniques for determining risk-adjusted return are based on the Sharpe ratio or some variation of it. For a given measurement period with a specified number of data points, the Sharpe ratio defines risk-adjusted return as the difference between a particular investment's average gain and a riskless investment's average gain, with the result being divided by the standard deviation of the specified investment's gains and losses (standard deviation is a statistical calculation that describes how much variation exists in a set of data).

When applying the Sharpe ratio to mutual funds, the usual approach is to use a monthly interval and to pick a period of time that goes back somewhere between 24 and 60 months. Suppose a growth and income fund has an average monthly gain of 0.9 percent over 24 months, and during the same period 90-day T-bills average 0.4 percent per month (90-day T-bills are considered a riskless investment). If the standard deviation of the monthly gains and losses is 1.84 percent, the Sharpe ratio would compute a factor of 0.27 for risk-adjusted return. By itself this figure is not significant. However, once calculated the same way for other funds, it can be used to identify funds that have higher risk-adjusted returns.

Generally speaking, funds that seem to migrate to the top of a risk-adjusted scoring system tend to be "sure and steady" performers. Many funds ranking high only on a total return basis often drop down on a risk-adjusted list because they take on too much risk in obtaining their high returns.

## OTHER MEASUREMENT TERMS

Aside from those already discussed, there are a few other technical terms that are used to describe mutual fund characteristics.

### Relative Volatility

Relative volatility is a measure of risk that is usually computed from the standard deviation of a fund's gains and losses and normalized to an index such as the S&P 500. For example, if the S&P 500 is assigned a relative volatility of 1, a typical growth fund might carry a score of 1.2, a growth and income fund could be 0.7, and an average bond fund would probably be around 0.4. A fund's price fluctuations are usually a pretty good indicator of how risky its portfolio is; a higher volatility means the fund has a greater risk of loss. Still, a relative volatility figure shouldn't be used to predict how much a fund will fall in a bear market. Market declines affect stocks and bonds differently; a particular fund's response to them cannot be reliably computed from a relative volatility number. Instead, use beta (discussed later in this section) to help understand bear-market risk.

### Turnover

Turnover indicates how actively a manager buys and sells securities in a fund. It is usually computed by dividing the dollar amount of securities sold (over a one-year period) by the fund's asset base. The result is then expressed as a percentage. Funds with turnover above 200 percent can expose shareholders to higher trading expenses, an effect that is particularly significant for foreign funds. They can also trigger larger capital gain distributions at year-end if the increased trading activity results in capital gains. By itself, high turnover is not necessarily bad. If the manager is doing a good job of selling high and buying low, a high turnover fund can provide superior long-term results. On the other hand, a fund with high turnover that has lagged behind its respective index for more than a year or two can be a sign of poor judgment on the part of its manager.

## Beta

To the extent that a fund moves with an index, beta measures the degree of the movement. Typically the S&P 500 is used; it is defined as having a beta of 1. If, on average, a fund moves up 2 percent when the index moves up 1 percent, it will have a beta of 2. On the other hand, if it moves up just 0.5 percent, it will have a beta of 0.5. Beta is useful for assessing the impact of a market sell-off (or rally) on a fund, but many investors incorrectly treat it as if it were an indicator of risk. Beta works like relative volatility if a fund correlates well with the S&P 500, but it can be deceiving at other times. As an example, an aggressive foreign fund or a gold fund may carry a beta of only 0.3 or 0.4 while maintaining a risk level twice as high as that of the S&P 500.

## R-Squared

This figure measures correlation between a fund and an index, typically the S&P 500. (It can also be used to compare one fund to another.) If a fund always moves up or down in direct proportion to the S&P 500, it has an R-squared of 1. If a fund never moves with the index, it has an R-squared of 0. If a fund moves opposite to the index more often than not, it will have a negative R-squared figure. Most funds range between 0 and 1 for most situations. Some investors use R-squared to build a portfolio. By choosing several funds that correlate loosely to each other (usually indicated by an R-squared of less than 0.7), it is possible to create a portfolio that has less overall risk than the funds it includes.

## DERIVATIVES

Simply put, a derivative is a financial instrument with returns linked to, or derived from, an underlying asset such as a stock, bond, commodity, or index. Options and futures, which have been around for decades and trade on established exchanges, are derivatives in their simplest form.

Many of these exchange-listed derivatives are more popular and more liquid than the underlying asset they are pegged to. Consider S&P Stock Index futures, which are a convenient way to obtain a diversified equity position. The alternative is to buy all of the individual stock positions and pay a lot more in brokerage commissions. Another kind of derivative commonly used is the foreign currency contract. These securities enable a fund manager to reduce the currency risk that exists whenever a foreign stock is purchased. For example, if a fund manager has 10 percent of his portfolio in Japanese stocks, he can protect against a decline in the yen by purchasing a contract to sell yen at some future date. If the yen declines, the contract will increase in value to offset the currency-related loss on the Japanese stock holdings. Suppose a fund manager buys $1 million of Sony stock when the yen is trading at 100 to the dollar. Then the manager hedges against a decline in the yen by purchasing $1million in contracts to sell yen at 100 to the dollar. Suppose the yen declines to 105 to the dollar and Sony stock remains unchanged in Japan. In dollar terms the manager has seen about a 5 percent decline on the Sony position, but the $48,000 loss is offset by a similar gain on the currency contract. In effect, foreign currency contracts allow a manager to match the performance of a stock in its home country (minus the cost of the currency contract).

Indexed securities, another kind of derivative, can add unique risks to a portfolio. Sometimes referred to as structured notes, these derivatives fluctuate in a defined way against a specified index. They are often used to profit from a particular viewpoint. For example, suppose a fund manager expects interest rates to decline in Canada. He or she could purchase a structured note indexed to the value of two-year Canadian bonds, multiplied by 8.5. If the view is correct and Canadian interest rates fall by one percentage point, this structured note would gain 15 to 20 percent. On the other hand, if Canadian interest rates go up one percentage point, it could lose 15 to 20 percent. A fund manager cannot lose more than the original investment with an indexed security, but because of high volatility, this type of derivative can add risk to a portfolio. Many funds lost money on indexed securities in 1994 because their manager's viewpoint was incorrect.

It was mortgage-backed derivatives and inverse floaters that gave derivatives a bad name when interest rates went up in 1994. Many of these exotic securities were held in what were supposed to be conservative funds. A few well-publicized bond funds and money market funds paid the price for excessive positions in these securities because many inverse floaters and mortgage-backed derivatives failed to follow their computer pricing models when markets for these securities became illiquid.

Business page headlines in 1994 brought a lot of stress to some mutual fund investors. Many reacted with alarm upon discovering that a fund they trusted owned some derivatives in its portfolio, as if any and all derivatives were a ticket to future losses.

The fact is that lots of money managers were betting on declining interest rates, and derivatives just happened to be the most efficient vehicle for doing it. If derivatives had never existed, 1994's headlines would probably have told tales of massive losses on zero-coupon bonds and the overuse of margin in bond-oriented portfolios.

You don't need to be excessively concerned about derivative use in mutual funds. Fund managers are now exercising more caution in their use of structured notes, mortgage derivatives, and inverse floaters after 1994's lesson. Public pressure has also forced mutual fund companies to be more forthcoming about their use of derivatives. In Fidelity's case, you can call and find out the current derivative exposure on any of its funds.

# **2**

# *Fidelity's Strengths and Weaknesses*

When you evaluate a mutual fund company, there are three basic factors to consider. In order of importance, these factors are performance, available choices, and service.

Most mutual fund companies do well in at least two of the three, or they don't stay in business very long. Fidelity and other successful firms in the industry have strengths in all three.

Fidelity's attractiveness has not gone unnoticed by the investing public. About one of every ten dollars in the mutual fund industry resides in a Fidelity fund—the largest market share in the industry. The company has a similar lead among 401(k) providers as well as in the variable annuity business.

Many companies tend to become less competitive as they get big, but Fidelity continues to search aggressively for new opportunities. The firm seems determined to be a key player in the brokerage business and is always trying to lure customers from key rivals such as Schwab. Becoming a leading financial services firm in overseas markets is also one of Fidelity's key goals, although trade barriers and cultural differences have kept the firm from growing very fast in foreign markets. The company is even testing its customer service advantage in some different domestic industries that complement its role in financial services. Two examples include corporate benefits administration and institutional software products.

But Fidelity's retail fund business remains its bread and butter, and the company hasn't stopped trying to improve. Current areas of internal focus include the use of company-specific financial models to improve earnings forecasting, increased investment in foreign research to boost performance in overseas markets, developing an advantage through quantitative techniques, and developing easy-to-use automated services for customers.

This chapter focuses on Fidelity's retail fund business and how it stacks up against the competition.

## FIDELITY PERFORMANCE

If you've had a chance to flip through *Morningstar Mutual Funds,* you may have noticed the higher concentration of five-star ratings that show up about five pages into the alphabetical listings. In the issue of February 6, 1999 (which lists data through December 31, 1998), a total of 232 out of 1,536 industry funds had earned the top badge for risk-adjusted performance. (Morningstar uses a bell curve to establish where each fund ranks relative to others in its class; only 15 percent of the funds listed in this issue were awarded five stars.) Skip to the Fidelity section, and you'll find that 26 percent (25 out of 98 Fidelity funds) receive the high honor. Clearly, Fidelity's emphasis on research produces statistically significant results in the real world.

There's nothing special about that particular issue of *Morningstar Mutual Funds;* it just happens to be the latest one available as of early 1999. You can probably find a similar ratio in Morningstar's latest issue, even several years after the fact.

## Comparison with the Industry Average

Fidelity's performance lead over the industry is not limited just to five-star ratings. It also shows up when you compare total return averages. Using the Morningstar database, I grouped Fidelity's funds into eight categories to compare performance against the industry-wide benchmarks that are published in each issue of *Morningstar Mutual Funds*. I used a trailing period of ten years, ending December 31, 1998 (funds without a ten-year history were excluded). Keep in mind that this period was bullish for stocks. In the future, rates of return are likely to be lower for the domestic stock, specialty stock, and hybrid categories.

*Domestic Stock*　This category, which includes domestic stock funds and stock-oriented growth and income funds, is one where Fidelity shows a strong advantage. The Fidelity funds in this group had an annualized return of 18.9 percent, versus 15.6 percent for the average industry fund with a ten-year return. A lead of just over 3 percentage points may not seem huge, but it is very significant when you consider that it was logged for an average of 15 funds over a ten-year period.

*International Stock*　The four Fidelity funds in this category returned 7.8 percent per year, trailing the industry average of 8.3 percent for funds with a ten-year history. Fidelity is investing heavily in international research, and the results in this category could improve with time.

*Specialty Stock*　Reserved mainly for sector funds, this category includes Fidelity's Select funds, a real estate fund, and a utilities fund. Most of these funds are domestic and many of them have a focus on smaller stocks, an area where Fidelity's research capability makes a bigger difference. The average of 33 Fidelity funds came out at a strong 17.3 percent per year, versus 11.9 percent for the industry funds in the category. Many of the first-time managers heading up the Selects started out as analysts, so these numbers are a testimonial to Fidelity's effective recruitment and promotion process.

*Hybrid*    This is the category Morningstar assigns to funds that blend stocks and bonds. The three Fidelity funds in this category averaged 14 percent annually, compared to 12.1 percent for industry funds that had a ten-year record. Generally speaking, it appears that Fidelity's advantage in this category comes mainly from stockpicking, whereas bond holdings appear to have played a less significant role.

*Specialty Bond*    For this category Morningstar tracks funds that mainly invest in junk bonds, convertibles, and foreign debt. Fidelity has a lead in this category owing to its research strength in junk bonds and convertibles. The average of three Fidelity funds came out at 10.8 percent per year, versus 8.7 percent for the industry average.

*Corporate Bond*    Fidelity could have done better here, but a tough 1994 took a heavy toll on funds that held foreign debt. As a result, the three Fidelity funds with a ten-year record had an average return of 8 percent annually, trailing the 8.3 percent return registered for the industry funds that Morningstar tracks.

*Government Bond*    The average of five Fidelity funds in this category was 8.5 percent per year, versus 8 percent for the industry funds. Fidelity's advantage seems to come from trading on short-term pricing inefficiencies in the government bond market, a practice that the company has refined over the years.

*Municipal Bond*    The 11 Fidelity funds with a ten-year history averaged 7.6 percent annually, compared to 7.4 percent for the industry funds. Four-star and five-star funds are common in this group, suggesting that Fidelity adds value in the form of risk reduction as well.

## How Fidelity Outperforms the Competition

Beating the industry performance averages in six of the eight major fund categories is no small feat, but for Fidelity it is business as usual. That's because performance is part of the Fidelity corporate culture, and the company's organization is set up to foster it. The way funds are managed and the way fund managers are supported is clearly results-oriented.

*Commitment to Research* Fidelity's hundreds of in-house analysts and the variety of markets that it covers are simply unmatched by any other mutual fund company. Many investors think the fund manager is the main factor that determines performance, but in Fidelity's case all fund managers are backed up by teams of analysts who have a vested interest in the quality and accuracy of their recommendations. In other words, Fidelity managers are set up for success because they pick and choose from a pool of securities that have been extensively researched.

*Knowing the Real Story* Fidelity analysts and managers meet with thousands of company executives every year to ask questions about sales, margins, competition, cost cutting, and industry trends. Some of the meetings occur when the fund managers or analysts go on the road; some occur on the phone (fund managers often call and chat with several company heads every day). Many company executives travel to Boston to tell their stories directly to Fidelity managers and analysts. On a typical day Fidelity managers and analysts can pick from an agenda of several different meetings without ever leaving their offices. All this communication is significant because it allows Fidelity managers to base investment decisions on information that is more up-to-date than the latest quarterly report. Company executives are surprisingly honest when discussing their situations. If they paint an overly rosy picture, they risk losing credibility with Fidelity down the road. If they downplay their situation, their stock price may not reach its full potential. As such, most give an accurate account of business just as they would to any major shareholder. Of course, there are a few companies that won't talk to Fidelity. But most public companies will not ignore a major (or potentially major) shareholder.

*Hard Work*   Fidelity managers, many of whom are young workaholics, put in the extra hours that make a difference. The more you know, the better your decisions are. Fidelity managers spend a lot of time trying to know as much as possible. In reference to working Saturdays at Fidelity, Peter Lynch (the former Magellan manager) often mentioned that there were usually enough fund managers for a game of basketball. Morningstar said in the March 1993 issue of *5-Star Investor* (now *Morningstar Investor*) that Fidelity managers are far more likely to be at the office during off-hours than their competitors are. This comment was based on Morningstar's firsthand experience trying to reach managers for telephone interviews.

*Hands-off Management*   Despite some new controls, Fidelity fund managers still have plenty of freedom to execute their strategies without facing management scrutiny every time they make a move. It makes a big difference when your bosses let you live with your own mistakes instead of second-guessing your decisions all the time. As a result, most Fidelity managers are highly motivated, independent thinkers.

*Performance-Based Hiring and Promotion*   Fidelity understands well that some people are naturally talented when it comes to picking securities. The ability to accurately assess opportunity and risk seems to be a personality trait, and regardless of education or background some are better at it than others. Accordingly, new hires usually start out as analysts. Once they prove their worth, they get a chance to run a Select portfolio or become an assistant at a larger fund. If they excel in that role, they may eventually run a mainstream fund. This system of promotion tends to weed out the candidates who are well-educated but would otherwise be less than successful at running a fund. It works particularly well at Fidelity because the managers of large, important funds are selected from a large base of analysts and smaller funds.

## Is Fidelity Getting Too Big?

The negative side of being big and successful is that at some point you become too big a fish for the pond. Fidelity is clearly a big fish. The company's stock fund assets are equivalent to about 3 percent of the U.S. market capitalization (as of late 1998). If the company's managed assets were 30 times greater, Fidelity funds could not outperform the market because they would *be* the market.

Here's how size can hinder Fidelity's fund managers:

- Large funds, such as Magellan and Contrafund, can't move too quickly when accumulating or liquidating a large position in a particular stock. If they do, they risk moving the stock's price in a way that works against the fund over the long run.
- Large Fidelity funds can't benefit when they find attractive small-cap stocks. Suppose Magellan buys $30 million of a small company stock that has a market capitalization of $300 million. Let's say this stock doubles over a one-year period. In a small fund a move like that would make for a good year. But in Magellan's $50 billion portfolio the total return for the period would increase by less than one-tenth of one percentage point.

The fund would have to find 100 such stocks just to boost its return by about six percentage points—and that's not a realistic scenario. In effect, larger funds are unable to realize gains from the small-cap arena. Instead, they must focus on finding the best large-cap and mid-cap investment opportunities.

- Fidelity funds that focus on small-caps are sometimes "shut out" of a stock by Fidelity's internal limits on ownership (these limits exist for liquidity reasons). The limits, which are usually set at 10 percent for smaller companies, stipulate the maximum percentage of a stock that all Fidelity funds can own. So if a given fund manager wants to buy a particular stock, but other Fidelity funds already own 10 percent of the company, the manager is forced to look for some other opportunity. In practice, Fidelity managers are usually not limited much on large-cap and mid-cap stocks, but in the small-cap universe there can be "lock-outs" on hundreds of stocks.

Together these constraints may seem somewhat alarming, but you have to realize that most Fidelity managers have been dealing with them for years. While there is clear evidence that size tends to hamper performance to some degree, there is no evidence to suggest that size *prevents* Fidelity funds from outperforming.

Consider Magellan, the fund of choice for the media to pick on. For ten years, article after article has criticized the fund's huge size, yet Magellan still outperformed the S&P 500 and beat more than 90 percent of industry growth funds as of December 31, 1998. Magellan is big, but Fidelity has always put strong managers in charge, and these leaders have done quite well focusing on mid-cap and large-cap stocks. Even as of late 1998, with the fund at about $80 billion, Magellan is less than 1 percent of the U.S. stock market capitalization. While Magellan may be too big for the kind of rapid industry moves that Jeff Vinik was making, there's no reason it can't beat the S&P 500 with Bob Stansky's sure and steady approach to picking large-cap stocks. (See Chapter 4 for more on Magellan.)

## AVAILABLE CHOICES

With about 160 retail funds directly available to the public, Fidelity quite clearly provides the largest selection of any mutual fund company. As of this writing, you can invest directly in any of 23 domestic growth funds, 18 growth and income and asset allocation funds, 39 sector funds (Select portfolios), 20 international and foreign funds, 20 taxable bond funds, 15 municipal bond funds, and 24 taxable and municipal money market funds. More than 50 funds are available with no front-end or back-end load, so no-load enthusiasts can find plenty of diversified funds to choose from.

If you decide to invest in a load fund, the most you will pay at the time of purchase is 3 percent, and your mutual fund shares will be tagged by Fidelity's computers so that you don't pay the 3 percent again on a future exchange involving those shares. All you have to do to retain the load credit is keep the investment in a Fidelity fund. (The details of Fidelity's load credit system are discussed in more detail in Chapter 12.)

Some investors would argue that you don't need a broad-based lineup from any one fund company now that mutual fund networks are available through Fidelity, Schwab, Jack White, and others. After all, if you can access hundreds of funds from your brokerage account, what does it matter?

It may not matter, but the mutual fund networks come with some drawbacks that can make them less attractive than staying with a single fund family. For one, the networks usually come with greater restrictions on trading if you plan to stay with no-load, no-transaction-fee funds. If you play the full field, you can pay multiple transaction fees and loads—something that doesn't usually happen in a single fund family. Finally, you may not help your performance.

Conventional wisdom says the more choices, the better. However, from the standpoint of probabilities you may be worse off in a network as opposed to confining your money to a research-advantaged group like Fidelity or a cost-advantaged group like Vanguard.

## FIDELITY SERVICE

Many American companies could learn a few lessons about customer service by observing Fidelity's practices. Many of Fidelity's competitors had to, whether they wanted to or not.

In the mid-1970s, Fidelity was the first fund company to make checkwriting available on money market funds, and by the end of the decade it was selling no-load funds directly to the public via newspaper and magazine ads. (Before then Fidelity funds were sold through brokers with a hefty 8.5 percent load to cover the commission.) By the mid-1980s Fidelity had expanded the staffing of its 800-number phone lines to provide around-the-clock coverage for exchange orders, quotes, fund information, and general questions. Fidelity also began a major initiative to establish investor centers in all major cities around the nation. By 1992 this network of investor centers had been expanded to most large cities, and automated phone systems were in place, allowing investors a faster way to get fund pricing and account balances and make exchange orders. More recently, Fidelity has introduced a web site (www.fidelity.com) and is courting on-line investors with a variety of conveniences and special electronic services.

Over the years Fidelity's competitors have matched many aspects of Fidelity's high level of customer service, but the large number of investor centers serve as a reminder that Fidelity is still ahead in the game. Walk into any of the 80 or so centers around the country, and you can talk with knowledgeable professionals who are willing to help—without the typical sales pressure. You can pick up a prospectus or attend an educational seminar. You can even get help with an application form or work directly with a representative to resolve a problem with your account, all without any extra charges.

The investor centers are particularly reassuring for first-time Fidelity investors who are a little nervous mailing off a check to a company they have never dealt with. For these investors, it's more comfortable to deal directly with Fidelity employees who live and work closer to home.

## One-Stop Shopping

One of the benefits of dealing with just one mutual fund company is that it can simplify your paperwork. One set of statements. One set of phone numbers. One set of money market checks. One set of year-end tax forms.

When you choose a mutual fund company with a wide array of financial services and products, you have the added advantage of going with one company for all of your financial needs. For example, with a Fidelity Brokerage Ultra Service Account (USA) you can consolidate your investments and perhaps even eliminate the need for a bank account. Following is a rundown on the many services available from Fidelity.

*Checkwriting on a Money Market Fund*   Writing a check on a money market fund is an easy and convenient way to redeem mutual fund shares, because it saves the time of waiting for Fidelity to send a check through the mail. A simple phone call can move money out of a stock fund and into your money market fund. At that point, all you have to do is wait a day, verify the trade was executed properly, then write the check. Most Fidelity money market funds have a checkwriting minimum of $500 and do not charge for the service, except for the Spartan funds—which stipulate a $1,000 minimum amount and a cost of $2 per check unless you maintain a high balance. Checkwriting is also available on bond funds, but I don't recommend it. Unlike a money market fund, each check written against a bond fund is a taxable transaction.

*The Bank Alternative* If you're out to replace your bank checking account, Fidelity Brokerage's cash management USA plan is the best bet. You get a variety of features for free—services that would probably cost a pretty penny at a bank. You need $30,000 in investments to establish a full-featured account, but you can satisfy the requirement if you have that much in nonretirement Fidelity fund accounts. It takes some time and paperwork to move these holdings into a USA brokerage account, but the fee structure and exchange privileges on Fidelity's brokerage side are virtually identical to its mutual fund group.

The core account in the USA plan is the one that works similar to an interest-bearing checking account. You get unlimited checkwriting at no cost. Bill payment, returned check images, stop payment, and wiring services are available for an added fee. The regular core account pays just slightly less than a money market fund. You can also get a Visa debit card, which allows you to get cash from an ATM or make purchases wherever Visa is accepted.

Of course, there are some drawbacks to substituting a Fidelity USA for a checking account. The main issues are ATM fees and the seven- to ten-day mailing and clearing time on deposited checks. In the latter case you can avoid the delay on paychecks by setting up direct deposit.

*Charge Cards and Credit Cards* If you have the USA plan, you can link a charge card (Visa or MasterCard) to your account. You can also use the charge card for getting cash at an ATM.

If you want a regular credit card for carrying a running balance, Fidelity offers these too (Visa and MasterCard). You don't even need a USA or other brokerage account to apply. Once established, you just mail in your payment each month as you would for any other credit card.

*IRA, Rollover IRA, Keogh, and SEP-IRA Accounts* Retirement accounts allow you to invest in the full range of Fidelity mutual funds (except municipals) while deferring any taxes until you start taking withdrawals (usually after age 59½). In these retirement accounts the front-end load is waived on all funds except Magellan, New Millennium, and the Selects. Also, the minimum initial investment on non-Spartan funds is reduced to $500 (as opposed to $2,500 for most funds in a taxable account). Retirement accounts are discussed in more detail in Chapter 11.

*Moneyline Transfers* The Moneyline service allows transfers between a given fund and a bank account, and these transactions usually take two to three business days to occur. For additional purchases of an existing fund, the minimum is typically $250 (except for Spartan funds, which have a $1,000 minimum). The Moneyline feature must be set up before you need it, because it can take about ten business days to be established.

*Automatic Purchases or Withdrawals* Automatic Account Builder piggybacks onto Moneyline and will transfer money from your bank account into a fund on a monthly or quarterly basis. (The minimum additional fund purchase drops to $100 with this program.) Automatic redemptions are also possible. The proceeds can be placed in another fund (such as a money market) or into your bank account via Moneyline, or they can simply be mailed to you in the form of a check.

*College Savings Plans* Fidelity recently started offering a tax-advantaged college savings plan called UNIQUE, which places your money in a pool that is managed by Fidelity professionals. The tax benefits are not yet recognized at the state level in most cases, but this will probably change if this type of investment vehicle becomes more popular over time.

Fidelity's traditional College Savings Plan, on the other hand, lets you and your child pick your own funds. Money is transferred to your child's own account under rules specific to the state in which you reside. Unfortunately, Fidelity no longer offers reduced minimums with this program.

*FundsNetwork*    Available with any Fidelity brokerage account, FundsNetwork allows you to purchase any of more than 3,000 industry mutual funds. There are three classes of funds: those with loads, those with a fixed transaction fee, and those with no load or transaction fee. FundsNetwork has been one of Fidelity's faster-growing programs, but as I have mentioned before, more choices does not necessarily mean better performance.

*Bill-Paying Service*    Available with a USA account, bill payments can be scheduled 24 hours a day and can be made to almost any party through a secure system using Fidelity's web site or a touch-tone telephone. Fixed payments, such as a mortgage, can be set up to occur at a specific time each month. One-time bill paying can be scheduled for a specific time in the future.

*Portfolio Advisory Service*    Fidelity's money management program, Portfolio Advisory Service (PAS), allows an investment team to choose your funds and make your trades for you. The cost can be up to 1 percent of assets per year, and the minimum account size is $200,000 for regular accounts and $100,000 for retirement accounts. A new tax-managed approach is available for larger accounts. The fee for PAS is probably less than you would typically pay for an independent money manager to manage your account, but the strategies are generally more diversified and may not offer as much growth for aggressive investors.

*Variable Annuities*    Discussed more in Chapter 14, variable annuities resemble mutual funds but are sold as life insurance in order to qualify for special tax treatment. They function somewhat like a nondeductible IRA account because investment gains are tax-deferred, but the options are limited and the fees are a bit higher than those of regular mutual funds. Nevertheless, Fidelity's lineup of variable annuities is more competitive than what most other insurance companies offer.

*Charitable Gift Fund*   Created by Fidelity, organization is recognized by the IRS as a public charity. As with a private foundation, your contributions are tax-deductible at the time you put money into an account. Once inside the Charitable Gift Fund, what happens to the money you donate is still your decision. You arrange how it is invested by allocating between four Fidelity mutual fund pools, and you (or a beneficiary) recommend grants to the charities themselves. The Gift Fund requires a minimum grant of $250 and will make payouts only to domestic IRS-recognized charities (this includes many educational institutions and other nonprofit organizations). Donations to the Gift Fund are irrevocable, and once in your Gift Fund account there is no tax liability on investment gains because the account is not considered part of your estate.

Some families may find the Charitable Gift Fund a simpler alternative to creating a private foundation because it eliminates the need for tax and legal filings. For others, it is a way to take a deduction on contributions now and pass on a legacy of charitable giving to heirs. The minimum to get started is $10,000, and additional contributions must be at least $2,500. The Gift Fund takes 1 percent of assets per year for services.

*Trust Services*   Available for large accounts in most states through the investor centers, Fidelity Personal Trust Services covers the full range of trusts, including living, revocable, irrevocable, and charitable trusts. The program provides fully tax-sensitive portfolio management for each individual account. In addition to mutual funds, Fidelity incorporates and manages the individual securities clients already own. Fidelity Personal Trust Services also manages general investment and rollover IRA portfolios.

*On-line Services* Fidelity's web site (www.fidelity.com) is state of the art, and the company continues to strive to make on-line investing friendly and easy to use for everyone. The web is likely to become the medium of choice in the future, and Fidelity actively encourages its customers to go on-line today. For Fidelity, the major benefits of conducting business on-line include a reduction in administrative costs (which may have a favorable impact on expense ratios), time savings, and fewer mistakes in providing information and executing transactions.

Like other on-line services, Fidelity's web site is rapidly changing as new services are added and the organization of existing features evolves. The following describes the services that are available as of early 1999.

- *Accounts and trading:* Shortly after you establish your on-line access PIN (which can also be done on-line), you can call up your account and view the total balance and the value of each position (based on the previous day's closing prices). If you wish to place a trade for $100,000 or less, it can done much faster than with a live phone rep (you'll need to know the ticker symbols of the funds involved, but you can find them on-line before you place the trade). You can even download a prospectus in PDF format, viewing or printing it with Adobe's Acrobat Reader. As with a telephone exchange, you are given a confirmation number for each trade order.

  If you set up a brokerage account for on-line access, you can pay your bills out of your core account (additional charges may apply). And a new host of notification and trading features allow you to monitor key events and place trades from a two-way pager and certain other portable electronic devices. When tax time comes, you can even access your tax forms on-line. If you want to set up a new account, you can get things started on-line.

- *News and quotes:* Obtaining daily fund prices on-line is easy, and Fidelity makes them available roughly two hours after the market closes. Monthly performance information can also be accessed, along with portfolio allocation, industry weightings, and the most recently disclosed top ten stock holdings. If you wish to look at a fund's complete list of holdings in its recent annual report, it can be downloaded in PDF format.

  If you invest in Fidelity's Variable Annuities, you can obtain quotes on-line. If your 401(k) or 403(b) account is part of Fidelity's Workplace Savings program, you can review your account on-line.

  Price charting, recent distributions, market news, and a calendar of events can also be accessed. Fidelity maintains an extensive list of domestic and foreign indexes for comparison. And if you like to track your investments during market hours, you can obtain real-time quotes on stocks or hourly pricing on the Select portfolios.

- *Research:* Fidelity provides a number of options for researching stocks as well as funds offered through Fidelity's FundsNetwork. Much of the information is free, but the most detailed reports require a fee. If you like to screen for specific stock fundamentals, Fidelity's Stock Evaluator allows you to narrow your stock search based on the parameters you set.

- *Planning and retirement:* An information center allows you to calculate how much money you'll need for retirement. You can pick a strategy and select a plan to help meet your goals (Fidelity provides extensive information on all of its retirement products). Information on tax planning is also available, and you can calculate how much money you'll need for a child's college tuition. There's also a life insurance calculator and information on estate planning.

Fidelity is constantly adding new features to its web site. The best way to find out what's available is to visit www.fidelity.com and take a look for yourself.

## Service Problems

Mistakes are rare when dealing with Fidelity, but they can be frustrating when they occur. It's easy to get edgy when significant amounts of money are involved, and Fidelity's phone system doesn't make it very easy to deal with a single person in resolving the problem. Often you end up waiting for someone at Fidelity to get back to you, and it can sometimes take longer than you would like. If things aren't going well, one option is to enlist the help of a Fidelity contact at your nearest investor center. This usually doesn't speed up the resolution of the problem, but it can relieve the stress because you have a key person who "owns" your problem.

The other service issue with Fidelity is mail volume. Even though the company has sharply reduced promotional mailings, a lot of material still arrives in your mailbox: annual reports, proxies, prospectuses, transaction statements, quarterly statements, tax statements, manager changes, Fidelity magazines, and more. Having a brokerage account or an annuity account can further increase the volume. Much of what is sent is legally required, meaning that Fidelity can't stop sending it even if it wanted to. In this respect, the volume of mail you get from Fidelity is no worse than what you would receive from any other fund company. I suspect that in future years fund companies will be allowed to post legal information on-line and avoid the costs of printing and mailing documents.

# 3

# Benefits and Risks of Long-Term Investing

The long-term return of the S&P 500 is shown along with other asset classes in Figure 1. This chart shows a period of 73 years, over which the S&P 500 returned 11.2 percent annually. During the same period, small stocks returned 12.4 percent per year. Clearly stocks have been one of the best long-term investments available, having outperformed inflation by more than 7 percent per year.

The total return from stocks exceeds inflation in a stable economy because corporations earn profits by providing goods and services. On average, those profits are used either for increasing revenue at a rate faster than inflation, increasing the value of company assets at a rate faster than inflation, or for paying dividends and buying back stock. In the latter case, shareholder return will usually exceed inflation if the company's revenue and profits grow with inflation. What all this means is that a diversified portfolio of stocks held for the long run will typically provide a total return that exceeds inflation.

The power of compounding at a rate faster than inflation is clearly illustrated by the results achieved by some of Fidelity's longer-running funds. The original Fidelity Fund,

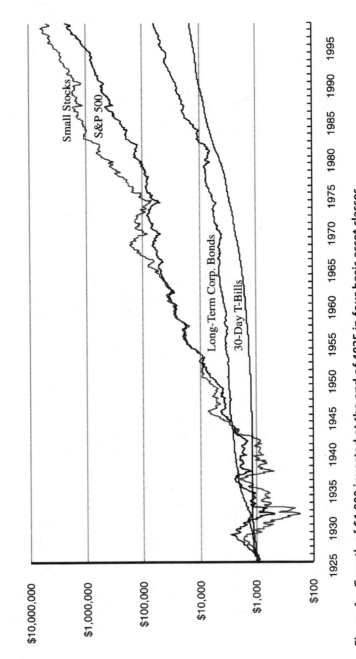

**Figure 1 Growth of $1,000 invested at the end of 1925 in four basic asset classes.**
*Source:* Ibbotson Associates, Inc.

started in 1930, has returned 11.3 percent annually for almost 69 years. Had retirement accounts been around back
then, $1,000 invested in Fidelity Fund at inception would
be worth about $1.5 million by the end of 1998. Or take
Puritan, which has gained 12.6 percent per year since 1947.
Over a period of nearly 52 years $1,000 would now be
worth $460,000. Trend has delivered an annual return of
13.5 percent since 1958; a $1,000 investment in Trend
would be worth $171,000 after 40.5 years. Even Equity-
Income, a relative newcomer of 32.5 years, would have
turned a $1,000 investment into $89,000 with its 14.8 percent annual growth rate. All of these examples illustrate the
potential benefits of long-term investing. While these growth
rates may be lower over the next 10 to 20 years, it is still
reasonable to expect that stocks will exceed inflation over
the long run.

## THE ARGUMENT AGAINST MARKET TIMING

If anyone asks you if the stock market is headed up or
down, always say up. You'll be right over two-thirds of the
time. Based on a 50-year monthly history of the S&P 500,
stocks have outperformed cash 72 percent of the time over a
one-year period. Increase the investment horizon to ten
years, and stocks exceed cash 86 percent of the time. Over
20 years the S&P 500 has always exceeded the return on a
cash investment.

Despite this reality, new investors often look at a historical chart of the market and reach the obvious conclusion
that holding cash during declines would have boosted returns. Along the same line of thinking, you could do better
at the racetrack if you would take care to bet on the winning horses. The whole idea of timing the market is based
on the false assumption that predicting the future will be as
easy as observing the past.

I estimate that over a ten-year period fewer than 5 percent
of market timers will actually exceed the S&P 500 return,

and those who do will beat it by only a small margin. Many first-time investors do not appreciate how hard it is to predict the market until they have tried it a few times. Here are the reasons I do not recommend jumping in and out of the market, either with stocks or stock funds:

- By their very nature, financial markets move in the direction that surprises or disappoints the maximum number of participants involved. If the majority wants to buy, prices are higher. If the majority wants to sell, prices are lower. If the majority are content, trading volume goes down, setting the stage for a surprise move up or down. The only way to win at this game is to ignore the short-term volatility and benefit from the long-term trend.

- Because stocks move up about twice as often as they move down, a cash position will be the wrong choice by a two-to-one margin when applied randomly over any long period of time. Many investors think they can make up for this statistical disadvantage by outsmarting the rest of the investment population, but over a long period of time no amount of intelligence can overcome such odds.

- More opportunity exists in picking funds than in timing the market. Imagine two farmers. The first tries to farm only during favorable weather patterns. The second plants every year but focuses on the crops that offer the most profit potential. Which farmer do you think will be better off in 20 years? Farmer number one may not suffer as many big losses, but farmer number two will be much better off in the long run. The same is true for investing. If you want to maximize your return, you have to keep your money in the game, not on the sidelines. Figure 2 compares the hypothetical return of perfectly timing the market versus perfect fund selection in Fidelity's domestic growth category. No one can do this well in the real world, but it shows how an

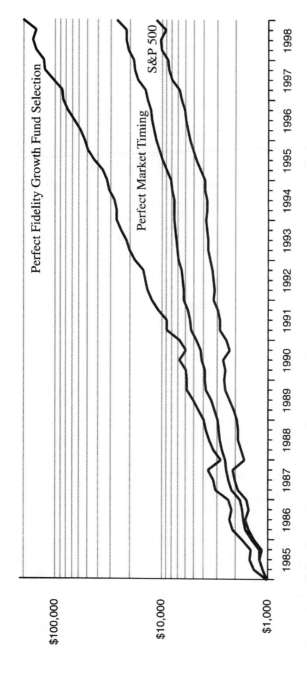

**Figure 2** Perfect fund selection versus perfect market timing, quarterly over a fourteen-year period.

investor who focuses on fund selection has a better shot at growth than one who ponders whether the investment should even be made.

## CHARACTERISTICS OF STOCKS

Stocks, or equities, represent ownership in a corporation—entitling the stockholder to a proportional claim on the corporation's net worth and its dividend payouts. Shareholders also have a right to influence the company's direction on strategic issues by participating in a shareholder vote, providing inputs to the board of directors, or expressing a point of view at the shareholders' meeting.

### Stocks and Stock Values

Stocks have value based on the corporation's earnings (or future earnings potential), dividends, and assets.

*Earnings*    In a mature company, earnings are necessary to continue paying out dividends and/or to repurchase existing shares of stock. In a growing company, earnings provide capital for expansion. In either case, a company's earnings (or anticipated future earnings) are a key indication of what future shareholder compensation might be. Many growth stocks do little to reward shareholders during their growing years, but shareholders anticipate that these firms will pay dividends or buy back shares at some point in the future.

*Dividends and Stock Buybacks*    Companies that are making money but are not growing usually reward shareholders with direct compensation because there isn't much potential to grow their business by reinvesting profits. In essence, shareholders are better off receiving dividends instead of having the company retain its earnings for internal use. The income stream of a dividend stock (or the ongoing increase in earnings per share for a company that is buying back its stock) can make it attractive even when earnings are flat or declining, provided the slump is not permanent and is not bad enough to force a dividend cut.

*Assets* A stock can have value without earnings or dividends if the company owns property, equipment, patents, licenses, or other valuable assets.

## Fundamental Indicators

Stocks are often compared on the basis of their price-to-earnings ratio (P/E ratio), which can often provide an indication of how expensive or cheap a particular company may be. For example, if a given stock has a $20 share price and earnings of $2 per share over the prior 12 months, it has a trailing P/E ratio of 10. Generally speaking, P/E ratios are lower for dividend/value stocks and higher for growth stocks. A stock with a P/E ratio of 45 may seem expensive on an absolute basis, but if the company can grow earnings at a 30 percent rate the stock can still be attractive. But stocks with high P/E ratios are vulnerable. At some point the earnings growth slows down, and the stock usually gets clobbered. Suppose a company with 30 percent annual earnings growth stumbles, and earnings growth suddenly slows to a 10 percent rate. If the change is permanent, the stock's P/E ratio could fall from 45 to 15—a potential decline in price of 67 percent.

A company's price-to-book ratio (which compares the stock price to the company's net worth per share on an accounting basis) can be a useful indicator, especially when earnings are depressed (P/E ratios are undefined if a firm is losing money, and they tend to be very high if the company is near breakeven). Generally speaking, a company that is doing the right stuff in a tough situation will exhibit a shrinking price-to-book ratio until the market takes notice. But book value for smaller companies tends to be less accurate than for large-caps, and foreign companies follow a different set of rules for establishing book value.

That's when the price-to-sales ratio can be useful. You can look at the price-to-sales ratio to see how cheap the stock is relative to current business levels. You can even compare the ratio to companies in the same industry to see what the stock might be worth with normal profits. Price-to-sales is also a dead giveaway for expensive stocks, which usually trade with ratios above 4. When evaluating foreign companies, price-to-sales cuts through the accounting differences that can cloud comparisons of P/E or price-to-book. The only problem with price-to-sales is that it isn't well defined for financial entities.

One other fundamental indicator for stocks is dividend yield, although this longtime indicator is less useful today. The increasing trend toward stock buybacks has prompted many companies to slow the growth of dividends and instead use the money to reduce the number of shares outstanding. Shareholders like it that way, because dividend income is taxed every year and can carry a higher tax rate than capital gains. Stock buybacks produce capital gains, the favored form of shareholder compensation.

Two fundamental indicators, P/E and dividend yield, are often calculated for stock indexes as well as individual stocks. Figure 3 shows how the two have varied over the years for the S&P 500 index. The lines clearly show that the S&P 500 is at the high end of its valuation range as of late 1998.

A high-priced S&P 500 does not mean a bear market is right around the corner. After all, there are several places along the chart where the index became expensive and stayed that way for many years. However, it does suggest that future gains may not be as robust as in the last 15 years.

Aggregate fundamental statistics are available for mutual funds. My favorite source is *Morningstar Mutual Funds*. Not only can you find a fund's overall P/E ratio and price-to-book ratio, but you can see how these figures compare to the major indexes and to other funds.

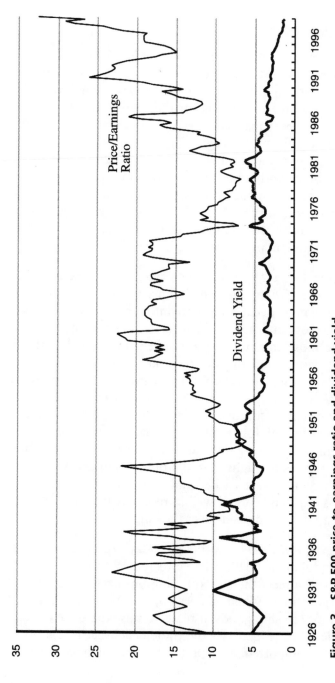

**Figure 3  S&P 500 price-to-earnings ratio and dividend yield.**
*Source:* Standard & Poor's

## Bear Markets

Fear of being caught in a bear market keeps many investors out of stocks. A typical bear market causes stocks to lose about one-third of their value, which may seem devastating to some. However, time is on the mature investor's side. Since 1925, bear markets have usually lasted about two or three years from the beginning of the sell-off until the market recovers and moves on to new highs. Such events usually occur with an economic situation that has a broad-based negative impact on corporate earnings for an extended period of time. Many bear markets are triggered by one or more of the following three factors: higher interest rates, surging oil prices, and trade restrictions.

*Higher Interest Rates*    When rates go up, the economy can slow and earnings can decline. Companies with debt suffer the most because they are hit with an increase in borrowing costs and a drop in revenue. Higher interest rates are the most common cause for bear markets, but this is widely known and the stock market is quick to adjust to changes that may affect corporate earnings. In the past, the Federal Reserve has set off many bear markets by raising short-term interest rates to fight inflation and then failing to wait long enough for results before making additional tightening moves. Usually the Fed had gone too far by the time there were visible signs that inflation was in check. Today's Fed is trying to act earlier and wait longer for results, a process that has worked well in recent years. Time will tell if this approach succeeds over the long run.

*Surging Oil Prices*    Although today's economy uses less oil per dollar of GDP (relative to the 1970s), the price of crude still affects the cost of doing business for just about all corporations. When oil goes up, it costs more to travel, it costs more to ship goods, it tends to raise the price of commodities, and it increases the trade deficit because most of our oil is imported. Except for wages, oil prices are the single most influential factor affecting inflation. In 1973–74 the price of crude quadrupled as the OPEC cartel took advantage of its dominant position in the world oil markets. In the United States, this caused the worst bear market in the last 50 years and set off an eight-year wave of inflation that caused the consumer price index (CPI) to double. By the mid-1980s, OPEC's pricing tactics had encouraged the development of other worldwide oil reserves, and competition finally broke the cartel's stranglehold. Still, as Iraq demonstrated in 1990, it is possible to see major worldwide supply disruptions. (Prices doubled after Kuwait was invaded and remained high until the Gulf War began.)

Today, the main concern for oil is the growing demand from emerging countries, which for many years was masked by sharp declines in Russian demand and later by the currency crisis. Technology has helped to expand supply and satisfy growing world demand. No doubt it will play a key role in keeping the price of crude from appreciating sharply over the long run. Still, there may be times when oil prices surge in the short term. During these periods the negative impact on the domestic stock market could be significant.

*Trade Restrictions*    Government policies can devastate an economy if exports or key imports are restricted in a major way. Country by country, national economies are good at some things and not so great at others. For example, the United States excels in developing and using new technology, providing financial services, and delivering top-notch entertainment. It also boasts the world's most productive farms and accounts for some 25 percent of global farmland. Japan's economy, with few natural resources, has emphasized high-volume manufacturing. Be it memory chips, photocopiers, cars, or VCRs, the Japanese have some of the world's best factories and can mass-produce with exceptionally high quality. China has low wages and can produce labor-intensive products at low cost. The list goes on: The emerging countries have low-cost oil; Canada has timber and minerals; Europe does well with industrial machinery, furniture, food products, fashion, and performance automobiles.

When trade is free, it raises the standard of living for everyone by allowing each country to profit from what it can do best. When trade is restricted, consumers lose out and corporate earnings are hit hard. The worst bear market of this century occurred in the early 1930s when isolationism was essentially legislated by Congress.

Imagine what our economy would be like if trade had been cut off 15 years ago. Gasoline would be over $4 per gallon, color TVs would cost $1,000, cars would be unreliable, and computers might still cost $5,000 for lack of inexpensive memory and other components. Food would be cheap, but interest rates and taxes would be much higher because no foreign capital would have been available to absorb the federal debt.

Especially in a global market, any disruption in trade can wreak havoc with the economy. These days a trade-driven bear market seems less probable, but skirmishes between the United States. and other major trading partners serve as a reminder that the risk is still there.

However bad they seem at the time, bear markets are temporary. Ultimately, things change for the better, and the financial markets are quick to react as the first evidence of recovery surfaces.

Many risk-averse investors buy only CDs or Treasury bills, feeling much better about a guaranteed 5 percent than about taking a chance on a 10 percent return with the possibility of a loss. With an investment horizon of less than three years it's hard to argue with this approach. However, if you don't have plans for your money for eight years or more, you're selling yourself short if you're not in the stock market. The long-term risk of owning stocks is much lower than the short-term risk. Over an eight-year period, there's about an 85 percent chance that stocks will do better than CDs or Treasury bills. Although a cash strategy might realize 35 percent growth over eight years, an equity-income fund could double over the same period.

## CHARACTERISTICS OF BONDS

When you buy a bond, you are lending money to either a corporation, a municipality, or to the government. In any case, you are purchasing a promise to return your principal with interest.

A bond's value is influenced by many factors, but interest rates and credit risk are the two dominant factors.

### Interest Rates

Because most bonds have a schedule of payments over a specified length of time, they have an inherent sensitivity to interest rates. If prevailing interest rates go up, a bond is worth less because its schedule of payments has become less attractive relative to the yield available on newly issued bonds. Other factors being equal, the value of the bond will fall until its yield-to-maturity (the yield of the remaining payments compared to the current value) is equal to prevailing market rates.

Suppose a ten-year bond pays a fixed coupon rate of 6 percent and is sold for $1,000. Later, the prevailing yield on similar ten-year bonds moves up to 7 percent. The market value of the bond would decline to about $950 so that a new buyer would realize an effective yield of 7 percent if the bond is held to maturity (the coupon rate is still 6 percent, but because the bond is bought at a discount the effective yield is higher). Conversely, a decline in prevailing interest rates will cause the value of the bond to rise until its yield-to-maturity is similar to the market rate.

The degree of a bond's interest rate sensitivity is determined by its repayment period. Long-maturity bonds fluctuate the most with interest rates because the schedule of interest payments goes on for a long time, leaving the bond holder with a substantial advantage or disadvantage, depending on whether rates go down or up. Short-maturity bonds, on the other hand, fluctuate less because the principal and interest will be available to reinvest at market rates in relatively short order.

## Credit Risk

The other significant factor affecting bond pricing is the ability of the bond issuer to repay (although this tends to be less significant in a bond fund). U.S. government bonds are considered to have near-zero credit risk because they are backed by the government's authority to raise taxes if push comes to shove. Top-rated corporate bonds and high-grade municipal bonds carry a little higher yield and a little more risk but are usually considered fairly safe. Investment-grade bonds, usually a broad range of corporate debt, are the next step down because business conditions can play a small role in the ability of the issuer to service its debt. At the bottom rung are high-yield bonds, otherwise known as junk bonds. In this group the default rate can be significant, and business conditions play a major role in the ability of the issuer to service its debt. Yields in this group are typically several percentage points higher than government bonds.

Bonds are often rated by agencies such as Standard & Poor's and Moody's. These firms review the health of the issuer and cast their judgment on credit risk. Standard & Poor's ratings (in descending order of risk) are AAA, AA, A, BBB, BB, B, and CCC. BB and higher are generally considered to be investment grade. Moody's ratings (again in descending order) are Aaa, Aa, A, Baa, Ba, B, and Caa. Ba and higher are considered investment grade. U.S. government bonds are considered to be at or above AAA or Aaa bonds.

Bonds usually carry less risk than stocks, but over the long run they have not exceeded inflation by as much. Since the start of 1926 (a period of 73 years), the annualized total return for long-term investment-grade bonds has been about 5.5 percent per year. Real growth (net of inflation) was about 2 percent for the period.

In modern years bond investors have done better. Starting in the early 1980s, investors began to understand how inflation factors into long-term returns. Since then, the inflation premium on long-term investment-grade bonds has risen to around three to four percentage points, almost double the long-term average. There are signs that this adjustment is a permanent one. It could mean that the difference in annual return between stocks and bonds may be only a few percentage points in the years ahead. Given the high premium on the S&P 500 (at the end of 1998), large-cap stocks may not provide as much of an advantage over bonds in the decade ahead.

There have been many bear markets for long-term bonds over the years, but most were only half as bad as a major sell-off in stocks (10 to 15 percent losses are typical). For short-term bonds, the sell-off was about half again as bad (usually 5 to 7.5 percent). Bonds are clearly safer than stocks, but they are far from being risk-free.

Bear markets usually occur at different times for stocks and bonds. In the typical economic cycle, interest rates will usually move upward as the economy expands and borrowing increases to meet expansion needs. Under these conditions, stocks usually benefit from earnings growth, but bonds slide as interest rates edge up. At some point the economy peaks, and growth begins to slow. Corporate earnings start to slide, causing stocks to decline. Borrowing demand slacks off, causing long-term interest rates to fall. This is a period when bonds benefit. Near the bottom of the cycle, stocks start to rise because of falling interest rates and future economic potential. Bonds continue to do well because there is not yet any upward pressure on long-term interest rates.

Because stocks and bonds are usually somewhat "out of phase," a portfolio that includes both is subject to less volatility. A mix of 60 percent stocks and 40 percent bonds is pretty close to ideal: It carries less risk than a bonds-only approach yet provides a higher total return. For this reason, the 60-40 mix has long been popular with conservative growth and income funds as well as balanced funds.

## CHARACTERISTICS OF CASH AND GOLD

Since 1926, cash-type investments (represented by the 30-day Treasury bill) have returned 3.8 percent per year, just slightly ahead of the long-term 3.1 percent rate of inflation. If government money market funds had been around since 1926, the advantage over inflation would have been offset by the management fee. When investing for the long term with a money market fund, the best you can hope for is to break even after inflation and taxes.

Investors who bought CDs and money funds in the early 1980s remember when risk-free double-digit returns were available. By contrast, today's rates seem low. They aren't. The 1980s were unique because short-term interest rates reflected the inflation rates of the late 1970s, yet inflation had subsided to less than 5 percent early in the decade. For about ten years, riskless cash investments delivered the kind of real returns that would normally be associated with long-term bonds. Then the recession in 1991 showed how low the return on cash can go in a soft economy. Short-term interest rates have risen since then, but it's unlikely that cash investments will ever again provide the kind of real returns that existed between 1981 and 1991.

Gold is sometimes considered the perfect inflation hedge. From the standpoint that it holds its value against inflation, it is. However, its real return over the long run is usually zero, just like cash investments. What is different about gold is that it tends to surge when inflation escalates and decline when inflation recedes. The volatility of gold is similar to the S&P 500, but the volatility of gold stocks (and gold funds) is typically twice as great as the metal itself.

Gold and gold stocks are sort of like inflation insurance. The long-term return usually isn't very good, but if inflation runs out of control (either in the United States or in other mature economies), gold-oriented investments tend to perform well.

Gold and bonds are somewhat inversely correlated, meaning that gold (and gold stocks) often move up when bonds are declining. A small 5 percent position in gold stocks or a 10 percent position in the metal itself can actually reduce the volatility of a bond portfolio because of this offsetting effect. However, it can also reduce the long-term return of the portfolio by a small amount.

The same is not true for stocks. When the economy is expanding and interest rates are edging up, cyclical stocks and gold are usually moving up together. If the Fed raises short-term interest rates too far, stocks and gold can both decline at the same time. Many investors ran for gold after the stock market crashed in 1987, only to see their gold holdings drop sharply a few days later.

Gold isn't like other commodities, where a large and growing shortfall would imply sharply higher prices. Most of the gold ever taken out of the ground is still around. With some 100,000 tons in "circulation" as jewelry, coins, and central bank reserves, the price of the metal doesn't need to rise very much to fill the void between supply and demand.

## INFLATION/DEFLATION

Over the last 70 years there have been two periods when inflation rose at an 8 percent clip for almost a decade. The first was right after World War II began, when the economy strained to support a massive military buildup. The second began right after the 1973 Arab oil embargo, when the price of crude quadrupled in U.S. dollar terms. Between those two unusual periods, inflation usually averaged about 2 to 3 percent per year.

Today, inflation has been put into remission because of advancing technology. Because of the nature of the forces at work, this is not a temporary situation:

- Big productivity gains are being realized because of cheap computing power. The impact can be compared to the steam engine, electric power, or the telephone, but this time the savings in labor is being realized over a shorter period of time. It's also a continuing process.
- Technology exerts a deflationary force on the economy by fostering competition. It does this by opening up new ways of doing things, which reduces barriers to entry and strips away monopoly powers. Companies today have very little ability to raise prices. That's a far cry from the 1970s, when firms like AT&T, Xerox, IBM, and Kodak could pass along increases whenever they wanted. Not even OPEC has much control today. Technology has dramatically lowered the cost of finding oil in the last 25 years, allowing non-OPEC countries to grab an increasing share of the world oil market. Today OPEC supplies just 35 percent of the world's oil, down from 60 percent in the 1970s.
- The internet is already driving down prices as on-line retailers undercut traditional stores in a bid to gain market share. But there are two other deflationary forces that will surface over a longer period of time. Increasingly, producers of goods and services are dealing directly with end customers. Over time this is likely to squeeze the margins of distributors and resellers, leaving only those who add value by dealing in high volume or by offering a huge selection of products. Also, the power of knowledge made available on-line will usher in a new era of consumer productivity, making it easier for people to take care of things on their own. Whether you avoid a doctor visit by self-diagnosing a simple ailment, make your own travel reservations, or

file your tax return electronically, the impact is deflationary because there is a net reduction in the goods and services demanded from the economy.

- Innovation and competition within the technology industry itself means that prices for technology-related goods and services will continue to fall, just as they have throughout the industry's 50-year history. In the general economy, most businesses are spending more on computers and telecommunications as time goes on. Over the long run, deflation in technology-related goods and services should have a greater impact on the overall economy.

As technology continues to play a bigger role in the economy, a deflationary period is likely to replace the inflationary era we are accustomed to. It will not be like the deflation of the 1930s, which was the result of an economic catastrophe. Instead, it will be the type of deflation that improves the standard of living by increasing the purchasing power of wage earners.

# 4

# *Domestic Growth Funds*

Growth funds aim for growth of capital, and most maintain portfolios that hold 80 percent or more in stocks. Some hold stocks that pay dividends, but generating dividend income is usually not a priority for this group. The typical fund in this group will have a lower dividend yield and higher P/E than the S&P 500. These funds usually carry more risk than the index, although there are a few exceptions. During a market decline, many of these funds may fall faster than the S&P 500. For this reason, you should invest only if your investment horizon is eight years or more and you are willing to accept a short-term loss of 25 to 30 percent if a bear market comes along.

Chances are you'll find Fidelity's best long-term performers in this group of funds. As I have mentioned, Fidelity's research advantage in domestic stockpicking puts it ahead in the game. Unlike the rest of the industry, many of Fidelity's domestic growth funds outperform the S&P 500 over a period of ten years or more.

Some funds in this group have a portion of their portfolio dedicated to foreign stocks, which is consistent with Fidelity's philosophy of looking for growth and value wherever it may exist. With a few exceptions, you can usually figure that foreign holdings will be less than 25 percent in a given fund.

## DOMESTIC GROWTH FUND CHOICES

Following is a fund-by-fund look at Fidelity's domestic growth choices. For all funds in this group, Fidelity reserves the right to block additional purchases after four trips in and out of the same fund in a 12-month period. Calendar-year performance for the group is listed in Appendix A. For suggested portfolios of growth funds, see Chapter 10.

### Aggressive Growth

Formerly called Emerging Growth, this fund was started near the end of 1990. The fund seeks capital appreciation by investing primarily in stocks of companies that offer the potential for accelerated earnings or revenue growth. Distributions are usually made in January and December. There is no front-end load, but a 0.75 percent redemption fee is charged on shares held for less than 90 days.

Aggressive Growth's price volatility alone qualifies it to be one of the riskier choices in Fidelity's diversified growth arena, mainly because of its heavy position in technology stocks. In short, it's not a fund for the faint of heart.

In theory, Aggressive Growth should wind up being one of the better long-term performers because it takes on more risk than most other funds. But it hasn't always worked out that way. An aggressive fund like this is more heavily dependent on the fund manager's stockpicking skills, and this fund has seen a few dry spells along with the good year. Still, this fund is an appropriate vehicle for investors who want to invest some of their long-term capital in fast-growing companies.

### Blue Chip Growth

Blue Chip Growth was started at the end of 1987. The fund's strategy is to invest primarily in a diversified portfolio of common stocks of well-known and established companies. Distributions can occur in September and December. The fund carries no load charges.

Blue Chip Growth is now one of Fidelity's largest growth funds. Former manager Michael Gordon once invested this fund in what he referred to as "tomorrow's blue chips." Gordon was replaced in March of 1996 and ultimately left Fidelity in a reorganization that reigned in managers who were straying too far from fund objectives. Under manager John McDowell, the fund has adopted a mainstream approach and has been a consistent performer. Still, I have a slight preference for Large Cap Stock over Blue Chip Growth. The two funds have nearly identical charters, but Large Cap Stock is a much smaller fund and could benefit from its ability to move faster during changing market conditions.

## Capital Appreciation

Capital Appreciation's objective is capital appreciation from a diversified portfolio of common stocks of domestic and foreign issuers. It may also invest in preferred stocks and bonds. Dividends and payouts of capital gains can take place in February and December. The fund is no-load.

Managers at this fund have always been free to pursue a wide range of investment styles. Ex-manager Tom Sweeney used to go after cheap, out-of-favor cyclical companies. *Forbes* magazine once described Sweeney's stockpicking approach as "roadkill with a pulse." Harry Lange took over in early 1996, focusing at times on consumer stocks and making outsized bets on the technology sector during other periods. As such, a fund like this is suitable mainly for aggressive investors who are looking for an investment vehicle that beats to its own drum.

## Contrafund

Like other funds in this group, Contrafund's objective is capital appreciation. It invests mainly in equity securities of companies where value is not fully recognized by the public. Distributions can occur in December and in February. It is sold with a 3 percent load, which is currently waived for retirement accounts. The fund is currently closed to new retail accounts.

Contrafund has been under the guidance of many different managers since it was started in May 1967. However, performance was subpar until Jeff Vinik became manager in 1988. Will Danoff, the fund's current manager, extended Vinik's winning streak after he took over in October 1990. Most of Danoff's great performance has been achieved while running Contrafund as if it were a traditional growth fund. The fund's objective was amended in 1997, stating a focus on under-recognized stocks as opposed to those that are out of favor. The difference may seem subtle, but the fund is now free to pursue a mainstream growth strategy without being in conflict with its charter.

Danoff occasionally adopts a major theme with his portfolio. A heavy concentration on the energy group held back performance in 1997, but betting on the companies that supply "bandwidth" for the internet was right on target in 1998.

Despite the closure, Contrafund can still be purchased by investors who already have an established account (it's also available to many 401(k) investors). Contrafund II offers a similar investing style and has the advantage of a smaller and more flexible portfolio.

## Contrafund II

Like Contrafund, Contrafund II also looks for companies where value is not fully recognized by the public. The fund was launched in 1998. Distributions can occur in August and in December. It is sold with a 3 percent load, which is currently waived for retirement accounts.

Contrafund II is currently managed by Jason Weiner. Throughout its first year of operation, this fund has been aligned closely with Contrafund, but as time goes on Weiner is likely to develop his own style. Time will tell, but I think this fund has a reasonably good shot at being a long-term winner. Weiner seems to emphasize growth without making any major bets on any one industry. Other Fidelity managers who have followed this recipe for success have generally reaped rewards in the long run.

One key advantage for Contrafund II is its smaller size. As market conditions change, this fund will have the flexibility to take on new positions without spending a lot of time unwinding stocks that have gone out of favor.

## Disciplined Equity

Disciplined Equity is headed up by Brad Lewis, who has been with the fund since it started in December 1988. The fund seeks long-term growth of capital by using computer-aided, quantitative analysis supported by fundamental research. Distributions occur in December; the fund is sold no-load.

Disciplined Equity has essentially matched the S&P 500's performance over the past ten years. Fidelity's goal with this fund has been to offer a better-performing alternative to a market index fund, but that's been a tough thing to do in recent years.

There are positive and negative arguments for screening stocks by computer. On the plus side, quantitative techniques take emotion out of the picture, and they are quick to detect changes in the market. They also evaluate all holdings on a continual basis. Unfortunately, today's market is looking beyond the numbers to judge a company by its ability to dominate its industry and export its brand into the global marketplace. Long-held assumptions about value and growth-rate multiples are falling by the wayside as investors try to visualize where a company will be 15 or 20 years in the future.

Ultimately, Fidelity's success with this fund will depend on how well Lewis can adapt his computer models to match the evolving thought patterns of today's market.

## Dividend Growth

Dividend Growth seeks capital appreciation by investing in stocks of companies that have the potential for dividend growth by either increasing their dividends or by commencing dividend payouts if none are currently paid. The fund was introduced in 1993 and has always been no-load. Distributions can occur in September and December.

Dividend Growth has posted strong results since inception, the result of having the right management style at the right time. In recent years it has benefited from its focus on large-cap stocks, which is where the largest dividend payers can usually be found (many of these companies are also buying back their stock). Just because this fund has the word "Dividend" in its title does not mean it is low risk. At times, current manager Charles Mangum has run a very concentrated portfolio. Still, if this fund can continue to focus on companies that are succeeding in the global economy, it could keep up its good performance. About the only concern is the fund's growing asset base, which reduces its mobility.

## Export and Multinational Fund

Introduced in late 1994 as Export Fund, this fund was renamed Export and Multinational in 1996. It invests mainly in stocks of U.S. companies that are expected to benefit from exporting or selling their goods or services outside the country Payouts of capital gains and dividends can occur in October and December. The fund carries a 3 percent front-end load, which is currently waived for retirement accounts.

Fidelity started this fund after a study showed that U.S. companies exporting a higher percentage of their business than the national average have outperformed the market on a historical basis. The theory is that any firm capable of delivering domestic products or services in foreign markets must be doing things right because it is able to overcome language barriers, shipping costs, and duties while still making a profit.

In recognition that larger companies have an advantage in serving global markets, Fidelity shifted Export's focus to include large-cap multinationals. With the appointment of manager Adam Hetnarski in late 1998, the fund has moved most of its holdings into global large-caps. Unless Hetnarski establishes a superior track record, I don't think that investors are getting anything that justifies the cost of a 3 percent load. Funds such as Blue Chip Growth, Growth Company, and Large Cap Stock will probably hold a similar mix of stocks.

## Fidelity Fifty

One of Fidelity's more unusual funds, Fidelity Fifty was started in September 1993. Its objective is capital appreciation; it normally invests in 50 to 60 stocks that the manager believes have the greatest potential for growth. A combination of fundamental and quantitative techniques are used to identify attractive stocks. Distributions can occur in August and December. It's sold with a 3 percent load, which is currently waived for retirement accounts.

Fidelity Fifty differs from other funds in that it runs a more concentrated portfolio. That means that the price swings of an individual stock have more impact on performance. Previous manager Scott Stewart used to choose stocks with limited correlation in order to keep volatility at bay. This made for a stable portfolio, but the performance he realized over his five-year tenure was not very exciting.

That's changing under new manager John Muresianu, who took over at the beginning of 1999. Muresianu added some highly volatile stocks to the fund's portfolio, causing the fund's short-term risk to score higher than even Aggressive

Growth. It's not clear if the fund is still following any quantitative stock selection criteria.

It's worth noting that Neal Miller of New Millennium has done well with high-priced, high-volatility stocks. If Muresianu proves to be an astute stockpicker, this fund could generate strong returns with its new strategy. However, if things go the wrong way, it could really hurt. Like Aggressive Growth, this fund is appropriate only for aggressive investors who want to invest a portion of their long-term capital.

### Growth Company

Introduced in January 1983, Growth Company invests mainly in stocks of companies that Fidelity believes have above-average growth potential. Known in its early years as Mercury Fund, Growth Company distributes dividends and capital gains in January and December. It is sold no-load.

One of Fidelity's mainstream growth funds, Growth Company usually emphasizes technology, pharmaceuticals, and other fast-growing segments of the economy. During the last ten years the fund has invested mainly in large-cap stocks.

Ex-manager Bob Stansky made this fund a winner by outperforming the S&P 500 by about three percentage points per year over a nine-year period. Performance under Larry Greenberg and current manager Steven Wymer hasn't been as strong in recent years but is certainly not disappointing.

Investors today are becoming increasingly growth-oriented, which should be a positive factor for this fund. But this fund is generally more volatile than the S&P 500 and should be considered only for long-term investments.

### Large Cap Stock

Started in June 1995, Large Cap Stock seeks long-term growth of capital, investing mainly in stocks with a market capitalization of $1 billion or more. The fund distributes dividends and capital gains in June and December. It is sold no-load.

This fund invests for growth and focuses on large-cap stocks. Its mainstream approach is very similar to Blue Chip Growth, except that Large Cap carries the advantage of smaller size. Even in the large-cap universe, this should provide for a small advantage when the market shifts focus.

Current manager Karen Firestone spent many years running Select Health Care and Select Biotechnology, and this experience is likely to make for a successful tenure at Large Cap Stock. Furthermore, Fidelity analysts know growth stocks pretty well. This fund should make a good fit for any long-term growth strategy.

## Low-Priced Stock

This fund was started in December 1989. Manager Joel Tillinghast has been running the fund since it started and has always focused on small-cap value stocks. Low-Priced Stock seeks capital appreciation by investing primarily in stocks that are priced below $35 at the time of investment. Dividend and capital gains payouts can occur in September and in December. The fund carries a 3 percent front-end load (currently waived for investors who add to existing retirement accounts), and there is a 1.5 percent redemption fee on shares held for less than 90 days.

Relative to the Russell 2000 universe, Low-Priced Stock has been an outstanding performer. Tillinghast and his team have delivered commendable performance considering the huge size of the fund and the 20 to 40 percent cash levels resulting from strong inflows that have occurred throughout much of the fund's history.

But today's market has changed, and the Russell 2000 universe may no longer offer the range of opportunities that exist in the mid-cap and large-cap segments of the market.

Increasingly, attractive small companies are being taken out of circulation by larger firms that seek growth through acquisitions. Fast-growing smaller companies that avoid becoming a takeover target often become large-caps in short order. Some initial public offerings (IPOs) have reached $1 billion in market capitalization in just 15 minutes, a process that used to take years. The result is that the companies remaining in the Russell 2000 are growing their earnings at a slower rate. Likewise, any fund that is confined to the Russell 2000 universe is also at a potential disadvantage.

To its credit, Low-Priced Stock carries significantly less risk than other growth-oriented funds, the result of broad diversification and a value-oriented portfolio. But over the long run it runs the risk of slipping behind other funds that focus on large-cap multinationals and growth stocks that command a premium price.

## Magellan

Magellan's objective is capital appreciation by investing primarily in common stocks and securities convertible into common stock. Distributions are paid out in May and December. It carries a 3 percent load, except for 401(k) and 403(b) plans, where the sales charge is usually waived. Magellan is now closed to new retail accounts but remains available in many 401(k) programs.

This famous stock fund got its start as Fidelity International fund in 1963, but shortly after inception Congress slapped a 15 percent tax on foreign investments, forcing the fund to change its charter. It was closed to new investors and did not reopen until 1981 after two other funds (Essex and Salem) were merged into it. Peter Lynch became manager in 1977, and his legendary stockpicking (coupled with the fund's small size at the time) resulted in about ten years of "golden" performance, in which annualized returns exceeded 30 percent. Investors took notice, and the fund grew by leaps and bounds after it reopened in 1981. By early

1986 it had crossed the $5 billion mark, and performance began to cool off, although it continued to do well.

By the late 1980s, Lynch's workaholic schedule had begun to take its toll. In April 1990 Lynch announced his plans to "retire," and Morris Smith took over. Smith navigated the fund for about two years, then announced plans to move his family to Israel. Jeff Vinik replaced Smith and outperformed the S&P 500 while running the fund between July 1992 and June 1996. Vinik was widely criticized by the media for his "gunslinger" style, his personal trading habits, and an upbeat comment on Micron that was made right before he sold out $20 billion in technology stocks (Micron included).

Current manager Bob Stansky took the helm amid widespread media speculation that Magellan was too big to outperform. He proved the pundits wrong in 1998 by exceeding the S&P 500 by five percentage points, a feat that was accomplished with the bottoms-up stockpicking approach that served him well at Growth Company.

For a decade the media has been saying that Magellan is too big, and during the same ten years Magellan beat the S&P 500 and outperformed 90 percent of domestic growth funds in the industry. Magellan may be too big for the massive sector moves that Vinik was making, but under Stansky it is not unreasonable to expect that Magellan will outperform the S&P 500 by two to three percentage points annually. After all, the fund is only about 0.7 percent of the U.S. stock market capitalization. If Stansky remains close to the S&P 500 and emphasizes a few long-term winners, he'll easily be ahead in the game. I continue to recommend Magellan for 401(k) investors. I think it's a better bet than an index fund.

## Mid-Cap Stock

Mid-Cap Stock was started in March 1994. It aims for capital appreciation by investing in companies with medium-size market capitalization. Distributions can occur in March and December. The fund is sold no-load.

This fund competes with the S&P Mid Cap 400 Index, and so far results have been mixed. Until recently, the fund focused mainly on value, missing out on some key growth stock opportunities.

As with small-caps, the mid-cap stock universe has been altered as a result of increased merger and acquisition activity. Larger firms, aided by enterprise software and other tools that make acquisitions easy to manage, are snapping up medium-size firms that show growth potential. What's left is a slower-growing group of companies. Unless Mid-Cap Stock can make a success of focusing on the dwindling pool of faster-growing companies that remain independent, it runs the risk of continuing to underperform the S&P 500 in the long run.

## New Millennium

New Millennium was started at the end of 1992. The fund's objective is capital appreciation, investing in all types of equity securities, favoring small- to medium-capitalization companies that show growth potential or that have the potential to exceed current earnings expectations. Distributions occur in January and December. The fund is currently closed to new retail accounts. Additional contributions for existing shareholders are subject to a 3 percent front-end load.

Manager Neal Miller is charged with using "change analysis" to identify stocks for his portfolio, the idea being to observe long-term trends in society and government and then figure out which companies will benefit. For example, much of the aging baby boom population will be entering retirement in about ten years, pushing up demand for travel and leisure activities. Ideally, change analysis would uncover such trends just before they become widely recognized by the market. To date, the fund's largest position has been technology stocks.

New Millennium has produced a good results while holding a unique blend of growth stocks, although some of the fund's strong 1995 gains appear to be a result of getting in on some attractive initial public offerings (IPOs). Still, Miller seems to keep overall risk lower than expected for a portfolio rich in high-priced stocks. And he has been able to gain significant exposure to the internet sector without any big increase in overall volatility. Over the long term New Millennium should continue to be a good match for investors who prefer an aggressive approach to growth.

If you aren't currently a shareholder but you like the New Millennium concept, keep an eye on Fidelity Fifty. If new manager John Muresianu remains at the helm, Fidelity Fifty is likely to have similar characteristics.

## OTC Portfolio

OTC Portfolio's objective is capital appreciation by investing in primarily in stocks traded in the over-the-counter (OTC) securities market. The fund was introduced right at the end of 1984. Distributions can occur in September and December. The fund is sold no-load.

The OTC market consisted mainly of small-cap stocks when this fund started in 1985, whereas today it is dominated by several large-cap technology firms that elected to stay on the NASDAQ exchange rather than switch to a New York listing (Microsoft, Intel, Cisco, and MCI Worldcom account for almost 40 percent of the NASDAQ index as of early 1999). Because OTC Portfolio competes with the NASDAQ index, it tends to hold a similar mix of stocks. That means heavy exposure to the technology sector, which typically accounts for 40 to 50 percent of this fund's holdings.

Technology stocks have been strong performers in recent years, but performance won't always be as consistent in future years. If you like to invest aggressively, Aggressive Growth provides more diversification and is less dependent on a handful of large-cap technology stocks.

## Retirement Growth

Formerly known as Freedom, Retirement Growth was started in March 1983 as a restricted fund available only for tax-deferred retirement accounts. The fund's objective is capital appreciation from investing primarily in common stocks, both domestic and foreign. Distributions occur in January and December, but in retirement accounts the payouts are simply reinvested with no tax impact. The fund is sold no-load.

The original concept behind Retirement Growth was to create a fund that could trade actively without creating large capital gain distributions, although Fidelity did not start to take advantage of this feature until 1998. After a period of following unique strategies that didn't pay off, Retirement Growth is now taking a mainstream approach under manager Fergus Shiel. His focus on large-cap growth stocks worked particularly well in 1998.

Like other funds following a similar strategy (Blue Chip Growth, Large Cap Stock, and Growth Company), Retirement Growth is likely to outperform the S&P 500 over the long run by focusing on stocks that can provide above-average earnings growth.

## Small Cap Selector

Small Cap Selector (known as Small Cap Stock before 1998) has an objective of long-term capital appreciation. It invests primarily in companies in the Russell 2000 universe. It was introduced near the end of June 1993 and can distribute dividends and capital gains in June and December. It has no front-end load, but there is a 1.5 percent redemption fee on shares held less than 90 days.

Small Cap Selector is one of Brad Lewis's quantitative funds, meaning that stocks are picked based on a computerized screen of financial statistics. In this particular version, the computer's eye is on domestic small-company stocks. Despite several revisions, this particular quantitative approach has not delivered on its promise. Picking stocks based on historical modeling has become more difficult in recent years because the market is no longer behaving in a traditional way. Today's investors are looking beyond the numbers and placing their money based on where they think a company will be 10 or 20 years from now.

Another problem is that the Russell 2000 universe no longer provides as many opportunities as it used to, as I mentioned in my discussion of Low-Priced Stock. If you want to invest in a quantitative fund, Disciplined Equity is a better alternative.

## Small Cap Stock

Small Cap Stock was introduced near the beginning of 1998. It invests in the stocks of companies with small market capitalizations; like Fidelity's other small-cap offerings it competes with the Russell 2000 universe. Dividends and capital gains are distributed in June and December. There's no front-end load, but a stiff 3 percent redemption fee applies unless shares are held for a full three years (1,095 days).

Small Cap Stock got off to a poor start, partly because the Russell 2000 universe lagged so badly in 1998, and partly because 20 to 25 percent of its assets were invested in foreign markets. Nevertheless, this fund has a better shot at success than Low-Priced Stock and Small Cap Selector because it is smaller and more focused on growth stocks.

Still, it may be an uphill battle for any fund that is limited to the Russell 2000. These days there aren't as many good stocks to choose from in the small-cap universe, a result of acquisitions and the tendency for attractive IPOs to become large-caps in relatively short order.

### Spartan Extended Market Index

Spartan Extended Market Index was introduced near the end of 1997. Its objective is to track the Wilshire 4500, an index that excludes the S & P 500 stocks from the Wilshire 5000. The fund is sold as no-load but there is a 0.75 percent redemption fee on shares held less than 90 days. There is a $15,000 minimum, and a $10 annual fee for account balances of less than $10,000. As of this writing, Fidelity is capping annual expenses at 0.25 percent.

This fund has the characteristics of a broadly diversified domestic mid-cap/small-cap fund. Like other index funds, its turnover is low because stocks are bought and sold only when the index holdings change. This minimizes annual distributions.

The omission of large-cap stocks could hold this fund back over the long run, since many of these stocks are global leaders and are acquiring smaller, fast-growing firms. If you want to index, go with Spartan Total Market Index, which tracks the entire Wilshire 5000.

### Spartan Market Index

Spartan Market Index was introduced in early 1990 as Market Index. Its objective is to track the S&P 500. The fund is sold no-load, but there is a 0.5 percent redemption fee on shares held less than 90 days. There is also a $10 annual fee for account balances of less than $10,000. Fidelity plans to cap annual expenses at 0.19 percent through the end of 1999. It is likely that the expense cap will be extended because Fidelity is in competing with Vanguard's Index 500 fund.

This fund has been an outstanding performer in recent years because the trend toward globalization has strongly favored the largest of the large-cap stocks. Also, the popularity of indexing has been a self-reinforcing trend because of market weighting. For every $100 going into this fund, roughly $6 is invested in General Electric and Microsoft (as of late 1998). Stocks that are added to the S&P 500 are subject to committee approval by a board of directors at Standard & Poor's, which can make mistakes. Despite strong growth, America Online was left out of the index for an extra year because the board wasn't convinced that the company was here to stay. By the time America Online was added to the index, it was the 30th largest stock in the country. Not surprisingly, many Fidelity funds that held America Online beat the S&P 500 during that year.

If you must index, consider going with Spartan Total Market Index, which tracks the entire Wilshire 5000. Another good alternative is Tax Managed Stock. Like an index fund, Tax Managed Stock is designed to keep distributions low. But like active funds, it is capable of outperforming the S&P 500 over the long run.

## Spartan Total Market Index

Spartan Total Market Index was introduced near the end of 1997. Its objective is to track the Wilshire 5000, an index that includes most of the stocks in the domestic market. This fund is sold no-load, but there is a 0.5 percent fee on shares held less than 90 days. There is a minimum investment of $15,000 and a $10 annual fee for account balances of less than $10,000. As of this writing, Fidelity is capping annual expenses at 0.25 percent.

The S&P 500 accounts for about 75 percent of this fund's behavior, with mid-cap and small-cap stocks accounting for the rest. Its turnover is low because stocks are bought and sold only when the index holdings change. Annual distributions are minimized as a result.

If you want to index, I think this fund is the best way to do it. It favors the global large-caps like the S&P 500, but it is more diversified and will benefit from smaller companies that are on their way to becoming large-cap stocks.

### Stock Selector

This fund is Disciplined Equity's more flexible cousin. Managed by Brad Lewis since its inception in September 1990, Stock Selector's objective is capital growth by investing in common stocks determined to be undervalued relative to their industries' norms. Distributions of dividends and capital gains occur each year in December. There is no load.

As with Disciplined Equity, Lewis runs a quantitative computer model to screen for attractively priced stocks. This fund, however, is allowed more latitude to overweight specific industry groups, and it can invest up to 35 percent of holdings in foreign stocks.

Stock Selector's extra freedom has been a mixed blessing. At times it has allowed the fund to deliver stronger performance than Disciplined Equity, but during other periods it has been penalized for straying too far from the large-cap universe. Since inception, both funds have performed on par with the S&P 500.

If you want to go with a quantitative fund, I recommend Disciplined Equity because it is less likely to get off track in future years.

### Tax Managed Stock

Tax Managed Stock was introduced in late 1998. Its objective is to seek long-term growth while reducing the impact of federal income tax on shareholder returns. The fund pays out dividends in October and distributes capital gains in December.

Fidelity created this fund as an alternative for investors who might otherwise buy an S&P 500 index fund to reduce the impact of annual fund distributions. By holding stocks for a longer period and trying to offset gains with losses, investors can expect index-like distributions while aiming to exceed the return of the S&P 500.

Although a fund like this does not make sense for IRA or Keogh accounts, it is an excellent choice for anyone who is trying to build up "tax-deferred" gains in a regular taxable account. The mix of stocks held will probably be similar to the S&P 500, but if manager Tim Heffernan can do a good job of picking long-term winners it may be possible to enjoy both index-beating performance and high tax efficiency.

## TechnoQuant Growth

TechnoQuant Growth is a quantitative fund that aims for long-term growth of capital. The fund's approach emphasizes technical factors such as price and volume information. The fund pays out dividends and capital gains in December. The fund is sold with a 3 percent front-end load and carries a redemption fee of 0.75 percent for shares that are held less than 90 days.

Unlike the quantitative approach used by Brad Lewis, computer programs used for TechnoQuant Growth look back through history and try to figure out which economic factors are bullish for each stock in the model. With current conditions plugged in, the computers then try to figure out a mix of stocks that are likely to outperform.

It's an interesting concept, but like other quantitative models this one is handicapped by a market that refuses to follow the patterns of the past. This particular approach also tends to make dramatic repositioning moves that result in high turnover. Among quantitative funds, Disciplined Equity is less likely to disappoint in the long run.

## Trend

Trend invests in securities of well-known, established companies as well as smaller well-known companies. It pays out dividends and capital gains in February and December. The fund is sold no-load.

Created in 1958, Trend is Fidelity's oldest growth-oriented fund. It was one of Fidelity's high flyers during the "go go" years of the 1960s, when it was run by Fidelity chairman Ned Johnson. In recent years it has been a poor performer, hampered by a string of managers who all had good ideas but picked a poor time to implement them.

The fund may finally be on the comeback trail under manager Nick Thakore. Thakore has adopted a mainstream growth-oriented approach similar to those of other successful funds. One key advantage for Trend is its relatively small size. With such a poor long-term track record it won't get big anytime soon—even if it does manage to post strong results.

## Value

Started in December 1978, this fund has also been known as Asset Investment Trust and Discoverer. Value seeks capital appreciation by investing in companies with valuable fixed assets or in companies believed to be undervalued based on company assets, earnings, or growth potential. Payouts of dividends and capital gains can occur in December. There is no load.

A cyclical fund by nature, Value has usually performed best during periods of strong economic growth. However, in recent years deflationary trends have made it tough for many of the industrial stocks in this fund's portfolio. Today's market is interested in firms that have long-term growth potential, which includes mainly growth stocks and large-cap multinationals. Unfortunately, Value seldom has much exposure to either group.

If you want to own a value fund, consider Equity-Income. This fund is part of the growth and income group discussed in Chapter 6. Equity-Income's large-cap portfolio is a more solid bet in the long run.

# 5

# International Funds

Foreign investing has not been a strong area for Fidelity, but that could change as time goes on. The company is investing heavily in foreign research, as evidenced by an increasing number of foreign analysts—many of whom are located in the countries they are covering. In some ways, this buildup of a solid "research infrastructure" resembles Fidelity's expansion of domestic research in the late 1980s. Over time it could favorably impact the performance of Fidelity's international funds.

The key reason many investors own foreign funds is that investing internationally adds an element of long-term diversification. About half the time the U.S. markets move with the major foreign markets, and about half the time they move in the opposite direction. Blending foreign and domestic stocks together incerases portfolio stability. (This is the same effect that occurs when you blend domestic stocks and bonds.) Studies show that a blend of 70 percent in the S&P 500 and 30 percent in the Morgan Stanley EAFE (Europe Australia Far East) index will result in less volatility than investing in either index by itself.

In recent years, however, an increasing number of investors are going with an all-domestic approach. Better performance is usually cited as the main reason, but an argument can also be made that foreign diversification is unnecessary, since many domestic corporations are globally diversified in their own right. Besides, expenses are generally higher for overseas mutual funds, and many foreign funds have a harder time staying ahead of their respective indexes.

Ultimately, the decision to include foreign funds in your portfolio comes down to one of personal preference. If you decide to invest internationally, start small and stick with broad-based funds as opposed to those that target specific regions or countries (broad-based funds allow Fidelity managers to focus investments where they find the best opportunities). Consider narrowing your scope only if you plan to make a long-term bet, because it's difficult to be successful when rotating through the world in search of hot countries or regions (even hedge fund managers find such strategies difficult to execute). You'll stack the odds of success more in your favor if you pick one or two favorites and stay with them for a while.

## INTERNATIONAL GROWTH FUND CHOICES

Following is a review of Fidelity's international choices. (Calendar-year performance is listed in Appendix A.) As with other equity fund groups, Fidelity reserves the right to block additional purchases after four trips in and out of the same fund in a 12-month period.

### Canada

Canada's objective is long-term capital growth; it invests primarily in common stocks of Canadian issuers. The fund was started in November 1987. Dividends and capital gains are paid out each year in December. The fund's 3 percent load is waived for retirement accounts. There is a redemption fee of 1.5 percent in the first 90 days.

Of all the single-country funds, Canada has the least currency risk because the U.S. dollar and the Canadian dollar have relatively high correlation (a natural result of proximity and the fact that the United States is Canada's largest trading partner).

Most of Canada's economy is based on natural resources, which makes this fund a good choice for a temporary bet on rising commodity prices. But Canada Fund lacks a necessary foundation of growth stocks, which in the long run could make for disappointing returns.

## Diversified International

Diversified International was started at the end of 1991 and seeks capital growth from investing primarily in countries that are included in the Morgan Stanley GDP-weighted EAFE index. Distributions are paid in December, and the fund is sold no-load.

Manager Greg Fraser has run the fund since inception at the end of 1991. Working with Brad Lewis, Fraser adapted the quantitative models used for Disciplined Equity and Stock Selector for use in this fund. Results have been mixed. Like Small Cap Selector, this may be one area where quantitative models have a tough time adding value.

If you are looking for a broad-based international fund, consider Spartan International Index.

## Emerging Markets

Emerging Markets started in November 1990 under the name International Opportunities. In early 1993 it was renamed Emerging Markets and began focusing specifically on developing countries. It seeks capital appreciation aggressively by investing in emerging markets, emphasizing countries whose GDP is relatively low compared to that of the world's major economies. Distributions can occur in December. The fund carries a 3 percent front-end load (currently waived for retirement accounts), and a redemption fee of 1.5 percent is charged on shares held for less than 90 days.

This fund is the most diversified of Fidelity's emerging market choices, but it hasn't always been that way. Heavy exposure to Malaysia in 1997 and an overweighted position in Latin America in 1998 resulted in unusually large losses. Only under current manager David Stewart (who took over in late 1997) has the fund made a serious effort to become more diversified both by country and by region.

By mid-2000 the regions of Latin America and Southeast Asia are likely to be on a solid path to long-term recovery. Whether stocks in these regions will reflect improving fundamentals remains to be seen, but you should still limit your stake to less than 15 percent of your portfolio.

### Europe Capital Appreciation

Europe Capital Appreciation was introduced at the end of 1993 and seeks long-term growth of capital from companies that have their principal activities in Eastern and Western Europe. Distributions occur in December. The fund carries a 3 percent front-end load (waived for retirement accounts) and charges a 1 percent redemption fee on shares held less than 90 days.

Originally this fund was slated to invest in the emerging markets of Europe, but today it looks a lot like Europe Fund. Longtime manager Kevin McCarey has done a reasonable job picking stocks but has trailed the Morgan Stanley Europe Index during his tenure. The fund holds about 30 percent of its assets in the United Kingdom, which (as of this writing) is not part of the common market.

This fund is suitable if you want exposure to Europe exclusively. Otherwise, consider Spartan International Index for broad-based international exposure.

### Europe Fund

Europe Fund is one of Fidelity's longer-running foreign funds, having started in October 1986. The fund seeks long-term growth of capital from companies that have their principal activities in Eastern and Western Europe. Dividends and capital gains are distributed each year in December. The fund carries a 3 percent front-end load (currently waived for retirement accounts), and a redemption fee of 1 percent is charged on shares held less than 90 days.

This fund is Fidelity's most successful foreign fund from the standpoint of long-term returns, but over its life it has lagged behind the Morgan Stanley Europe Index. Like Europe Capital Appreciation, this fund holds about 30 percent of its assets in the United Kingdom, which (as of this writing) is not part of the common market.

This fund is a reasonable choice if you want to invest only in Europe. Otherwise, consider Spartan International Index for broad-based exposure.

### France Fund

Introduced in November 1995, France Fund seeks long-term growth of capital by investing in equity securities of French issuers. Annual payouts can occur in December. The fund is sold with a 3 percent load (currently waived for retirement accounts), and there is a 1.5 percent redemption fee on shares held less than 90 days.

Like other European countries, France's economy has been constrained by high tax rates, too many government regulations, and an abundance of government-provided or government-mandated social services. To succeed in the common market, French companies must become more competitive with or without the help of government deregulation. Many have already shown a surprising ability to adapt.

This fund could make sense as a bet on the success of EMU, but otherwise you may want to consider a more diversified fund such as Europe Fund or Spartan International Index.

## Germany Fund

Germany Fund began in November 1995. Its objective is long-term growth of capital by investing in equity securities of German issuers. Annual payouts can occur in December. The fund carries a 3 percent load (waived for retirement accounts at this time), and there is a 1.5 percent redemption fee on shares held less than 90 days.

Germany's banks could be winners in the common market. Unlike other industries, banking firms aren't as negatively impacted by excessive regulation. Not surprisingly, Germany Fund has a heavy emphasis on financial services. Other German firms have escaped restrictive labor laws by moving their operations out of the country, giving them a head start in becoming global competitors.

This fund could also make sense as a bet on the success of EMU, but otherwise you may want to consider a more diversified fund such as Europe Fund or Spartan International Index.

## Global Balanced

Global Balanced was started in February 1993. The fund seeks high current income with preservation of capital, and it aims for broad diversification by investing in dividend stocks and bonds issued anywhere in the world. Dividends are paid annually in December. Payouts of capital gains can take place in September and December. The fund is sold no-load.

This fund invests around 50 percent in foreign markets, with the balance in domestic securities. Bond holdings usually account for 25 to 30 percent of assets.

Global Balanced has the potential for good performance when conditions are favorable in foreign markets, but it can also lag when things go the wrong way. Unless you prefer the international diversification, consider Balanced fund (discussed in Chapter 6). The domestic approach might offer slightly higher long-term returns.

## Hong Kong and China

Introduced in November 1995, Hong Kong and China seeks long-term growth of capital by investing mainly in equity securities of Hong Kong and Chinese issuers. Distributions can occur in December. There is a 3 percent load (currently waived for retirement accounts), and a 1.5 percent redemption fee applies on shares held less than 90 days.

Almost all of this fund's assets are currently invested in Hong Kong, owing to the liquidity problems and foreign restrictions of China's small stock exchange. That means a sizable investment in real-estate firms, which make up a substantial portion of Hong Kong's market.

It would seem that an economy that revolves around real estate and distributors would be under pressure from global deflationary forces. Then again, Hong Kong remains the gatekeeper for most of the goods that flow in and out of China. And someday, China's stock market will open up to foreigners, which could present some opportunities.

As emerging market funds go, this one is not very diversified. I don't recommend investing more than 5 percent of your portfolio. Southeast Asia offers a broader base of emerging market stocks

## International Growth & Income

One of Fidelity's longer-running funds, International Growth & Income was introduced at the end of 1986. The fund's objective is capital growth and current income consistent with reasonable investment risk. Dividends and capital gains can be paid out in December. The fund is sold with no load.

This fund has relatively little exposure to the domestic market. Under a recent charter change, it now invests mainly in stocks. The idea is to mirror the strategy behind Growth & Income fund (see Chapter 6) in the foreign markets.

The new strategy may prove to be a solid long-term approach, but until that's clear I think investors should stick with Spartan International Index.

## International Value

Introduced in November 1994, this fund seeks long-term growth of capital by investing in stocks of foreign companies believed to be undervalued in the marketplace. Distributions can occur annually in December. The fund is sold no-load.

International Value is managed by Rick Mace, who also runs Overseas and Global Balanced. With the exception of a three-month lag during the 1998 sell-off, Mace has done well with this fund. He is willing to bet on the stocks that he believes in, even if it means a significant deviation from EAFE index. So far his bets have been right more often than wrong.

With Mace at the helm, this fund has a reasonable shot at outperforming the EAFE index over the long run. However, it may be a bit more volatile than Fidelity's other diversified international funds.

## Japan Fund

Japan Fund was started in September 1992, and it seeks long-term capital growth by investing primarily in stocks of Japanese issuers. Payouts for the fund usually occur in December; it carries a 3 percent load and a 1.5 percent redemption fee for the first 90 days. The load is currently waived on retirement accounts.

The Japanese economic contraction appears to be over. After eight years of falling stock prices and a near-collapse of its financial system, the Japanese government and its private sector are reluctantly allowing American-style financial reforms to take hold. Depending on the rate at which these reforms are adopted and the degree of monetary and economic stimulus, the Japanese stock market could begin a long, slow recovery that lasts many years, or it could quickly make up for lost time. With American and European firms now being allowed to acquire Japanese companies (or their assets), it seems very unlikely that Japan's stock market will ever get any cheaper than it was in mid-1998.

The value of the yen continues to be a key driver of the Japanese economy, since it determines the worldwide competitiveness of the nation's factories. Over time this may become less of an issue as globalization takes hold, with foreign companies owning more Japanese assets and Japanese firms owning more factories in Europe and North America.

Japan is the one place where Fidelity seems to be doing well with its foreign research. In recent years this fund has strongly outperformed the Tokyo Stock Exchange Index.

## Japan Small Companies

Japan Small Companies began in November 1995, and it seeks long-term capital growth by investing mainly in equity securities of Japanese companies with a market cap of 100 billion yen or less at the time of investment. Distributions occur in December, and the load structure of this fund is identical to Japan Fund.

Many of my observations about Japan Fund hold true for this fund as well. Although this fund may not perform as well as Japan Fund in the long run, it stands to benefit more from the country's heavy-handed economic and monetary stimulus programs. It should also perform better during periods in which the yen appreciates against other world currencies, a result of having fewer export companies in its portfolio.

Fidelity's research efforts are paying off in this segment of the Japanese market as well. In recent years Japan Small Companies has strongly outperformed Tokyo Stock Exchange (2nd section) Index.

## Latin America

This fund was started in April 1993 and seeks high total investment return. The fund invests primarily in stocks of Latin American issuers, which include Argentina, Brazil, Chile, Colombia, Ecuador, Mexico, Panama, Peru, and Venezuela. The fund carries a 3 percent load (currently waived for retirement accounts), and there is a 1.5 percent redemption fee on shares held less than 90 days. Distributions typically occur in December.

This fund has been through a rocky period over the last six years, as Mexico devalued in 1995 and Brazil was forced off its link to the U.S. dollar in early 1999. By midyear 2000, most of the damage from Brazil's austerity measures should be water under the bridge. The stage could then be set for a longer-lasting period of stability and growth.

Still, the risks of investing in this region will remain high. There may be periods of strong growth, but there will also be sharp sell-offs. As an emerging market, Latin America is one of the more volatile regions. If you invest in this fund, consider limiting it to less than 10 percent of your portfolio.

## Nordic

Introduced in November 1995, Nordic seeks long-term growth of capital by investing mainly in stocks of issuers in Denmark, Finland, Norway, and Sweden. Distributions can occur in December. There is a 3 percent load (currently waived for retirement accounts), and a 1.5 percent redemption fee applies on shares held less than 90 days.

The companies in this region are generally further along in adopting American-style incentives for rewarding shareholders. Fidelity has managed to outperform its benchmark with this fund.

The only problem is that Nokia and Ericsson account for about 25 percent of the Nordic market capitalization, and they carry a similar weighting in Nordic fund. Being more growth-oriented may be a good thing, but having such a heavy weighting in two stocks could be a problem if either company stumbles in the world market.

If you invest, keep in mind that Nordic fund carries risks that are comparable to a sector fund.

## Overseas

Introduced in December 1984, Overseas was Fidelity's first international fund. Its objective is long-term capital appreciation from investing stocks of issuers whose principal activities are outside of the United States. Payouts are made in December. The fund is sold no-load.

Overseas is managed by Rick Mace, who also runs International Value and Global Balanced. Overseas is significantly more diversified than International Value. Mace has generally outperformed more often than not with this fund, but he was set back by a three-month sell-off in 1998.

With Mace running the show, this fund could modestly outperform the EAFE index over the long run. Still, an argument can be made for simply matching the EAFE index through Spartan International Index, especially if Fidelity continues to cap Spartan International's expenses at the current 0.35 percent level.

## Pacific Basin

Pacific Basin started in October 1986. The fund aims for long-term growth of capital, investing primarily in common stocks of Pacific Basin issuers. Countries within the fund's charter include Australia, Hong Kong, Indonesia, Japan, South Korea, Malaysia, New Zealand, China, the Philippines, Singapore, Taiwan, and Thailand. Distributions can occur in December. The fund has a 3 percent load, and a redemption fee of 1 percent applies to purchases of less than 90 days.

Because this fund competes with the Morgan Stanley Pacific Index, around 75 percent of Pacific Basin's assets tend to be invested in Japanese stocks. As such, the comments for Japan Fund apply here as well.

I see no reason to favor this fund over Japan Fund, as I have doubts that diversifying into Australia, Hong Kong, and other Pacific Rim countries will enhance long-term returns or reduce risk in any meaningful way.

### Southeast Asia

Started in April 1993, Southeast Asia seeks long-term growth of capital by investing in common stocks of Southeast Asian issuers. This includes Hong Kong, Indonesia, South Korea, Malaysia, the Philippines, China, Singapore, Taiwan, and Thailand. Developed countries such as Japan, Australia, and New Zealand are generally not included. Dividends and capital gains are typically paid out in December. A 3 percent front-end load applies (it's currently waived for retirement accounts), and a redemption fee of 1.5 percent is charged on shares held less than 90 days.

As an emerging-market fund, Southeast Asia is more diversified than Hong Kong and China but more narrowly defined than Emerging Markets. This particular region was hit hard by the currency crisis in late 1997. By mid-2000 many of these countries will probably be on a solid path to recovery, but a lot depends on how quickly Japan recovers and how well China deals with problems at its state-run institutions.

As an emerging market, Southeast Asia is less risky than Latin America but remains far more volatile than the EAFE index. If you invest in this fund, consider limiting it to less than 10 percent of your portfolio.

### Spartan International Index

Spartan International Index was introduced near the end of 1997. Its objective is to track the EAFE index, a benchmark that includes most large stocks in the major markets of the world. The fund is sold no-load, but there is a 1 percent redemption fee on shares held less than 90 days. The minimum investment is $15,000, and there is also a $10 annual fee for account balances of less than $10,000. As of this writing, Fidelity is capping annual expenses at 0.35 percent.

With its current expense cap, Spartan International Index is almost a full percentage point ahead of most other diversified international funds. Furthermore, its low turnover minimizes trading expenses (trading costs are not included in the expense ratio, but the drag on performance can be significant in a foreign fund).

Unless you want to target a specific country or region, this fund may be your best bet for gaining international exposure in a Fidelity portfolio.

## United Kingdom

Fidelity's original United Kingdom fund was introduced in November 1987 and merged into Europe Fund in 1989. Today's United Kingdom fund was introduced in November 1995. The fund seeks long-term growth of capital by investing mainly in equity securities of British issuers. Distributions can occur in December. There is a 3 percent load (currently waived for retirement accounts), and a 1.5 percent redemption fee applies to shares held less than 90 days.

So far, this fund hasn't caught investor interest any more than it did the first time around. Its asset base is a tiny $6.5 million at the end of 1998—the smallest fund in this group. It's a good thing expenses are still being capped at around 2 percent.

The United Kingdom has elected to take a rain check on EMU, which could be a good strategy. If the EMU countries end up struggling with slow economic growth, Britain can stay outside the fray, cutting interest rates to keep its own economy humming along. If EMU revs up economic growth, the country can become a member and enjoy access to lower interest rates. Because Britain's economy is larger than those of other EMU countries, it is unlikely to be turned away if it meets budgetary requirements.

Nevertheless, investors may be better off in Europe Fund or Europe Capital Appreciation. Both of these funds keep around 30 percent in British firms but are free to invest their remaining assets in other regions of Europe. Over the long run this could translate into higher returns.

## Worldwide

Worldwide was started in May 1990, and it seeks growth of capital by investing in securities issued anywhere in the world. The fund invests primarily in common stocks issued by companies of all sizes in all parts of the world. The fund competes with the Morgan Stanley World Index. Distributions occur in December, and the fund is sold no-load.

Penny Dobkin, the fund's manager since inception, has maintained a highly diversified portfolio and has often focused on value stocks. In the past, she has even taken on large cash positions. Worldwide's weighting in U.S. stocks has grown to roughly one-half of the portfolio as of late-1998. However, performance has trailed the Morgan Stanley World Index because Dobkin's value-oriented approach has been out of sync with today's growth-oriented markets.

Dobkin boosted Worldwide's exposure to growth stocks in 1998, so it's possible that this fund could post better results in future years. If you don't want to take that chance, you can obtain global diversification by investing 50 percent in Spartan International Index and 50 percent in Spartan Total Market Index (see Chapter 4).

# 6

# Growth and Income Funds

Compared to growth funds, growth and income funds seek growth in moderation. A higher percentage of their holdings are dedicated to income-producing securities, which are more stable and tend to reduce overall risk. The resulting lower level of volatility means that growth and income funds, on average, do not suffer as much in a down market.

The trade-off is that growth and income funds generally grow at a slower rate than their growth-oriented cousins. Historically, the long-term difference between growth funds and growth and income funds has ranged from one to three percentage points per year. But that figure could widen as a result of deflation and globalization.

When choosing a growth and income fund, you don't have to worry as much about being in the right fund. There is less variation in long-term performance in this group because of the greater focus on income-producing securities. Fund manager ability, while still important, is not going to make or break a growth and income fund the way it can for a growth fund.

The way this group achieves income depends on the type of fund. Stock-oriented and equity-income funds generate income by emphasizing dividend stocks. Balanced funds earn income by investing in bonds as well as dividend stocks. Asset allocation funds earn current income by devoting a portion of their portfolios to cash and bond positions.

Most of Fidelity's growth and income funds have quarterly dividend payouts in addition to their annual distributions of capital gains. Investors often set up their accounts to reinvest this income, but some retirees use it to help cover living expenses. Although the yield is not large (1 to 3 percent is typical), the amount of income obtained should increase as long-term gains in share price raise the value of the investment. Some investors view a growth and income fund as an income source that grows at a faster rate than inflation when distributions of capital gains are reinvested.

More often, however, investors choose a growth and income fund simply because it's more conservative than a stock fund. With reinvested distributions, the long-term growth rate of most funds in this group is likely to range from 7 to 10 percent per year.

## GROWTH AND INCOME FUND CHOICES

Following is a fund-by-fund review of Fidelity's growth and income and asset allocation funds. For all funds in this category, Fidelity reserves the right to block additional purchases after four trips in and out of the same fund in a 12-month period. For calendar-year performance, see Appendix A. For suggested portfolios of growth and income funds, see Chapter 10.

### Asset Manager

Asset Manager was started at the end of 1988, and it seeks high total return with reduced risk by allocating assets among stocks, bonds, and short-term instruments of U.S. and foreign issuers. Dividends are paid quarterly in March, June, September, and December. Capital gains are usually distributed in December. The fund is sold no-load.

This fund has a neutral mix of 50 percent stocks, 40 percent bonds, and 10 percent short-term. (Bonds with less than a three-year maturity are considered "short-term," as are cash-type holdings.) Asset Manager has limits for each of these asset classes as well as for foreign holdings: stocks must be in the range of 30 to 70 percent of holdings; bonds must be 20 to 60 percent of assets; and short-term securities may be up to 50 percent of the fund.

Fidelity implemented a team approach for this fund when it replaced manager Bob Beckwitt. Stockpicking is currently the responsibility of Tom Sprague. The asset allocation mix is the job of Dick Habermann. Charles Morrison selects income holdings. Under this team, Asset Manager resembles a more traditional growth and income fund and is not likely to experience unusually good or bad years, as it did under Bob Beckwitt.

Compared with similar risk funds like Puritan and Balanced, Asset Manager has slightly more emphasis on growth stocks and a higher weighting in cash. It's a solid choice for investors who prefer a conservative approach, and it seems capable of a long-term growth rate in excess of 10 percent per year.

## Asset Manager: Growth

Introduced on the coattails of Asset Manager's success, Asset Manager: Growth was introduced at the end of 1991. It offers a more aggressive approach to asset allocation. Its objective is maximum total return over the long run by allocating assets among stocks, bonds, and short-term instruments of U.S. and foreign issuers. Dividends and capital gains are usually paid out once a year, in December. The fund is sold no-load.

This fund is run by the same team that leads Asset Manager, except that Brad Lewis is in charge of stock selection. Asset Manager: Growth has a neutral mix of 70 percent stocks, 25 percent bonds, and 5 percent short-term. The range for stock holdings is 50 to 100 percent. For bonds it is 0 to 50 percent, and for short-term investments it is also 0 to 50 percent.

Asset Manager: Growth generally plays the value side of the large-cap universe, and its income holdings provide a modest cushion that helps to reduce risk in a sell-off. It's a good choice for investors who want long-term growth without taking on as much risk as the S&P 500.

## Asset Manager: Income

Introduced in October 1992, this fund was the last of the Asset Manager trio. Asset Manager: Income seeks a high level of current income by allocating its assets among stocks, bonds, and short-term instruments of U.S. and foreign issuers. Dividends are paid out monthly, but usually January is skipped. Unlike bond funds, all income earned is reflected in the share price until the monthly distribution date. The fund pays out capital gains in December. There is no load.

The most conservative fund in Fidelity's growth and income group, this fund has slightly more risk than that of an intermediate bond fund. Run by the same team that manages Asset Manager: Growth, Asset Manager: Income has a neutral mix of 20 percent stocks, 50 percent bonds, and 30 percent short-term. Stock holdings can range from 10 to 30 percent, bonds can be 40 to 60 percent of assets, and short-term instruments can range from 10 to 50 percent of the portfolio.

This portfolio is heavy in cash and bonds, but a small weighting in growth stocks helps boost performance. Over the last five years, Asset Manager: Income has significantly outperformed most bond funds while taking on just slightly more risk. The fund's income stream is not as high as those of most bond funds, but the difference should be made up in share price appreciation. For investors who are uncomfortable with losses, Asset Manager: Income is an excellent choice.

## Balanced

Launched in November 1986, Balanced seeks high income with preservation of capital. The fund invests in a broadly diversified portfolio of high-yielding securities, including common stocks, preferred stocks, and bonds. Dividend payouts occur in March, June, September, and December; distribution of capital gains usually takes place in September and December. There is no load.

Balanced usually holds a mix of roughly 35 percent bonds and 65 percent value stocks. Foreign stocks no longer play much of a role in this fund, but current manager Stephen DuFour has managed to boost performance by allocating about 15 percent of the fund to growth stocks that pay dividends.

Balanced is a good choice for investors who want a conservative approach to growth. With just 60 percent of the S&P 500's risk, Balanced is likely to hold up better than stock-oriented funds in a sell-off. Yet over the long run it seems capable of delivering returns in excess of 10 percent per year.

## Convertible Securities

Convertible Securities was started in January 1987. It seeks a high level of total return through a combination of current income and long-term capital appreciation. The fund normally invests at least 65 percent in convertible securities. Dividends occur in March, June, September, and December. Capital gains can occur in January and December. The fund does not charge a load.

The convertible securities market is somewhat of a hybrid that bears some resemblance to both the stock market and the high-yield bond market. After slipping a bit during the 1995–97 period, this fund seems back on track under manager David Felman. Convertible Securities carries about 80 percent of the S&P 500's risk and can be expected to follow whenever the stock market makes a major move up or down.

Although this fund would not be considered a core holding by most growth and income investors, it may be worth considering. Fidelity's research commitment is significant in this segment of the market, and Convertible Securities is capable of providing an attractive return for its risk level.

## Equity-Income

Equity-Income was started in May 1966. It aims for reasonable income by investing in income-producing stocks. The fund seeks a yield that exceeds that of the S&P 500. Capital appreciation is a secondary objective. Dividends are paid in March, June, September, and December. Capital gains can occur in March and December. The fund is sold no-load.

As evidenced by this fund's lifetime return of 15.7 percent annually, Fidelity's equity-income strategy is one that has stood the test of time. This fund has had a string of successful managers, including Bruce Johnstone, Beth Terrana, and present manager Stephen Petersen (who has run the fund since August 1993).

Nevertheless, today's market is changing in response to deflationary pressures. Traditional value stocks are being marked down as investors allocate more of their portfolio toward growth stocks. And dividends seem less desirable with a tax code that favors stock buybacks and long-term capital gains.

About 25 percent of Equity-Income's portfolio consists of old economy stocks in the energy, commodity, and industrial sectors. Because many of these companies will not be able to grow their earnings in a deflationary environment, there is some risk that Equity-Income's performance will be held back relative to the S&P 500. But as value funds go, Equity-Income has the best shot at success owing to its large-cap focus.

## Equity-Income II

Equity-Income II began in August 1990. The fund seeks income that exceeds the S&P 500 yield by investing primarily in income-producing stocks while considering the potential for capital appreciation. Dividends are paid out in March, June, September, and December. Capital gains usually occur in January and December. There is no load.

Like Equity-Income, this fund invests mainly in large-cap stocks. Unlike Equity-Income, growth stocks usually account for more then 25 percent of assets. The difference is Equity-Income II's yield guideline, which isn't as rigid compared with Equity-Income. The added flexibility allows manager Bettina Doulton to bias this fund a bit more toward long-term growth.

This fund is a solid choice for the equity portion of a growth and income portfolio. However, if your goal is to exceed the S&P 500, you'll probably need to take on more risk.

## Fidelity Fund

The original Fidelity Fund got its start back in April 1930. Its current objective is to achieve long-term capital growth with current income by investing in common stocks and convertibles. Dividends are distributed in March, June, September, and December. Capital gains are typically paid out in August and December. It is sold with no load.

Fidelity Fund has exceeded the S&P 500 over the last 66 years, providing an annual return of 10.7 percent versus 9.9 percent for the index. The fund seemed to be slipping in the 1980s and early 1990s, but under Beth Terrana it has been a strong performer since she assumed responsibilities in mid-1993.

With a broad base of blue-chip stocks and a balanced industry mix, Fidelity Fund is likely to maintain a risk level similar to that of the S&P 500. And with Terrana picking the stocks, there's a reasonable chance that Fidelity Fund will stay ahead of the S&P 500 in future years.

## Freedom Funds

Fidelity's Freedom funds are actually funds of funds. Each fund invests in 10 to 20 other Fidelity funds, using an asset allocation model that picks an appropriate mix based on the year that retirement is anticipated. The mix is adjusted to become a bit more conservative each year. The funds do not mature when the actual date is reached; rather they revert to a conservative income-oriented approach deemed appropriate for investors who are living off their investments.

The current group of funds includes Freedom 2000, Freedom 2010, Freedom 2020, Freedom 2030, and Freedom Income, which is designed for investors who are in retirement. Each fund charges a low 0.1 percent expense ratio because investors are already paying the underlying expense ratios of the funds that are held in the portfolios. Dividends and capital gains are usually paid in December, except for Freedom Income, which makes a dividend payout monthly. The funds are sold with no load, and there is no redemption fee if you decide not to go the full term.

As of this writing, the benchmark for Freedom 2030 is 70 percent Wilshire 5000, 15 percent EAFE, 6 percent domestic bond, and 9 percent domestic high-yield bond. Freedom 2020 is currently measured against 68 percent Wilshire 5000, 12 percent EAFE, 13 percent domestic bond, and 7 percent domestic high-yield bond. Freedom 2010 is benchmarked against 55 percent Wilshire 5000, 9 percent EAFE, 27 percent domestic bond, 7 percent domestic high-yield bond, and 2 percent cash. Freedom 2000 aims at 37 percent Wilshire 5000, 4 percent EAFE, 40 percent domestic bond, 4 percent domestic high-yield bond, and 15 percent cash. Freedom Income tries to exceed a mix of 20 percent Wilshire 5000, 40 percent domestic bond, and 40 percent cash.

These funds are convenient for investors who prefer to buy one broadly diversified investment pool and leave the ongoing management up to Fidelity. The overall fees are modest, and the "no-surprises" approach should provide respectable returns.

## Growth & Income

Growth & Income was started at the end of 1985. It seeks high total return through a combination of current income and capital appreciation. The fund invests mainly in stocks of companies that pay current dividends and that offer potential growth of earnings. Dividends are paid in March, June, September, and December. Capital gains can be distributed in September and December. There is no load. The fund is currently closed to new retail accounts, but remains available in many 401(k) programs.

Like Fidelity Fund, this fund is one of the more aggressive in the group. It owes its attractive long-term performance to a string of strong managers, including Beth Terrana, Jeff Vinik, and current manager Steven Kaye. Despite the fund's title, there has never been much of an income focus with this fund. As of mid-1996, bond holdings are near zero and the dividend yield on stock holding is around 1 percent.

With Kaye's growth-oriented style, there's a reasonable chance that this fund will outperform the S&P 500 over the long run. If you are looking for an alternative fund that is not closed, consider Fidelity Fund.

## Growth & Income II

Introduced in early 1999, this fund's charter is the same as Growth & Income. Dividends are paid in March, June, September, and December. Capital gains are likely be distributed in August and December. There is no load.

Fidelity introduced this fund as an alternative for investors who were locked out of Growth & Income when it closed in 1998. Although its objective is the same, it has a different manager: Louis Salemy.

This fund's smaller size could turn out to be an advantage, but until Salemy establishes a track record it probably makes sense to go with Fidelity Fund (led by manager Beth Terrana).

## Puritan

Puritan was started in April 1947. It seeks high income consistent with preservation of capital. It invests in a broadly diversified portfolio of high-yielding stocks and bonds. Dividends are paid in March, June, September, and December. Capital gains are usually paid out in September and December. The fund has no load.

Puritan has invested in a conservative mix of stocks and bonds for over 50 years, and it has provided a 12.6 percent annualized return since inception. The fund generally holds around 65 percent in stocks and 35 percent in bonds. Bettina Doulton has been in charge of stockpicking since early 1996 and has posted solid returns with about 60 percent as much risk as the S&P 500.

Puritan is a good choice for investors who prefer a conservative approach to growth. Like Asset Manager and Balanced, it should hold up better than stock-oriented funds in a sell-off. And over the long run it seems capable of delivering a long-term return in excess of 10 percent per year.

## Real Estate

Real Estate's inception was in November 1986. The fund seeks above-average income and long-term capital growth. It invests mainly in equity REITs (Real Estate Investment Trusts), both domestic and foreign. Dividends occur in March, June, September, and December. Capital gains can occur in March and December. The fund does not carry a front-end load, but there is a 0.75 percent redemption fee on shares held less than 90 days.

Classified as a growth and income fund because of its income stream, this fund actually behaves more like a conservative sector fund. The loss of a key tax break and recent deflationary fears resulted in significant losses in 1998. In years past, the current situation might be interpreted as a buying opportunity. This time may be different.

As the internet reshapes the domestic economy, rates of appreciation in commercial real estate could go flat in the coming years. On-line shopping and an increasing number of employees that work out of their home could reduce demand for both retail and office space. Competition in the hotel industry could erode margins and reduce the value of existing properties. Rising productivity and higher wages could mean more home owners and fewer apartment dwellers.

Because of the negative implications of the growing deflationary trends in the economy, this fund may not make sense for most growth and income investors. If you invest, consider limiting your position to less than 10 percent of your portfolio.

### Utilities Fund

Utilities Fund (previously known as Utilities Income) was started in November 1987. The fund seeks high total return through a combination of current income and capital appreciation. The fund normally invests 65 percent of total assets in utility stocks. Dividends are paid out in March, June, September, and December. Distributions of capital gains can occur in March and December. There is no load.

This is not your father's utility fund. Fidelity is investing mainly for growth in the telecommunications industry. The main focus is local and long-distance telephone companies, but recent holdings even included a modest stake in cable companies.

As a result, Utilities Fund is now looking more like a conservative sector fund as opposed to a defensive high-yield stock fund. That may be a good thing from a total return standpoint, but in a down market this fund will probably decline almost as much as the S&P 500.

If you are looking for a no-load fund that invests in telecom stocks, this fund is a solid bet. If you are looking for a conservative growth and income fund that will hold up well in a sell-off, consider Asset Manager, Balanced, or Puritan.

# 7

# *Bond Funds*

Most bond funds provide little or no capital appreciation over the long run. Instead, they focus on providing a monthly income stream. Over time, their total return is determined primarily by the accumulation of monthly dividends. Bond funds are generally considered to be a conservative investment, but they are far from risk-free. An intermediate-term bond fund has roughly 30 to 40 percent of the volatility inherent in the S&P 500. While a growth fund might fall 25 percent from its peak in a major sell-off for stocks, an intermediate-term bond fund might decline 10 percent in a similarly negative period for bonds.

Whereas corporate earnings are the dominant factor for stock valuations, bond funds are affected mainly by interest rates and inflation expectations. If interest rates are moving down, bond funds will usually rise in value. Conversely, if interest rates are edging up, you can expect a loss in principal.

## SHORT-TERM VERSUS LONG-TERM INTEREST RATES

Changes in the yield curve (a plot of interest rates versus maturity) can affect different bond funds in different ways. The Federal Reserve more or less controls short-term interest rates, whereas long-term rates are set by supply-and-demand forces. When the Fed is trying to promote economic expansion, it will reduce short-term rates, increasing the spread between short-term and long-term rates; when the Fed is trying to fight inflation or slow the economy, it will raise short-term rates, which can cause the yield curve to become flat or even inverted. A short-term fund will be more affected by what the Fed does, but intermediate- and long-term funds are affected more by market forces. Suppose the Fed raises short-term rates to fight inflation. Long-term rates may increase as well if inflation concerns remain, but they can decline if the Fed's actions result in an economic slowdown (when expansion-related credit demand declines, it usually causes long-term rates to fall). In the latter situation, long-term bond funds can actually benefit from a rate hike on the short end.

## INTEREST RATE SENSITIVITY

In general, the degree of interest-rate risk in a bond fund increases with the fund's weighted-average maturity (usually referred to as average maturity). Thus, a fund with a three-year average maturity will usually fluctuate very little, whereas a 20-year fund can be many times as risky.

A more exact measure of a fund's interest rate risk is duration. A fund's duration tells you how much it would gain or lose in value for a one percentage point "across-the-board" change in interest rates, assuming that other factors such as credit risk remain constant. For example, a fund with a duration of 5 would experience a 5 percent increase in principal if interest rates declined one percentage point, or it would lose 5 percent if rates went up one percentage point. Fidelity calculates both average maturity and duration figures for most of its funds.

## CREDIT RISK AND EXCHANGE-RATE RISK

Credit risk, or risk of default, is another factor that can affect some types of bond funds. In U.S. government bond funds, this risk factor is usually negligible because the government has the power to raise taxes to meet obligations. Bond funds that invest in corporate debt carry some elements of credit risk, but most are diversified enough that a default by a single bond issuer would have only a minor impact on the fund. Once in a while a slowdown in the entire economy will cause investment-grade funds to lag slightly behind government funds, but interest rates are still the dominant risk factor. In the junk bond universe, a diversified fund is routinely impacted by credit risk perceptions. If the economy starts to slow, the junk bond market usually declines as investors anticipate a higher default rate. If the economy is getting stronger, junk bonds can rally (provided interest rates are not on the rise). The same effects can occur in emerging-market bond funds, where entire countries can be perceived as improving or deteriorating credit risks.

Exchange-rate risk, or currency risk, is a third factor that can affect bond funds that include foreign investments. Unless these positions are denominated in dollars (or hedged), they will fluctuate with exchange rates, resulting in price swings that can be greater than fluctuations caused by interest rates or credit-risk perceptions. Even if the fund is hedged, meaning that it purchases currency-forward contracts to offset the exchange rate fluctuations, it can still lose out over time because the cost of hedging reduces the fund's income stream.

## YIELD

A bond fund's 30-day yield, which is calculated based on the SEC's definition of yield-to-maturity, is usually a reasonable indicator of what a bond fund is capable of earning when interest rates are flat. The 30-day yield is recalculated each day because it fluctuates with market conditions. Usually it goes up when a fund's net asset value (principal) declines, and it goes down when a fund gains value from falling interest rates. A bond fund's actual income stream can be higher or lower than its 30-day SEC yield. The actual income stream (sometimes called the dividend yield or the distribution rate) can be higher or lower than the 30-day yield figure if the fund holds bonds that were purchased at premium or discounted prices. A fund's income stream can also lag behind its stated yield if the fund engages in hedging activity on its foreign holdings. New Markets Income has gone through periods where its SEC yield was two to three percentage points higher than the actual dividends paid out.

Bond funds usually don't reflect the accumulation of regular income in their share price, but it is tracked daily and posted once a month based on the fund's net income. The dollar amount of the dividend can be figured by multiplying the fund's monthly mil rate (a figure Fidelity calculates) by the number of shares in the account. When buying or selling in mid-month, bond fund shareholders receive a partial month of income based on what has accumulated when you leave the fund. The accumulation of income is based on the daily mil rates, which are figured for each day of the year. The only time you ever lose out on any bond fund income is when you buy a Spartan fund on a Friday. In this particular case, you don't start accruing income until the following Monday.

## TAXABLE VERSUS MUNICIPAL

One of the first decisions you should make before buying a bond fund is whether to go with a taxable fund or a municipal fund. The income stream from a taxable fund is usually higher but is taxed along with your other income sources, whereas the income from a municipal fund is lower but is not taxed in most cases (although distributed capital gains and gains or losses from the sale of a muni fund are taxable events).

Generally speaking, regular taxable bond funds will offer a higher after-tax income stream if your federal tax bracket is below 36 percent. Nobody likes to pay taxes, but from a rational point of view it is best to go with the choice that will maximize your after-tax income.

Municipal funds avoid tax on their income stream, but the gain or loss in share price is taxed just like a regular fund (as are distributions of capital gains). In general, investors with a federal tax bracket of 36 percent or higher will realize a higher after-tax return with a muni fund. If you are subject to Alternative Minimum Tax (AMT), you may owe tax on some of the income stream, depending on how much AMT paper the fund holds. Most of Fidelity's municipal bond funds hold less than 10 percent AMT paper, but some of its municipal money market funds have large AMT positions.

With the exception of Spartan Short-Intermediate Muni, all of Fidelity's municipal funds take on a significant amount of interest-rate risk. Most have a duration of between 6 and 8, meaning that a one percentage point increase in interest rates can wipe out more than a year's worth of income. For that reason, I recommend a minimum investment horizon of three years. Over that period of time, the income stream usually dominates over fluctuations in principal. If you'll be needing your money in less than three years, play it safe and go with Spartan Short-Intermediate Muni.

If you want to make an apples-to-apples yield comparison between a taxable fund and a municipal fund, first pick two funds with similar maturities. If you are considering Spartan Short-Intermediate Muni, compare it to Short-Term Bond. If you are looking at an intermediate- or limited-term muni fund, benchmark it to Investment Grade Bond.

Next, compare the yield of the muni fund to the taxable fund by computing a "taxable equivalent yield." The equation is:

**Tax-Free Yield ÷ [(1 − Fed Bracket) × (1 − State Bracket)] = Taxable Equivalent Yield**

Fed Bracket is your federal tax bracket in decimal form, and State Bracket is your state tax bracket in decimal form. (Use 0 for State Bracket if you are not evaluating a state-specific fund.) The formula takes into account the fact that state taxes are deductible at the federal level; that's why the federal and state brackets aren't simply added together. An example follows:

### Frank

Frank has a federal tax rate of 28 percent and is trying to decide between Short-Term Bond (a taxable fund) and Spartan Short-Intermediate Muni. His taxable equivalent yield for Spartan Short-Intermediate Muni is:

$$4.06\% \div [(1 - 0.28) \times (1 - 0)] = 5.64\%$$

Because Short-Term Bond is yielding 5.94 percent, Frank will probably realize more after-tax income by staying on the taxable side.

The remote possibility exists that a change in the tax code may someday grant taxable bonds the same tax-free status that municipal bonds now enjoy. If the playing field is ever leveled, most municipal funds would face a one-time lag of 10 to 15 percentage points relative to taxable funds. It would be like losing two years of tax-free income.

### TAXABLE BOND FUND CHOICES

In early 1995 many domestic funds in this group adopted restrictions on foreign holdings and began to maintain a stable duration. As a result, these funds are unlikely to see a repeat of the poor performance that occurred in 1994.

Following is a recap of Fidelity's taxable bond fund choices. Except where noted, dividends are declared daily and paid out monthly. All of these funds are sold no-load. Those that have redemption fees are noted in the discussion.

For all funds in this group, Fidelity reserves the right to block additional purchases after four trips in and out of the same fund over a 12-month period. Calendar-year performance is listed in Appendix A. For suggested bond fund portfolios, see Chapter 10.

## Capital & Income

Originally known as High Income when it started in November 1977, Capital & Income seeks to provide a combination of income and capital growth, focusing on low-quality debt and common and preferred stocks. Capital gains and excise dividend distributions can occur in June and December. The fund carries a 1.5 percent redemption fee on shares held for less than 365 days.

About 75 percent of Capital & Income is run like a traditional high-yield bond fund, and Fidelity draws on more than 20 years of experience in the junk bond universe. Its analysts often figure out which companies are getting healthier before the rest of the market does. In 1992, Capital & Income and High Income loaded up on Chrysler debt when it was still classified as junk, because Fidelity analysts were confident from discussions with Chrysler execs that the company was going to survive the recession. Both funds benefited from the high yield on Chrysler bonds and also realized a nice capital gain when the rating agencies upgraded Chrysler many months later. Time and again fund managers have played this game, almost always to the benefit of Capital & Income and High-Income shareholders.

Up to 25 percent of Capital & Income can invest in the stocks or bonds of distressed firms, usually companies with a heavy debt load. For about five years Fidelity had an entire "vulture investing" team that would buy up a majority stake in a distressed bond issue, then meet with the company's management to do a deal. It worked well for three years, but after some unexpected complications with two deals (Macy's and El Paso Electric), Fidelity decided to abandon the vulture investing approach. Manager David Glancy now focuses mainly on high-yield stocks and convertibles for this portion of the fund.

The junk bond market is very sensitive to the economic cycle. Although high-yield bonds perform well when economic growth is strong, these securities can perform poorly if signs of a slowdown emerge. Usually the yield premium on junk bonds (compared to government bonds) is about three to four percentage points, but at the onset of a recession it can go significantly higher as junk bonds decline in value.

Since inception, Capital & Income has returned 12 percent per year with about half of the S&P 500's risk. Fidelity's ability to assess risk has made its junk bond funds among the industry's best long-term performers. Compared with High Income fund (discussed later), Capital & Income is slightly more aggressive and has a higher redemption fee.

## Ginnie Mae

Ginnie Mae seeks high current income and invests primarily in mortgage-related securities issued by the Government National Mortgage Association. The fund began in November 1985; distribution of capital gains can occur in September and December.

Like other funds that deal in mortgage securities, this fund typically earns a higher yield than a broad-based government securities fund. However, mortgage funds usually lag behind traditional bond funds when interest rates decline—an effect that occurs because borrowers can pay off their old mortgages early and refinance at lower rates. With stable or rising interest rates, however, these types of funds tend to perform relatively well.

## Government Income

Government Income seeks high current income free from state and local taxes; it invests only in U.S. government securities and instruments related to government securities. Capital gains are usually paid in December. Most states allow you to avoid state and local income tax on the portion of income generated from U.S. Treasury holdings, but you still have to pay federal income tax on the full income stream.

Government Income has essentially no credit risk, but it is one of Fidelity's more interest rate–sensitive funds. With a duration that is usually close to 5, the fund can gain or lose 5 percent with a one percentage point change in interest rates. Over the long run, this fund is likely to provide a total return that's higher than Intermediate Government Income but less than Investment Grade Bond. If you can meet the higher minimum, go with Spartan Government Income to earn a slightly higher yield.

## High Income

Originally known as Spartan High Income, this fund started in August 1990. It invests mainly in high-yield bonds, with an emphasis on lower-quality securities. Capital gains and any excise distributions can occur in June and December. There is a 1 percent redemption fee on shares held less than 270 days.

High Income offers more of a pure play on junk bonds than Capital & Income does. Recently, however, manager Thomas Soviero has put a portion of the fund in preferred stock and convertibles. Like Capital & Income, this fund should benefit from Fidelity's expertise in the junk bond universe (see the previous section on Capital & Income).

In the long term, High Income is likely to perform almost as well as Capital & Income, perhaps around 10 percent per year over the long run. That's a good return for a fund with less than half the risk of the S&P 500, but keep in mind that performance can be poor when evidence of an economic slowdown first surfaces.

## Intermediate Bond

Intermediate Bond was started in May 1975; before 1988 it was known as Thrift Trust. It seeks high current income by investing in investment-grade debt with a weighted average maturity of between three and ten years. Payouts of capital gains can occur in June and December.

Overall, Intermediate Bond carries slightly more credit risk than government funds but less than Fidelity's investment-grade funds. Interest-rate risk is average with a duration of around 4.

The fund is a good choice for bond investors who don't want any fancy footwork—just good solid performance that won't bring any surprises when times get tough.

## Intermediate Government Income

Formerly known as Spartan Limited Maturity Government, this fund was started in May 1988. It seeks high current income with preservation of capital; it normally invests in U.S. government securities and related instruments. Capital gains can be paid out in September and December.

I favor Short-Term Bond for obtaining the best yields without much interest-rate risk. If you want to avoid credit risk too, this fund probably is the best choice among short-maturity funds. Over the long term, it should do slightly better than a money market fund.

## International Bond

Formerly known as Global Bond, this fund seeks high total return by investing principally in foreign debt securities, including securities rated below investment grade. The fund was started at the end of 1986. Capital gains are distributed in February or December.

Being subject to both currency risk and credit risk in developing and mature markets, this fund has been one of

Fidelity's more volatile bond funds and has been on the wrong side of too many strategy changes by prior managers. I'm not sure this fund offers any long-term advantage compared with domestic bond funds.

## Investment Grade Bond

Investment Grade Bond seeks high current income, investing mainly in investment-grade securities. The fund was started in August 1971; before 1992, it was known as Flexible Bond. Capital gains can be paid out in June and December.

Investment Grade Bond is broadly diversified and focuses almost entirely on the domestic market. It's a good all-around choice for those who want to add some bond exposure to their portfolios. If you can meet the higher minimum, go with Spartan Investment Grade Bond to earn a slightly higher yield.

## New Markets Income

New Markets Income was started in May 1993, and it seeks high current income with capital appreciation as a secondary objective. The fund invests mainly in debt securities and other instruments issued in emerging countries. There is a 1 percent redemption fee on shares held less than 180 days.

With a focus on emerging-country debt, New Markets Income is by far the most risky fund in this group; it's even more risky than many stock funds. Since inception, the fund has invested primarily in Latin America, where political uncertainty and dramatic capital flows have resulted in a roller coaster ride for investors. Mexico's financial crisis in late 1994 and early 1995 caused this fund to lose over 30 percent, but it recovered in 1996. Russia's financial collapse in 1997 resulted in a short-term loss of almost 20 percent. More recently, Brazil's decision to float its currency caused the fund's share price to fall 42 percent.

By mid-2000 this fund will have survived all the worst-case scenarios and may even be worth consideration as a high-risk, high-yield vehicle. Manager John Carlson has done a pretty good job of steering this fund through a minefield of financial calamities and could deliver good results in a more conducive market environment. If you invest, don't bet the farm. Limit New Markets Income to no more than 15 percent of your income-oriented holdings and be willing to see results over the long term.

### Short-Term Bond

Short-Term Bond was started in September 1986 and seeks high current income consistent with preservation of principal. It normally invests in investment-grade securities, maintaining an average maturity of three years or less. Capital gains are usually small if they occur at all; they can be distributed in June and December.

Short-Term Bond is essentially a short-maturity version of Investment Grade Bond. The fund has always kept interest-rate risk low but in the past has ventured out on the credit risk side. Its small position in Latin American debt was largely responsible for its 4 percent loss in 1994.

These days Short-Term Bond is maintaining a high-quality portfolio and is focusing mainly on the domestic market. As such, it remains one of my favorite alternatives for investors who would otherwise keep their dollars in a money market fund.

### Spartan Government Income

Spartan Government Income began in December 1988 and seeks a high current income by investing in U.S. government securities and related instruments. Capital gains can be distributed in June and December.

This fund is essentially the same as Government Income, except that its expenses are lower because of the higher minimums that are required. As such, it earns a slightly higher yield.

## Spartan Investment Grade Bond

Spartan Investment Grade Bond was introduced in October 1992, and it seeks high current income by investing in investment-grade debt. Capital gains can be paid in June and December.

Like Investment Grade Bond, this fund is a good all-around choice for a domestic bond fund. The main difference is that this fund's expenses are lower because of the higher minimums that are required. As such, it earns a slightly higher yield.

## Target Timeline Funds

The Target Timeline funds seek an annual total return within 0.5 percent of the quoted yield at the time of purchase—assuming the fund is held to maturity and all distributions are reinvested. These funds focus on investment-grade corporate bonds. Timeline 1999 and Timeline 2001 are closed to new accounts, but as of this writing Timeline 2003 is still open. Capital gains are distributed in September and December. At the end of the investment period (for example, in September of 2003 for Timeline 2003), you can have your shares redeemed or you can "roll over" your capital into another fund. There is a 0.5 percent fee if you redeem shares in the first 90 days.

Fidelity introduced the Timeline funds for investors who would normally buy an individual bond instead of a bond fund, and from a performance standpoint it has delivered on its promise. However, the concept has been something less than a smashing success, and these funds will probably not be replaced after they reach their "maturity" date.

## MUNICIPAL BOND FUND CHOICES

Following is a recap of Fidelity's municipal bond fund choices. Except where noted, dividends are declared daily and paid out monthly. All of these funds are sold with no front-end load. Some have redemption fees, which are noted in their respective section. For all funds in this group, Fidelity reserves the right to block additional purchases after four trips in and out of the same fund in a 12-month period. Calendar-year performance is listed in Appendix A. For suggested bond fund portfolios, see Chapter 10.

### Spartan Arizona Municipal Income

This fund began in October 1994, and it seeks high current tax-free income for Arizona residents. Capital gains can be distributed in October and December. There is a redemption fee of 0.5 percent on shares held less than 180 days.

Although this fund's total return has been a bit weaker than other funds in this group, it's still likely to offer the highest after-tax return for Arizona residents.

### Spartan California Municipal Income

Formerly known as California Municipal Income, this fund was introduced in July 1984. It seeks high current tax-free income for California residents. The fund invests primarily in investment-grade municipal securities. Payouts of capital gains can occur in April and December.

This fund boasts a high-quality portfolio and a solid long-term record. It's a good choice for Californians.

### Spartan Connecticut Municipal Income

Spartan Connecticut was started in October 1987. It seeks high current tax-free income for Connecticut residents. The fund invests primarily in investment-grade municipal bonds. Payouts of capital gains may occur in January and December.

There is a 0.5 percent redemption fee on shares held for less than 180 days.

Like Fidelity's other state-specific funds, this fund has a good long-term track record and is a solid choice for high-bracket Connecticut investors.

## Spartan Florida Municipal Income

This fund was started in March 1992. It seeks high current tax-free income and exemption from the Florida intangible tax. The fund invests primarily in investment-grade municipal bonds. Capital gains payouts can occur in January and December. There is a 0.5 percent redemption fee on shares held less than 180 days.

This fund has a solid record and a high-quality portfolio. It's a good long-term choice for high-bracket Florida investors.

## Spartan Intermediate Municipal Income

Formerly known as Limited Term, this fund was started in April 1977, and it seeks high current income (free from federal income tax) with preservation of capital. The fund invests primarily in investment-grade municipal securities. Payouts of capital gains can occur in February and December.

Despite the "Intermediate" title, this portfolio still carries considerable interest-rate risk and usually maintains a duration of about 5. If you want a low-risk municipal fund, go with Spartan Short-Intermediate Municipal Income.

This fund is a good all-around choice for investors who have no state income tax or do not have a state-specific fund to choose from.

## Spartan Maryland Municipal Income

Spartan Maryland started in April 1993, and it seeks high current tax-free income for Maryland residents. The fund invests primarily in investment-grade municipal bonds. Capital gains distributions may occur in October and December. There is a 0.5 percent redemption fee on shares held less than 180 days.

Spartan Maryland has performed on par with Fidelity's other single-state funds and is a viable long-term choice for high-bracket Maryland investors.

### Spartan Massachusetts Municipal Income

Formerly known as Massachusetts Municipal Income, this fund started in 1983. It seeks a high level of current income exempt from federal and Massachusetts state personal income tax. It invests primarily in investment-grade municipal bonds. Capital gains can be paid out in March and December.

This is a good long-term performer that can provide relief from Massachusetts's relatively high maximum tax bracket.

### Spartan Michigan Municipal Income

Formerly known as Michigan Municipal Income, this fund started in November 1985. The fund seeks high current tax-free income for Michigan residents. It invests primarily in investment-grade municipal bonds. Capital gains can be paid in February and December.

Like most of Fidelity's other state funds, this fund has a solid record. Its investment-grade portfolio often includes 10 to 15 percent lower-grade issues.

### Spartan Minnesota Municipal Income

Formerly known as Minnesota Municipal Income, this fund started in December 1985. It seeks high current tax-free income for Minnesota residents. The fund invests primarily in investment-grade municipal bonds. Capital gains can be distributed in February and December.

Minnesota Municipal Income has less latitude than other state funds, partly because the state's muni bonds tend to be high-quality issues and partly because the state allows only a 5 percent stake in issues from other states. As such, the fund's total return tends to be slightly less than Fidelity's other state-specific funds. Still, it is probably a better bet than Spartan Municipal Income, which is not tax-free at the state level.

### Spartan Municipal Income

Formerly called High Yield, this fund was started in December 1977 and seeks high current income free from federal income tax. The fund invests normally in investment-grade municipal bonds. Payouts of capital gains can occur in January and December.

This fund is the closest match to a state-specific fund in terms of interest-rate risk and long-term return potential. A good choice for high-bracket investors with no state income tax or for those who have no state fund available. If you prefer a little less interest-rate sensitivity, go with Spartan Intermediate Municipal Income.

### Spartan New Jersey Municipal Income

Spartan New Jersey was started in January 1988, and it seeks high current tax-free income for New Jersey residents. The fund invests primarily in investment-grade municipal bonds. Payouts of capital gains may occur in January and December. There is a 0.5 percent redemption fee on shares held less than 180 days.

This fund has a solid long-term record. Its portfolio often includes 15 to 20 percent lower-grade issues.

### Spartan New York Municipal Income

Formerly known as New York Municipal Income, this fund began in July 1984. It seeks high current tax-free income for New York residents. The fund invests primarily in investment-grade municipal securities whose interest is free from federal income tax and New York State and City income taxes. Distributions of capital gains can occur in March and December.

This fund is a good choice for high-bracket New York investors.

### Spartan Ohio Municipal Income

Formerly known as Ohio Municipal Income, this fund was started in November 1985. It seeks high current tax-free income for Ohio residents. The fund invests primarily in investment-grade municipal bonds. Capital gains distributions can occur in February and December.

This fund has a respectable long-term record and should be a good choice for high-bracket Ohio investors.

### Spartan Pennsylvania Municipal Income

This fund began in August 1986, and it seeks a high level of current tax-free income for Pennsylvania residents. The fund invests primarily in longer-term, investment-grade municipal bonds. Capital gains distributions can occur in February and December. A 0.5 percent redemption fee is charged on shares held less than 180 days.

This fund has a good track record and represents the best choice for high-bracket Pennsylvania investors.

### Spartan Short-Intermediate Municipal Income

Spartan Short-Intermediate Muni was started in December 1986, and it seeks high current income free from federal income tax. It invests primarily in investment-grade municipal securities, maintaining an average maturity of two to five years. Although capital gains are rare (1 cent in 1993 is the only distribution on record), it is possible for the fund to make payouts in October and December.

This fund is Fidelity's only municipal choice that I would characterize as low-risk. With a duration that's typically about three years, the fund has less than half of the interest rate exposure of Fidelity's other muni bond funds. As such, it is not likely to suffer a loss over a 12-month period.

The disadvantage, of course, is a lower yield. Spartan Short-Intermediate Muni usually doesn't offer an after-tax advantage when compared to a taxable fund like Short-Term Bond—unless you are in one of the highest federal tax brackets.

# 8

# *Money Market Funds*

Money market funds have been around since the 1970s, and Fidelity was the first company to offer checkwriting as an option. Competitors followed suit, and in the 1980s money market funds were a very popular alternative to keeping money in the bank. Back then, of course, short-term interest rates were abnormally high while the Fed wrestled to get inflation under control.

A money market fund is essentially a bond fund with a high-quality portfolio and a very short average maturity, typically less than 90 days. The fund is managed to hold the share price stable at one dollar, resulting in the number of shares in the account being equal to the dollar value of the account.

Money market funds operate with a different structure than other cash-type investments such as bank CDs (certificates of deposit) and Treasury bills:

- A money market fund is not insured by the FDIC. This bothers some investors, but you have to remember that money market funds are managed for a high degree of safety. Many invest in government notes, which have near-zero credit risk, and the ones that invest in corporate debt are broadly diversified. Although a default by a single institution or a rapid increase in short-term interest rates could cause the one dollar share price to drop by a penny or two, this is an unlikely event. (Even if it happened, you wouldn't lose your dividend income the way many CD owners lost their interest when their banks failed.) In a Fidelity money market fund, you have the skills of Fidelity analysts working in your favor. With top-notch risk-assessment abilities, chances of a Fidelity money market fund ever "breaking the buck" are pretty minimal.

- Your rate is not locked in. A money market fund's seven-day yield varies based on market conditions and is only an estimate of the dividend income you will earn in the coming 12 months. The actual amount of income you receive may be higher or lower, depending on whether short-term interest rates move up or down.
- There are no penalties or loads. Except for Select Money Market, Fidelity's money market funds have no front-end or back-end charges, and there is no minimum amount of time you must invest. Dividend income you earn is computed daily and credited to your account on a monthly basis. It doesn't matter when you take the money out of your account; you still earn a prorated amount of income for the time your money was held.

## A MONEY MARKET FUND AS HOME BASE

Unless you plan to establish a Fidelity brokerage account, a money market fund can be a good way to get started with Fidelity. Once your account is set up with a money market fund, you can exchange into other funds over the phone (although you will have to order and read the prospectus for each fund before you call in any switches). With checkwriting or Fidelity's Moneyline service in place, a money market fund provides a fast and easy way to redeem shares. Suppose you want to sell $15,000 of your Puritan shares to purchase a vehicle. Just call in a switch from Puritan to your money market fund, wait until the close of the next business day, and then write a check after verifying that the funds are in your money market account.

If you do have a Fidelity brokerage account, a money market fund can boost the return on the money that would otherwise remain in your core account (money market funds usually pay 0.25 to 0.5 percent more than the core account rate).

A money market fund is suitable as a place to keep money you need for near-term living expenses or to maintain an emergency reserve for unexpected events. In either case, the rate you earn will probably be better than what you can obtain from a bank.

## TAXABLE VERSUS MUNICIPAL

Unless your federal tax bracket is 36 percent or higher, a taxable money market fund is probably the best bet. You can verify this by comparing taxable equivalent yields (detailed in Chapter 7). To avoid getting a distorted comparison, you should compare taxable and tax-free yields at different times over a three-month period. Also avoid taking the municipal yield figures too seriously around the end of December and early January, when year-end liquidity demands tend to raise the yield on municipal money market funds.

A state-specific money market fund can often be a better bet than a national fund. While there is more exposure to state-related credit problems, Fidelity's state-specific money market funds have relatively high credit quality and the risk is pretty minimal.

## SPARTAN VERSUS NON-SPARTAN

Spartan money market funds provide about 10 to 15 basis points more income than their non-Spartan counterparts.

However, the Spartan advantage can easily be erased by checkwriting and exchange redemptions. In a Spartan fund, checks cost $2 and redemptions run $5 (unless your balance is above $50,000, in which case both are free). With an account balance below $50,000, two checks per month or one exchange redemption per month will more than wipe out the typical yield advantage of a Spartan money market fund.

Even if your transaction frequency is low, Spartan money market funds may be less attractive because of their minimums. The checkwriting minimum is $1,000 versus $500 for most non-Spartan funds, and to open an account it takes a significant sum ($20,000 for Spartan taxable money markets and $25,000 for Spartan Municipal money markets). All things considered, a regular non-Spartan money market is probably your best bet unless you expect your balance to stay above $50,000 and you aren't concerned about a higher checkwriting minimum.

## TAXABLE MONEY MARKET FUND CHOICES

Even here Fidelity offers many choices, but for most funds the results are pretty similar. Cash Reserves is probably as good as any other fund, and it usually carries a competitive yield. If your account balance will be over $50,000, Spartan Money Market is a viable option. When trading the Selects, keep your loaded Select money in Select Money Market and keep your no-load money in a no-load money fund to avoid paying extra fees (more on this in Chapter 12). A fund-by-fund recap follows; calendar-year performance is listed in Appendix A.

### Cash Reserves

Fidelity's most popular money market fund seeks as high a level of current income as is consistent with preservation of capital and liquidity by investing in money market instruments. Yield will fluctuate.

It takes $2,500 to open a Cash Reserves account, and a $2,000 balance is required to maintain it. (IRA accounts can be opened with just $500.) There is no charge for writing checks, although they must be made out for $500 or more.

Cash Reserves provides a good combination of yield, features, and investment minimums. It is my favorite money market fund except for investors who expect to maintain a balance over $50,000. In that case, Spartan Money Market could be a better choice for investors who don't mind a higher checkwriting minimum.

### Fidelity Daily Income Trust

Fidelity Daily Income Trust (FDIT) seeks income while maintaining a stable share price. It invests in high-quality short-term money market instruments of domestic issuers. The fund's yield will fluctuate.

FDIT differs from Cash Reserves in investing in domestic-only notes and in requiring twice as much to open an account ($5,000 for regular accounts). Yield is usually a bit less than Cash Reserves.

Writing checks for less than $500 is permitted with this fund, but there is a $1 charge in each case.

### Select Money Market

Seeking high current income consistent with preservation of capital and liquidity, Select Money Market invests in a broad range of high-quality money market instruments. The fund is managed as a diversified portfolio.

Intended only as a cash option for money invested in Fidelity's Select family (see Chapter 9), this fund carries a 3 percent load if the money being invested hasn't already paid a 3 percent load at some point in the past. Checkwriting is not available.

Investors trading the Selects can choose other money market funds when they want to get out of the market, but this can sometimes result in unintended load fees. Suppose you just invested $10,000 in Spartan Money Market and then you sell $10,000 of Select Automotive and add the proceeds to the same account. A few months later you purchase $10,000 in Asset Manager shares, not realizing that you just used up your loaded Spartan Money Market shares. Later you move $10,000 back into Select Biotechnology. Surprise! You'll pay $300 in load fees. (See Chapter 12 for more on avoiding load fees.)

Using Select Money Market to "quarantine" your loaded shares prevents such a situation from occurring. Granted, Select Money Market yields about 20 to 50 basis points less than Spartan Money Market, but in the preceding example you would have had to stay in Select Money Market for many years to lose $300 from a yield standpoint.

## Spartan Money Market

Spartan Money Market seeks income while maintaining a stable share price. The fund's yield will fluctuate with interest rates.

This fund is typically Fidelity's highest-yielding money market, and I recommend it for investors who expect to maintain a balance of $50,000 or more. (Fidelity waives all checkwriting and exchange fees if the account balance is above that threshold.) For an account between $20,000 and $50,000, it can sometimes make sense to hold the fund, but only if your checkwriting and redemption activity is low. Otherwise, go with Cash Reserves instead.

Additional investments and checks drawn on the account are both subject to a $1,000 minimum.

## Spartan U.S. Government Money Market

This fund seeks income while maintaining a stable share price. The fund invests in high-quality, U.S. government short-term money market securities and repurchase agreements for those securities. The fund's yield will fluctuate.

Spartan U.S. Government has the same structure as Spartan Money Market, except that it runs a slightly higher-quality portfolio and produces a slightly lower yield. I think it amounts to splitting hairs. Spartan Money Market's portfolio is also high in quality and risk is minimal. You might as well enjoy the extra yield that Spartan Money Market provides. If you want maximum safety, go with Spartan U.S. Treasury Money Market, where you might be able to offset the lower yield by avoiding state income taxes on a portion of the income stream.

### Spartan U.S. Treasury Money Market

This fund seeks income while maintaining a stable share price. It normally invests in high-quality, U.S. Treasury short-term money market securities whose interest is free from state and local income tax. Yield will fluctuate.

This fund offers portfolio quality that's about as safe as you can get, but a large jump in interest rates could still threaten the $1 share price in an extreme situation. The yield from this fund is usually a bit lower than others in the group.

Most states allow some or all of the income from this fund to be exempted from state and local income taxes (although you still have to pay federal taxes).

The features and minimums for this fund are the same as for Spartan Money Market.

### U.S. Government Reserves

U.S. Government Reserves seeks a high level of current income as is consistent with the security of principal and liquidity; the fund invests in repurchase agreements secured by obligations issued or guaranteed as to principal and interest by the U. S. government or by any of its agencies or instrumentalities. The fund may also enter into reverse repurchase agreements. The fund's yield will fluctuate.

Basically, this fund is similar to Cash Reserves, except for a slightly higher-quality portfolio and a yield that's a bit lower. I prefer Cash Reserves—it provides a higher yield with about the same amount of interest rate risk that higher-quality funds are exposed to.

## MUNICIPAL MONEY MARKET FUND CHOICES

For investors subject to Alternative Minimum Tax (AMT) on their federal taxes, these municipal money market funds may not have any advantage over a taxable fund. As of this writing, all but the Massachusetts funds carry a significant amount of AMT paper in their portfolios.

Following is a breakdown of the Fidelity choices available. The non-Spartan funds require $5,000 to open an account; Spartan funds have a $25,000 minimum. Calendar-year performance is listed in Appendix A.

### California Municipal Money Market

California Municipal Money Market seeks current income exempt from federal and California state personal income tax while maintaining a stable share price; the fund invests in high-quality, short-term municipal securities. Yield will fluctuate.

### Connecticut Municipal Money Market

Connecticut Municipal Money Market seeks a high level of current income exempt from federal income tax and, to the extent possible, Connecticut taxes on dividends and interest income taxes. The fund invests primarily in high-quality, short-term Connecticut municipal obligations. Yield will fluctuate.

## Massachusetts Municipal Money Market

This fund seeks a high level of current income exempt from federal income tax and Massachusetts personal income tax as is consistent with preservation of capital and liquidity. It invests normally in municipal money market securities so that at least 65 percent of income distributed is tax-exempt at the state level and 80 percent is exempt at the federal level. Yield will fluctuate.

## Michigan Municipal Money Market

Michigan Municipal Money Market seeks a high level of current income exempt from federal and Michigan state personal income tax as is consistent with preservation of capital. It invests normally in municipal money market securities so that at least 80 percent of income distributed is tax-exempt at both the state and federal levels. Yield will fluctuate.

## Municipal Money Market

Municipal Money Market (formerly Tax-Exempt Money Market Trust) seeks a high level of interest income that is exempt from federal income tax as is consistent with a portfolio of high-quality, short-term municipal obligations selected on the basis of liquidity and stability of principal. Yield will fluctuate.

Among the non-Spartan money market funds, Municipal Money Market is a good choice for investors who have no state income tax or do not have a state-specific fund to choose from. Its minimum initial investment is $5,000.

## New Jersey Municipal Money Market

New Jersey Municipal Money Market seeks a high level of current income exempt from federal income tax and the New Jersey gross income tax as is consistent with the preservation of capital. The fund invests in high-quality, short-term municipal obligations so that at least 80 percent of the fund's income is tax-exempt at both the state and federal levels. Yield will fluctuate.

### New York Municipal Money Market

This fund seeks high current income exempt from federal, New York state, and New York City income taxes. It aims for a stable share price and invests in high-quality, short-term municipal obligations. Yield will fluctuate.

### Ohio Municipal Money Market

Ohio Municipal Money Market seeks a high level of current income exempt from federal and Ohio state personal income tax, as is consistent with preservation of capital. The fund invests in high-quality, short-term municipal money market securities so that at least 80 percent of the fund's income is tax-exempt at the state and federal levels. Yield will fluctuate.

### Spartan Arizona Municipal Money Market

This fund seeks high current tax-free income for Arizona residents while maintaining a stable share price. It invests in high-quality, short-term municipal money market securities whose interest is tax-exempt at the state and federal levels. Yield will fluctuate.

### Spartan California Municipal Money Market

This fund seeks a high level of current income exempt from federal and California state personal income tax while maintaining a stable share price. The fund invests in high-quality, short-term California municipal obligations. Yield will fluctuate.

## Spartan Connecticut Municipal Money Market

This fund seeks a high level of current income exempt from federal income tax and, to the extent possible, from Connecticut personal income tax, as is consistent with preservation of capital and liquidity. The fund invests normally in high-quality, short-term municipal money market securities so that at least 65 percent is tax-exempt at the state level and 80 percent is tax-exempt at the federal level. Yield will fluctuate.

## Spartan Florida Municipal Money Market

This fund seeks a high level of current income exempt from federal income tax, as is consistent with the preservation of capital and liquidity. It invests normally in high-quality, short-term municipal money market securities so that at least 65 percent of income is exempt from Florida's intangible tax and 80 percent is exempt from federal taxes. Yield will fluctuate.

## Spartan Massachusetts Municipal Money Market

This fund seeks a high level of current income exempt from federal income tax and Massachusetts personal income tax as is consistent with capital preservation and liquidity. The fund invests primarily in high-quality, short-term municipal money market securities. Yield will fluctuate.

## Spartan Municipal Money Market

Spartan Municipal Money Market seeks a high level of current income free from federal income tax as is consistent with the preservation of capital and liquidity by normally investing in high-quality, short-term municipal money market securities of all types. As with other funds in this group, the fund seeks to maintain a stable share price.

This fund has the benefit of national diversification, and it is one of Fidelity's best-yielding municipal money funds. At times it even exceeds the after-tax return of state-specific funds. However, if your balance is less than $50,000 and you expect to do more than one transaction per month, you should consider Municipal Money Market instead.

### Spartan New Jersey Municipal Money Market

This fund seeks a high level of current income exempt from federal income tax and, to the extent possible, from the New Jersey gross income tax, as is consistent with the preservation of capital. The fund invests normally in high-quality, short-term municipal money market securities so that at least 65 percent of income is tax-exempt at the state level and at least 80 percent of income is tax-free at the federal level. Yield will fluctuate.

### Spartan New York Municipal Money Market

This fund seeks high current income exempt from federal, New York state, and New York City personal income tax while maintaining a stable share price. It invests in high-quality, short-term municipal money market securities. Yield will fluctuate.

### Spartan Pennsylvania Municipal Money Market

This fund seeks a high level of current income exempt from federal and Pennsylvania state personal income taxes, as is consistent with preservation of capital. The fund invests normally in municipal money market securities so that at least 65 percent of income is tax-exempt at the state level and at least 80 percent is tax-free at the federal level. Yield will fluctuate.

# 9

# Select Funds

Fidelity's family of Select funds is intended for venturesome mutual fund investors. Each portfolio concentrates on stocks in a particular industry group, casting away the concept of diversification and concentrating instead on providing opportunities. Not surprisingly, many Selects have price volatility that more closely resembles individual stocks than diversified mutual funds.

Studies have shown that industry trends account for roughly 30 percent of the price movement in individual stocks, with broad market and company-specific factors accounting for the rest. Stocks in similar industry groups tend to move together because economic factors that affect a particular stock are likely to have a similar impact on others in the same industry.

The Selects are an attractive way to trade industry trends. In addition to having Fidelity's research skills working in your favor, trading expenses are much lower than if you were covering the stock commissions and price spreads yourself. Fidelity's web site and phone quote system make it easy to check hourly prices during market hours, and there are no limits on the number of trades you can make (although trading inside of 30 days is not cheap because of the 0.75 percent redemption fee).

## SELECT HISTORY

Fidelity started its Select family in July 1981 with Energy, Health Care, Precious Metals, and Technology. Financial Services and Utilities were added in December 1981. Investor interest in the Selects was slow to catch on in the beginning, but after Select Technology's 50 percent plus gains in 1982 and 1983, investors took notice. Fidelity responded by adding additional portfolios for other industries. By 1987 there were 35 sectors and a money market option and Fidelity had introduced hourly pricing to allow investors to buy and sell throughout the day instead of waiting for close of the market for their transactions to take place.

In 1988, however, investor interest stalled. At that time the Selects generally held smaller stocks, and the 1987 crash hit them harder than it hit diversified funds (which hold a higher percentage of blue chips). Mutual fund investors also became wary of program trading (computerized stock selling and buying by large institutions), which was blamed for creating such a large one-day decline.

Fidelity also faced tough times. Congress had eliminated the IRA deduction for many investors, and this took away a lot of Fidelity's business. Facing staff cuts, Fidelity killed plans to introduce additional Selects. About the same time, existing sectors became more difficult to manage because large investors, aided by hourly pricing, were increasingly trading for the short run. Technology funds struggled most; there were times when $50 million disappeared in a matter of hours. In late 1989, Fidelity imposed a 0.75 percent redemption fee on trades of 29 days or less to restore order to its internal trading operation. The fee did the trick, but it alienated many of the more active traders.

Things began to come together in 1991. A rally in small stocks breathed new life into the Select funds. A large boost in research spending helped Fidelity's Selects begin delivering performance that outstripped their rivals at other fund companies. Nevertheless, the majority of assets in the Select family remained heavily concentrated in just a few sectors. At the end of 1991, about 50 percent of the $4.2 billion in Select assets was in just two sectors: Select Biotechnology and Select Health Care.

Good performance has kept the group alive and well since then. As of December 31, 1998, 15 out of 31 equity Selects have exceeded the S&P 500 over a trailing ten-year period. That's perhaps the best record in the industry for any large group of funds. Select assets are now over $17 billion and are now more evenly distributed throughout the various portfolios. In a mutual fund universe where high-performance funds usually don't stay small for very long, the Selects continue to offer a wide range of nimble and attractive funds.

Fidelity tends to rotate managers frequently in the Select family. This helps broaden skill levels and identify candidates who have the right set of skills for managing one of Fidelity's larger diversified stock funds. From a statistical standpoint this practice has had very little effect (if any) on the group's long-term performance.

## INVESTING IN SELECTS

Picking the winning Selects is tougher than it looks. As with any aggressive growth strategy, it's a balancing act between taking on enough risk to be rewarded but not going so far that it's difficult to recover from losses. When trading Selects, you should avoid margin and short selling. These strategies involve too much risk. Sooner or later, you'll be in the wrong place at the wrong time, and you might erase over a year's worth of gains (or more) in just a few days.

Based on comments from my subscribers, I'm convinced that some investors set their expectations too high. My Select System model in *Fidelity Monitor* has returned 22.4 percent annually during the last ten years (as of December 31, 1998), meaning that it placed ninth out of 31 Selects and exceeded the S&P 500 by three percentage points per year. According to data from the *Hulbert Financial Digest,* it was the best mutual fund newsletter portfolio for the period. But judging from the feedback I received, there was no shortage of disappointment along the way. In the early years I would often get mail comparing the model to the top year-to-date performer. "Why aren't you in it?" would be the common question. Around the middle of the decade, I received a barrage of e-mails criticizing my lack of exposure to the technology group. More recently, while holding some of the top performing financial and media sectors, the discussion has revolved around the losers: "Why on earth are you still holding that?"

If you decide to get involved in the Selects, you need to be realistic. Over the long run, you may score a few home runs, but you won't be in the top fund every year. (The odds of doing that for five years in a row are about the same as winning the state lottery.) You'll also have your share of losers. And even if you are really good, you'll probably still lag behind the S&P 500 at least 25 percent of the time.

## Basic Strategies

Following are three different strategies (industry analysis, short-term price momentum, and undervalued sectors) that can be used to invest in the Selects. I've used all three methods at different times over the years, and I've included my thoughts about each approach.

*Industry Analysis* With this approach you try to identify the industries that are best positioned for long-term growth, and you buy and hold. This now seems to be the most popular way to invest in the Selects, and it is working increasingly well as the stock market splits into two basic groups: old economy firms that struggle in a deflationary era, and new economy stocks that are poised to deliver above-average earnings growth for many years to come. Because most of the

Selects line up in either one group or the other, it's relatively straightforward to construct a portfolio of winning sectors, allowing Fidelity managers do the hard work of picking the right stocks. At any rate, it helps to have a long-term investment horizon and to have some background on the choices that are available. My discussion of each Select portfolio (following this section) should be helpful in this respect.

*Short-Term Price Momentum*   This is also a popular Select strategy, partly because it is used by many newsletters and also by software programs that make it easy to design and back-test your own trading system. Unfortunately, the market is becoming more efficient, making it increasingly difficult to outperform with this approach. Back-testing with data from before 1996 can lead you to believe that you've got a winning system, but going forward such an approach is getting tougher by the day. Five years ago good news in a particular industry would be reflected by rising prices over a period of about two weeks. Now it takes just one or two days. A few years from now it may be just one or two hours. Systems that track prices on a daily basis run the risk of doing little more than responding to yesterday's news.

*Undervalued Sectors*   I have developed a relative-value model that compares each sector's current price-to-book ratio against its historical average. By ranking the Select family based on each fund's discount (or premium), it's possible to identify "under-recognized" sectors. In *Fidelity Monitor,* my Select System combines this approach with industry analysis to construct a portfolio capable of outperforming the S&P 500.

## THE SELECT PORTFOLIOS

Following is a review of each Select portfolio. These funds are sold with a 3 percent load, but the load is paid only once when you first buy in and not on subsequent switches. The minimum investment is $2,500 per fund or $500 in retirement accounts. There is no limit on exchanges, but there is an exchange fee of $7.50 and a redemption fee of $7.50 for trades of 30 days or more (0.75 percent of assets is charged for short-term trades of 29 days or less). The fees do not apply when switching out of Select Money Market. Fidelity is currently waiving the $7.50 exchange fee if you use an automated approach to execute your trades. All of the following portfolios seek capital appreciation by investing primarily in the equity securities of the specific industry sector they are named for. Distributions can occur in April and December.

### Select Air Transportation

A classic cyclical sector, Air Transportation tends to perform well during periods of economic growth and not so well when the economy is sliding into a recession. It is also negatively affected by rising oil prices, since fuel is a key cost component of the industry. The fund invests mainly in equity securities of companies engaged in the regional, national, and international movement of passengers, mail, and freight via aircraft.

In the long run, advancing technology is more a threat than a benefit to this sector. Over time barriers to entry will fall, making it easy for new entrants to lease a plane, do business over the web, and contract out everything else. Labor unions will make it difficult for existing firms to cut costs, since wages are the dominant cost factor for the industry. Another negative is that passenger airlines, which have long retained rights to operate under their own rules, may be subject to new regulations and disclosure requirements.

### Select Automotive

This fund invests mainly in the equity securities of companies engaged in the manufacture, marketing, or sale of automobiles, trucks, specialty vehicles, parts, tires, and related services.

Select Automotive tends to be an "early" cyclical because auto sales are one of the first things to pick up when the economy recovers from a down cycle and consumer confidence comes back. It is one of the more predictable cyclical sectors because once it starts to outperform the market, it tends to stay in that trend for a number of months.

It isn't clear if this group will win or lose in the long run. A lot of labor costs will be taken out of car assembly, either by building major components in emerging markets or by producing entire vehicles there (General Motor's Brazilian factories are a good model for what's to come). But competition will also push down car prices as the global players seek market share everywhere on the planet. And the coming conversion from internal combustion to the efficient and clean-burning fuel cell design will cost billions in research and development. Only a few large companies will be able to pull it off.

## Select Biotechnology

Biotechnology invests mainly in equity securities of companies engaged in the research, development, and manufacture of various biotechnological products, services, and processes.

Many of the companies in this fund have the potential to be acquired by pharmaceutical companies in search of bolstering their new product pipelines, but right now most of them are spending heavily on research and development and may not have income-producing products for several years. Some firms may never get off the ground. Others that come up with blockbuster products may be worth 10 or 20 times their current valuation a few years down the road.

This industry is likely to be one of the faster-growing segments of the economy over the next 20 years. Although most biotech firm are geared toward health care solutions, genetically engineered products also have broad-based potential in other industries. Yield-boosting seeds are already popular in the agricultural industry, and the potential has barely been tapped in other areas. Fidelity seems to understand this sector reasonably well, making it one of the better bets for long run.

## Select Brokerage & Investment Management

Select Brokerage & Investment Management invests mainly in equity securities of companies engaged in stock brokerage, commodity brokerage, investment banking, tax-advantaged investment or investment sales, investment management, or related advisory services.

Barring a long-lasting bear market, this sector has considerable potential for growth here at home and in the global markets. Money management companies are benefiting from the aging baby boom population, which is saving for retirement and stands to inherit a large sum of money over the next 20 years. Advancing technology has created a boom in on-line trading, which can be expected to catch on overseas as well. The big domestic players in this market will be favorably positioned to duplicate their success in other countries.

## Select Business Services & Outsourcing

Select Business Services & Outsourcing invests mainly in equity securities of companies that provide business-related services to companies and other organizations.

As other companies focus increasingly on what they do best and farm out the rest, these firms will be presented with opportunities for long-term growth. Fidelity appears to be emphasizing higher margin service providers that offer a unique service that may have global potential. On the downside, margins in many of the fastest growing businesses are thin and a focus on productivity is necessary to survive and prosper.

## Select Chemicals

Select Chemicals invests mainly in equity securities of companies engaged in the research, development, manufacture, or marketing of products or services related to the chemical process industries.

This industry is another broad-based cyclical sector like the automotive group. Many of these companies supply raw materials and are often the last to see a pickup in demand during an economic recovery cycle. (Product and factory inventories are consumed first before chemical commodities such as plastic make the turn upward.) Compared with other "late cyclical" sectors, chemical companies tend to be among the more profitable compared with other commodity producers.

This sector stands to benefit from advancing technology, but some segments of the market may suffer from competitive pressures. Companies that focus on plastic will see growth as this commodity increasingly replaces metal (in appliances and cars) and wood (in furniture and home construction). Other companies are gaining a foothold in Agribiotech and may have the opportunity to export successful products worldwide. Traditional commodity-based producers, however, will be subject to pricing pressures as production shifts into low-wage countries.

## Select Computers

Investing mainly in the computer industry, Select Computers looks for equity securities of companies engaged in research, design, development, manufacture, or distribution of products, processes, or services that relate to currently available or experimental hardware technology.

As a technology sector, Select Computers is one of the riskiest and least predictable sectors in the Select family. Technology stocks often move to the beat of a different drummer, and it is not uncommon to see this sector gain or lose 10 to 15 percent in a matter of days. A correction of 20 percent or more often occurs at least once during the course of a typical year.

It won't always be easy to figure out who the winners are in this sector, but Fidelity has done a great job analyzing this group of companies. The standard PC has become somewhat of a commodity, and it will be tough to find profits in this area. But the internet is spurring a transition back toward powerful workstations and mainframes, and there should be many long-term opportunities in this area. Still, because of the volatility in this sector it may make sense to seek out a more broadly based fund like Select Technology.

## Select Construction & Housing

Formerly called Housing, Select Construction & Housing invests mainly in equity securities of companies engaged in the design and construction of residential, commercial, industrial, and public works facilities as well as those of companies engaged in the manufacture, supply, distribution, or sale of products or services to those construction industries.

As a cyclical sector, this fund has characteristics similar to those of the automotive group, except that it is more sensitive to long-term interest rates.

Material costs are falling in this sector as appliances and other commodities are produced in low-wage countries. Technology is automating other tasks, such as design and project management. Pricing pressures are forcing less efficient producers out of business. Only a few companies in this industry will benefit by producing on a global scale. Long-term earnings growth stands to be lackluster at best in this sector.

## Select Consumer Industries

Formerly known as Consumer Products, Consumer Industries invests mainly in equity securities of companies engaged in the manufacture and distribution of goods to consumers, both domestically and internationally. That covers a lot of ground. The fund owns stocks in sectors such as automobiles, telecommunications, food, household products, retailers, broadcasters, and casino resorts.

Most of the companies in this group are in relatively mature industries, but many are building a global presence and should benefit from above-average long-term growth. Brands that enjoy success in the United States are proving to be relatively easy to export to other countries. Success in toothpaste, fast food, discount retailing, and even on-line services has been duplicated overseas, and as the world's standard of living goes up there will continue to be many opportunities.

## Select Cyclical Industries

Cyclical Industries invests mainly in equity securities of companies engaged in the research, development, manufacture, distribution, supply, or sale of materials, equipment, products, or services related to cyclical industries.

This sector has usually been a mix of commodity producers, automakers, chemical companies, and other economically sensitive firms. This group will probably not see much growth over the long run but could be a good short-term bet when the economy is in a slump and the Fed is in the process of cutting short-term interest rates.

## Select Defense & Aerospace

This fund invests mainly in equity securities of companies engaged in the research, manufacture, or sale of products or services related to the defense or aerospace industries.

In recent years this fund has shifted away from defense contractors and has focused more on aerospace companies. It isn't clear whether this group will benefit over the long term. On the one hand, the world's appetite for aircraft and satellite launching will expand dramatically. But on the other hand, advancing technology will also lead to big cost reductions and more competition.

## Select Developing Communications

This fund invests in equity securities of companies engaged in the development, manufacture, or sale of emerging communications services or equipment. Being a technology sector, Developing Communications is subject to the same roller-coaster price trends that occur with other technology sectors like Electronics and Computers. However, Developing Communications doesn't have quite as much volatility.

This fund invests mainly in the equipment makers that provide the infrastructure for the internet and wireless communications. Picking the winners in this group is not easy, but Fidelity seems to be doing well. The opportunity for long-term growth is significant, as these companies represent one of the faster-growing areas in the technology group.

## Select Electronics

Select Electronics invests in equity securities of companies engaged in the design, manufacture, or sale of electronic components as well as those of companies that sell electronic components, electronic component distributors, and vendors of electronic instruments and electronic system vendors.

The fund's primary emphasis is on chip makers, otherwise known as integrated circuit manufacturers. Chips provide the brains and memory for products such as computers, consumer electronics, cellular phones, and automobiles. This sector behaves a lot like other technology sectors such as Computers, Technology, and Software, but it is affected more by global economic factors. It is a cyclical sector, but it has much more growth potential than other cyclical groups.

The companies that are likely to benefit most in this group are those with relatively limited competition that can sell on a worldwide basis. Fidelity has done an excellent job focusing on such firms and has also profited by investing in companies that provide the high-tech equipment necessary for chip-making factories.

## Select Energy

Investing mainly in equity securities of companies in the energy field, Select Energy's portfolio includes the conventional areas of oil, gas, electricity, and coal as well as newer energy sources such as nuclear, geothermal, oil shale, and solar power.

As a commodity sector, this portfolio tracks investor expectations for the price of oil. In the short run it is very difficult to predict, since the price of oil is in a constant state of flux. In the long run, however, cheap oil is probably here to stay. Advancing technology has dramatically lowered the cost of finding oil reserves over the last decade. In some parts of the world it now costs less than a dollar a barrel to identify new deposits. Furthermore, new techniques are making it easier to get it out of the ground. The currency crisis of 1997 and 1998 will accelerate the development of oil production in emerging markets, since crude is one of the few things these countries can readily export to improve the balance of trade. This means OPEC will continue to lose its grip on the global markets, and oil will remain a low-margin commodity even with expanding world demand. There may be some long-term benefit as large oil companies consolidate, but in the long run this sector will struggle to deliver anything more than single-digit earnings growth.

## Select Energy Services

A more aggressive portfolio than Select Energy, Select Energy Services invests mainly in equity securities of companies in the energy service field, including those that provide services and equipment to the conventional areas of oil, gas, electricity, and coal as well as to newer areas such as nuclear, geothermal, oil shale, and solar power.

These types of firms help oil and gas producers locate new reserves and to handle the drilling of new wells. Advancing technology allows these firms to play a more significant role in the industry, both in locating oil and by improving the output of existing wells. And many of these firms have become global players. Still, business levels in this group are tied to the price of oil, which makes for a "feast or famine" environment. As such, Energy Services is a volatile fund. It provides the most leverage if oil prices are moving up, but if you bet wrong you can lose a lot of money in a short period of time.

Long term, companies in this group should deliver higher earnings growth than those in Select Energy but will probably lag behind other growth-oriented sectors.

## Select Environmental Services

Introduced in June 1989, Select Environmental Services invests mainly in equity securities of companies engaged in the research, development, manufacture, or distribution of products, processes, or services related to waste management or pollution control.

When Fidelity initiated this fund, it was widely expected that increasingly strict environmental laws would create a boom for these types of companies. However, the boom went bust when recycling programs and other measures created more landfill capacity and industrial companies took their own initiative to reduce air and water pollution. It's also proving to be tough to make money in waste management. Incinerating garbage opens up other environmental issues, and deregulation of electric markets has reduced the profit potential of power generation.

It seems unlikely that this group of companies will have much success in delivering long-term earnings growth.

## Select Financial Services

Concentrating on banks, S&Ls, insurance, credit cards, mortgage lenders, and brokerages, Select Financial Services invests mainly in equity securities of companies providing financial services to consumers and industry.

Today's deflationary forces are providing a key advantage for financial institutions: The value of money that is loaned out is no longer eroding like it was in the 1970s, 1980s, and early 1990s. Furthermore, this sector has also benefited more than other groups from advancing technology. Computers have allowed these firms to automate in a major way. They've also helped to reduce fraud and manage credit risk.

Today the United States boasts some of the most productive and profitable banks in the world. Over the long run many of these firms should be able to provide solid earnings growth as they continue to expand their role in the global economy.

## Select Food & Agriculture

This portfolio invests mainly in equity securities of companies engaged in the manufacture, sale, or distribution of food and beverage products, agricultural products, and products related to the development of new food technologies.

Select Food & Agriculture has the characteristics of a growth and income fund, mainly because the food and beverage business changes very little under varying economic conditions. The fund also makes for a good defensive play when the market outlook is bleak. It usually holds up well in a correction or bear market, yet it can participate if market conditions turn bullish.

It isn't clear if advancing technology and globalization will help or hurt this sector. Some of these companies have already established a global presence and are enjoying robust overseas growth. Others are focusing only on the U.S. market and could be hurt as new competition enters the market. This sector can also have exposure to tobacco firms, which could be held back by long-term liability exposure.

## Select Gold

A classic gold fund, Select Gold invests mainly in equity securities of companies engaged in exploration, mining, processing, or dealing in gold or—to a lesser degree—in silver, platinum, diamonds, or other precious metals and minerals. The fund may also invest directly in the metal itself, although traditionally its bullion position has been small.

Gold stocks don't usually follow the stock market because mining company profits are tied directly to the price of the metal. Because of the fixed cost of getting gold out of the ground, mining profits (and so mining stocks) tend to fluctuate about twice as much as does the metal itself. Despite their low beta, which is due to a lack of correlation with the general market, gold stocks are among the most risky equity securities around.

Unlike other commodities, very little gold is needed for industrial uses other than jewelry production. Most of the gold that has ever been mined is still around in various forms. As such, most supply shortages can usually be resolved with only a modest increase in the price. Gold can sometimes make a major move up, but only if a large portion of the world population is trying to acquire it to protect against potential losses in purchasing power that might result from holding paper currencies. Except as a Y2K safeguard, it is difficult to envision such a situation in a world where deflationary forces continue to gain the upper hand.

In the long run, advancing technology is likely to be negative for this group of companies. Over time, new ways of extracting gold are bound to be uncovered, creating downward pressures on the price of the metal.

## Select Health Care

Select Health Care invests mainly in equity securities of companies engaged in the design, manufacture, or sale of products or services used for or in connection with health care or medicine. Throughout its history, the fund has focused mainly on pharmaceutical stocks.

In the long run an increasing number of ailments will be managed by taking pills, meaning that this sector is likely to command a greater share of the money spent on health care. In the developed world, an aging population is also a favorable demographic trend. In emerging countries, rising standards of living will bring modern medical treatment to the general population, and prescription drugs will see rising demand first.

Until now, most blockbuster drugs have been identified either by screening thousands of substances or by observing side effects during trials for other conditions. In future years, however, a higher percentage of revenue will come from drugs that are engineered based on a more complete understanding of our genetic sequence and the chemical signals and responses that take place. These new pills could be far more effective and will probably generate less severe side effects. They will also cure ailments for which no effective treatment currently exists. This will create new sources of revenue.

A few potential negatives exist. Competition within the industry could increase if it becomes possible to develop several effective solutions for each ailment. Some of today's blockbusters may lose patent protection before the era of engineered drugs takes hold. And biotech firms are further ahead in the race to develop a complete understanding of human DNA, although acquisitions and license agreements will eventually level the playing field.

## Select Home Finance

Originally known as Select Savings & Loan, Select Home Finance invests mainly in the equity securities of companies that provide mortgages and other consumer-related loans.

From 1991–97 this fund provided exceptional returns. The institutions that survived the savings and loan crisis early in the decade enjoyed a great run after their weaker competitors were liquidated. (It also helped that Fidelity and former manager David Ellison had a thorough understanding of how this industry works.)

But going forward this group may lose ground relative to the big banks. The small guys are at a disadvantage when it comes to on-line banking, ATM networks, economy of scale, and global growth potential.

Even though deflation is somewhat favorable for this group, these institutions may not grow earnings fast enough to outperform over the long run.

## Select Industrial Equipment

Formerly known as Industrial Technology (and before that as Capital Goods), Select Industrial Equipment invests mainly in equity securities of companies engaged in the manufacture, distribution, or service of products and equipment for the industrial sector. These companies include integrated producers of capital equipment, parts suppliers, and subcontractors.

A classic cyclical sector, this group of companies has the potential to perform well when the economy is rebounding from a period of poor performance. In the long run, however, advancing technology is a threat to many of the companies in this group. New competition could push down prices, and many of these firms do not have the ability to cut costs or conquer global markets.

## Select Industrial Materials

Select Industrial Materials invests mainly in equity securities of companies engaged in the manufacture, mining, processing, or distribution of raw materials and intermediate goods used in the industrial sector.

This portfolio concentrates on deep cyclical stocks—producers of plastics, chemicals, paper, mining, energy, and steel. These types of companies usually pick up when an economic recovery is far enough along that inventories have been depleted and factories need raw materials to produce new goods. Industrial Materials can also benefit in the short run when the market worries about inflation, which usually means rising prices for industrial commodities.

Long term, many of these companies may lose market share to firms that operate in countries where labor costs are low. Those that don't could still find it tough to grow earnings as advancing technology lowers barriers to entry and creates new sources of supply, resulting in downward pressure on pricing.

## Select Insurance

Previously known as Select Property & Casualty Insurance, Select Insurance invests mainly in equity securities of companies engaged in underwriting, reinsuring, selling, distributing, or placing of property and casualty, life, or health insurance.

It isn't clear if this group will benefit from advancing technology. The internet is likely to educate consumers and create greater price competition, but the result could be a new group of leaders that have potential to expand globally. If Fidelity does a good job of researching this sector, and it has in the past, Insurance may have the potential to outperform.

## Select Leisure

Select Leisure invests mainly in equity securities of companies engaged in the design, production, or distribution of goods or services in the leisure industries. Typical investments include broadcasters, cable TV operators, on-line services, beverages, restaurants, publishing, hotels and motels, casinos, and other entertainment companies.

The long-term outlook appears positive for this group. An aging population in the United States points toward increasing demand for leisure activities, and some of these companies stand to benefit from the growth of the internet (Fidelity considers on-line services to be part of this group). Over time advancing technology is likely to open up new opportunities without creating too much competition in the process.

## Select Medical Delivery

Known as Health Care Delivery before 1987, Select Medical Delivery invests mainly in equity securities of companies engaged in the ownership of hospitals, nursing homes, and health maintenance organizations as well as in other companies specializing in the delivery of health care services. The fund usually maintains a position in medical equipment suppliers as well.

The aging U.S. population would seem to be a positive factor for this group, but an increasing share of health care profits are being earned by the drug companies. For HMOs in particular, this means an ongoing struggle to contain costs. Advancing surgical techniques and better pills will also make for shorter hospital stays, forcing some institutions to downsize. Cost pressures could also result from new regulations that are aimed at expanding patients' rights. It seems unlikely that this sector will see much profit growth over the long run.

## Select Medical Equipment & Systems

Select Medical Equipment & Systems invests mainly in equity securities of companies engaged in the research, development, manufacture, distribution, supply, or sale of medical equipment and devices and related technologies.

Unlike Medical Delivery, this sector should be able to provide respectable long-term growth—although earnings may not grow as fast as the pharmaceutical and biotech groups. Generally speaking, these companies are providing the equipment and the devices that are making surgical procedures less invasive, resulting in shorter hospital stays and faster recovery times. In some cases, these new procedures are able to offer a more effective solution.

## Select Multimedia

Formerly known as Broadcast & Media, Select Multimedia invests mainly in equity securities of companies engaged in the development, production, sale, and distribution of goods or services used in the broadcast and media industries. Typical groups include cable TV, broadcast TV, content-based web sites, book publishers, newspapers, and magazine companies.

Many of the companies in this group are the ones providing the actual content for web sites, television, books, and magazines. In some respects these companies can be considered the software side of the World Wide Web. The on-line revolution is likely to drive demand for more (and better) content, and many firms in this group are in a good position to deliver it. Over the long run this group will benefit from advancing technology. Television is edging closer to the quality of film, and high-speed internet connections will allow moving pictures and sound to become commonplace on the web. Content providers will have many opportunities for long-term earnings growth.

## Select Natural Gas

Select Natural Gas invests mainly in equity securities of companies engaged in the production, transmission, and distribution of natural gas and involved in the exploration of potential natural gas sources as well as of those companies that provide services and equipment to natural gas producers, refineries, cogeneration facilities, converters, and distributors.

Even though natural gas has its own supply-and-demand factors, it experiences price trends similar to Select Energy and Select Energy Services. Part of the reason is that many companies produce both oil and gas, and their equity values tend to move as a group. The other reason is that some businesses and electric utilities can use either oil or gas and will choose the one that is less expensive. If oil prices fall, for example, some users may switch to oil, and the resulting decline in natural gas demand will bring down natural gas prices as well.

Even though natural gas burns cleaner than other fossil fuels, advancing technology is still a long-term negative for this commodity. While pumping oil, a lot of natural gas is burned or pumped back in the ground because there is no economical method for transporting it. Technology is likely to create cost-effective transport mechanisms, and as with oil it is becoming easier to locate new deposits.

## Select Natural Resources

Select Natural Resources invests mainly in equity securities of companies that own or develop natural resources or that supply goods and services to such companies, and it may also invest directly in precious metals.

This portfolio is essentially a blend of Energy, Energy Services, and Industrial Materials. Except for periods where rising global demand triggers a short-term rally, the long-term prospect for this portfolio is somewhat bleak. Advancing technology and other worldwide deflationary forces are likely to exert downward pricing pressures on most global commodities, making it tough for these companies to grow earnings.

## Select Paper & Forest Products

Select Paper & Forest Products invests mainly in equity securities of companies engaged in the manufacture, research, sale, or distribution of paper products, packaging products, building materials, and other products related to the paper and forest products industry.

Select Paper & Forest Products focuses mostly on paper and lumber companies, which have deep cyclical characteristics similar to those of Select Industrial Materials.

A few of these companies have vast timber resources that may become more valuable over time, but like other commodity sectors this portfolio is not likely to produce the kind of returns available from growth-oriented sectors. Paper companies are part of a mature market in which competition exists worldwide. Global deflationary forces can be expected to force prices lower over the long run, making it difficult to grow earnings. Except for the occasional short-term rally (which is hard to predict in this group), there is no compelling reason to own this portfolio.

## Select Precious Metals & Minerals

The group's longest-running gold fund, Select Precious Metals & Minerals invests mainly in equity securities of companies engaged in exploration, mining, processing, or dealing with gold, silver, platinum, diamonds, or other precious metals and minerals; it may also invest directly in precious metals. (See my discussion of gold characteristics in Chapter 3.)

This is essentially a gold fund, and my comments about Select Gold apply here as well. Select Precious Metals differs from Select Gold in that it invests more on a global basis, which involves slightly more risk. It also tends to invest a greater percentage of assets in precious metals other than gold. Under normal conditions the two funds usually move in tandem.

## Select Regional Banks

This fund invests mainly in the equity securities of companies engaged in accepting deposits and making commercial and principally nonmortgage consumer loans.

From 1991–97 this fund provided unusually good returns. The banking crisis early in the decade reduced the number of competitors and forced many of the survivors to adopt a more profit-minded focus. Today's deflationary forces are also positive for this group, and advancing technology has allowed these firms to cut costs and better manage fraud and credit risk.

Still, most of these banks focus mainly on the domestic market, and many of them have already achieved some degree of market dominance. Over time the earnings growth in this group should be respectable, but it may not keep up with the global financial institutions that are held in the Brokerage and Financial Services portfolios.

## Select Retailing

Select Retailing invests mainly in equity securities of companies engaged in merchandising finished goods and providing services primarily to individual customers.

Today's deflationary environment appears to be positive for this group. Consumers are enjoying significant growth in purchasing power, and much of it is being spent at the shopping mall. There is some downward pressure on prices, but most of these firms are seeing their costs fall just as fast. On-line shopping is a cause for concern for some, but many stores will embrace the web and use it as a tool to augment sales and to help keep traffic in their traditional stores. A number of companies in this group also have the potential for significant global growth. Fidelity has done a good job with this sector and should be able to sort out the winners from the losers as the new economy takes hold.

### Select Software & Computer Services

This fund invests mainly in equity securities of companies engaged in research, design, production, or distribution of products or processes that relate to software or information-based services.

This fund is a subsector of the volatile technology group. Software companies tend to have characteristics different from those of electronics manufacturers and computer makers, but their stocks are still quite volatile because small mistakes can quickly become big problems in the high-tech universe.

There may be many large corrections along the way, but this sector should continue to provide good long-term earnings growth. As Microsoft becomes less dominant, many new opportunities will emerge. The internet poses some concerns for traditional software firms, but Fidelity is likely to focus increasingly on web-based software companies.

### Select Technology

Select Technology invests in equity securities of companies that Fidelity believes have developed (or will develop) products, processes, or services that will provide or will benefit significantly from technological advances and improvements.

In practice, this portfolio invests in a broad-based group of technology firms, including software developers, chip makers, communications equipment manufacturers, and on-line services.

Despite the fact that this portfolio is more diversified than other tech sectors, it is still one of the riskier choices in the Select group. Its price trend can change abruptly in response to a seemingly minor hiccup relating to earnings or the economy. Still, if you have the patience to ride out the big short-term swings, this fund is likely to deliver solid long-term earnings growth. Fidelity seems to do especially well at identifying the winners in this group.

## Select Telecommunications

This fund invests mainly in equity securities of companies engaged in the development, manufacture, or sale of communications services or communications equipment.

Select Telecommunications has traditionally invested most of its assets in telephone companies, both the regional Bells and the long-distance carriers. In recent years, cellular companies and communications equipment manufacturers have been commanding a larger share of the portfolio.

This sector has the opportunity to profit from the growth of on-line services and wireless communications. Advancing technology will allow many of these firms to offer new services such as high-speed internet access. But the conversion from voice circuits to packet-based data transmission could create a lot of excess capacity, particularly if the Bell companies are allowed into the long distance market during the transition. The result could be a big decline in long-distance pricing.

This sector could provide reasonable earnings growth if Fidelity does a good job at stockpicking. Developing Communications offers the potential for higher earnings growth, but the trade-off is an increase in overall risk.

## Select Transportation

A more broadly based portfolio than Select Air Transportation, Select Transportation invests mainly in equity securities of companies that provide transportation services or companies that design, manufacture, distribute, or sell transportation equipment.

Select Transportation usually invests in railroads, airlines, and trucking companies. This is an economically sensitive group. Competitive pressures are not as great a concern as they are for other cyclical groups, but the opportunity for earnings growth is below average. A heavy investment in capital equipment makes it difficult for these companies to cut costs, and the potential for global growth is relatively limited.

## Select Utilities Growth

Formerly known as Select Utilities, Select Utilities Growth invests mainly in equity securities of companies in the public utilities industry and companies deriving a majority of their revenues from their public utility operations.

This portfolio generally holds mostly telephone companies, but it also has some exposure to electric utilities and gas suppliers. It isn't likely to provide much downside protection in a sell-off, but it is one of the least risky Selects and it will normally exhibit less volatility than the S&P 500.

It isn't clear if this sector will survive and prosper in the new economy. Phone companies usually make up the bulk of this portfolio's holdings. For these firms, the internet offers growth, but long distance pricing may see significant downward pressure in the years ahead. As for electric power producers, some are venturing into overseas markets, but it's too early to tell how successful they will be. And deregulation may still hold some surprises here at home.

Fidelity has done a commendable job of identifying the winners in this group, and it has delivered excellent long-term performance for its risk level.

# 10

# *Designing a*
# *Suitable Portfolio*

One of the key challenges for many investors involves developing an overall portfolio strategy. In this chapter, I describe a relatively straightforward approach that is flexible enough for a wide variety of situations.

You may already be familiar with Fidelity's approach to portfolio allocation, which involves answering questions about your investment experience, risk tolerance, investment horizon, age, and financial situation. I think this point-scoring system is straightforward and the questions are appropriate. Still, this approach considers a lot of variables, and those in retirement may have trouble defining their investment horizon accurately.

My approach, on the other hand, emphasizes the investment horizon as the major factor. I also consider personal risk tolerance, but unless you are highly risk-tolerant or very risk-averse I prefer to let the investment horizon be the key driver. What follows is an approach used successfully by many *Fidelity Monitor* subscribers. I have made some refinements over the years, but the basic four-step process is unchanged.

## PUTTING TOGETHER YOUR FIDELITY PORTFOLIO

I'll start with an overview of the process and then go into detail.

1. Decide whether your risk tolerance is low, medium, or high, based on how you feel about investment losses and your preference for income versus growth.
2. Make reasonable estimates of when you will need to spend the principal. These estimates are based on your income sources, living expenses, and the timing of major financial expenditures. You then break up your spending needs into three time periods. (You can skip this step if all your investments are long-term and you don't expect to spend the money for eight years or more.)
3. Apply the suggested fund categories to the dollar amounts in each time period and come up with a suggested overall mix. More details and a chart to help you can be found later in this chapter under "Determining an Appropriate Mix."
4. If you have existing investments, review them to see how your current portfolio stacks up. You can then adjust your portfolio to move it closer to the suggested mix. If you are a first-time investor or if all of your current holdings are in a cash position, you can purchase funds to fit the suggested mix. (In this situation, the merits of a dollar cost averaging approach for purchases of growth-oriented funds are discussed later in this chapter.)

### Determining Your Risk Tolerance

Try not to let any preconceived notions get in the way when deciding whether your risk tolerance is low, medium, or high. Unless your feelings about risk are very strong one way or the other (or if you have a strong preference for conservative or aggressive holdings), you should consider your risk tolerance to be medium. The idea here is to simply decide on an appropriate category for your general disposition.

Consider your risk tolerance low if you are very uncomfortable with sustaining losses or if you are the type who has a strong preference for a predictable income stream. Suppose you knew that bank CD rates would be 5 percent and inflation would be 3 percent for the rest of your life. Would you be tempted to cash in all your investments for this "worry no more" investment strategy? If the answer is yes, you're definitely in the low category.

Consider your risk tolerance to be high if you are willing to ride through the ups and downs of the market in order to grow your portfolio at a faster rate. Suppose you just added a large sum of money to a successful growth fund you've been in for ten years, and the fund declines 25 percent along with the overall market. If you would be disappointed but not worried, you probably have a high tolerance for risk. Investors who can roll with the punches would not lose much sleep in such a situation and would probably make only minor changes in their portfolio.

If neither of these two examples describes your situation, you're probably in the medium group, as are the majority of investors. Investors with medium risk tolerance don't like losses but are willing to live with them to build wealth over the long run. They understand that some exposure to stock-oriented investments is necessary to grow their portfolios, but they don't want to take unnecessary risk.

You may want to consider your spouse in selecting a risk level, particularly if there's a big difference in the way the two of you look at risk. Even when dealing with combined assets, it can often be less stressful to run a split portfolio with each half tailored to the individual's own level of risk tolerance.

If you're picking investments for friends or relatives, it's a good idea to use their threshold for risk tolerance, especially if it's lower than your own. You may understand long-term investing, but those who trust you might tend to view any significant short-term loss as an error in judgment on your part.

## The Trade-Offs of Time

Figure 4 illustrates why the length of time you plan to invest is so important in determining how to structure your portfolio. This chart, which is based on 50 years of market behavior, shows how $1,000 grows with different classes of assets over various periods of time. These figures are adjusted for inflation to give a clear picture of real growth. Inside each box, the figure at the top shows what $1,000 would be worth after the best-case gain for the period indicated. The middle figure is the typical value of an initial $1,000 investment, based on the average return for the period. The bottom figure is the worst-case result over the time frame indicated.

As you might expect, investment returns increase as you take on more risk. This is evident for all time periods and is consistent in both the averages (the middle figures) and the best-case figures (shown at the top). A cash strategy represented by 30-day T-bills was just ahead of inflation (1.1 percent per year real return) for the 50 years ending December 31, 1998. An income approach, represented by a portfolio of 70 percent bonds (50 percent intermediate-term government bonds and 20 percent long-term corporate bonds) and 30 percent stocks (S&P 500 index), provided a real 50-year return of 4.5 percent annually. A growth and income approach using 60 percent stocks (S&P 500) and 40 percent bonds (intermediate-term government bonds) delivered an after-inflation growth rate of 6.7 percent. A growth strategy with 100 percent stocks (S&P 500) averaged a real return of 9.3 percent. Finally, an aggressive growth strategy holding 100 percent in small stocks grew 10.4 percent after inflation.

More interesting, however, is how the worst-case numbers vary. For an investment horizon of more than a year,

| Asset Allocation | | 1 Year | 3 Years | 5 Years | 8 Years | 12 Years | Real Growth |
|---|---|---|---|---|---|---|---|
| Aggressive Growth: 100% Small Stocks | Best Case | $ 1927 | $ 2518 | $ 3610 | $ 5787 | $ 8875 | 10.4% |
| | Average | $ 1104 | $ 1347 | $ 1644 | $ 2214 | $ 3295 | |
| | Worst Case | $ 510 | $ 458 | $ 390 | $ 529 | $ 1080 | |
| Growth: 100% S&P 500 | Best Case | $ 1570 | $ 2300 | $ 3150 | $ 4591 | $ 6749 | 9.3% |
| | Average | $ 1093 | $ 1305 | $ 1559 | $ 2035 | $ 2904 | |
| | Worst Case | $ 545 | $ 575 | $ 593 | $ 697 | $ 748 | |
| Growth & Income: 60% S&P 500, 40% Int. Gov't Bonds | Best Case | $ 1430 | $ 1837 | $ 2487 | $ 2773 | $ 3662 | 6.7% |
| | Average | $ 1067 | $ 1213 | $ 1380 | $ 1675 | $ 2167 | |
| | Worst Case | $ 674 | $ 702 | $ 752 | $ 732 | $ 819 | |
| Income-Oriented: 50% Int. Gov't Bond, 20% Corp LT Bond, 30% S&P 500 | Best Case | $ 1362 | $ 1673 | $ 2187 | $ 2619 | $ 3544 | 4.5% |
| | Average | $ 1045 | $ 1142 | $ 1247 | $ 1423 | $ 1698 | |
| | Worst Case | $ 762 | $ 772 | $ 738 | $ 701 | $ 782 | |
| Money Market Equivalent: 100% 30-Day T-Bills | Best Case | $ 1071 | $ 1182 | $ 1310 | $ 1392 | $ 1516 | 1.1% |
| | Average | $ 1011 | $ 1034 | $ 1057 | $ 1093 | $ 1143 | |
| | Worst Case | $ 924 | $ 776 | $ 735 | $ 612 | $ 564 | |

Legend:
Best Case
Average
Worst Case

**Figure 4** After-inflation growth of $1000 for five asset allocation classes; tested over 50 years.
*Source:* Ibbotson Associates, Inc.

taking on additional risk actually reduces the odds of a loss (indicated by increasing worst-case numbers). At some point, however, your risk of loss jumps up significantly. This is why the investment horizon is key to helping you decide on the appropriate asset class. **For a given investment horizon, there exists an investment strategy that represents the best overall trade-off in terms of risk and total return.** (This is indicated by shaded boxes in Figure 4.)

For a one-year investment period, the risk of loss goes up with any strategy involving more risk than cash. While higher average returns are available, you're taking more of a chance with such a short time period.

For a three-year horizon, an income-oriented approach is the best bet. Notice how the bottom number is actually worse with cash—that's because the higher income stream stands up to inflation better than a cash investment can.

Over five years, a growth and income strategy is the best fit. Notice how the bottom number goes up when moving from cash up to growth and income. Once you take on more risk than a growth and income mix, the potential of bear market losses begins to offset the benefit of taking on more risk.

For an eight-year horizon, the worst-case numbers tend to suggest growth and income again. Looking closely, however, the risk of loss between growth and income and growth is only slightly higher, whereas the after-inflation average return is better by more than two full percentage points. Stocks win out here when you weigh the odds.

For very long-term investments it pays to be aggressive. In the 50-year test period small stocks never lagged inflation or cash investments over a horizon of 12 years or more. If you can stand the year-to-year fluctuations, the long-term risk of holding growth-oriented small stocks is very low.

Cash was actually more "risky" than stocks during certain periods of time. The worst-case figure shows how a cash approach lagged inflation in the 1970s. A portfolio in 30-day T-bills would have lost almost half of its purchasing power during the 12 most inflationary years of the last half century. A repeat of this scenario seems unlikely, but it is worth noting that cash investments have frequently lagged behind inflation on an after-tax basis.

## Your Investment Horizon

Most investors do not invest for a certain period of time and then spend their savings all at once. Putting a son or daughter through college may come close to this scenario, but even then you spend the money over a period of several years. To do a good job of designing a suitable portfolio, you need to characterize your investment horizon.

Unless your investment portfolio is large relative to your annual living expenses, you should consider setting aside three to six months' living expenses as an emergency reserve. A higher amount could be appropriate if your job security is low or if the chance of unexpected medical expenses is high. The emergency fund should be kept in a liquid cash investment such as a money market fund or a savings account.

Now, let's determine the investment horizon for the balance of your investment savings. You don't have to be precise; just try to make some rough estimates based on a likely scenario with no surprise events.

For each of the following periods, estimate your gross income from sources other than your investment holdings. Then figure approximate living expenses, including all major expenses such as housing, food, utilities, insurance, travel, cash outlays for vehicles or property, college expenses, taxes, and medical costs.

The amount by which total expenses exceed income sources is the amount of money needed from your portfolio in the specified period.

***The Next Three Years*** If you are employed and anticipate no major expenses, this figure will probably be $0. If you expect major expenditures, such as a home, car, or college expenses, include any outlays that will exceed your regular income sources. If you are in retirement or if you expect to retire in the next few years, include the amount by which your next three years living expenses will exceed income sources such as social security, pensions, rental income, etc.

*A Period Starting Three and Ending Eight Years from Now*   As with the previous step, figure the amount by which your expenses will exceed noninvestment income sources. Investors expecting to work during this period may end up with $0 in this period as well. Investors in retirement should make allowances for higher costs. Assuming inflation averages 2 percent per year, living expenses that aren't fixed are likely to be about 10 percent higher in this five-year period.

*A Period of Eight Years in the Future and Beyond*   This is the easiest amount to figure, because you simply take your total investment holdings and subtract the previous two figures. Those age 50 or less may find that most or all of their investment holdings are in this category. Retirement investors with a substantial asset base may also end up with a high percentage of their assets in this group. This category is appropriate for investments that may eventually be passed on to heirs or donated to charitable causes (money that may not ever be needed for living expenses).

You may be retired and find that your portfolio will not cover eight years of living expenses. This may be okay depending on your age and health, but you should meet with a fee-based financial planner to review the situation.

## Determining an Appropriate Mix

At this point, you are ready to apply the allocation table shown in Figure 5. This matrix takes into account your risk tolerance and your investment horizon.

| Risk Tolerance | Years Before Money Is Needed for Living Expenses | | |
| --- | --- | --- | --- |
| | Less than 3 Yrs. | 3 - 8 Years | 8 Years or more |
| Low | Money Market | Income-Oriented | Growth and Income |
| Medium | Income-Oriented | Growth and Income | Growth-Oriented |
| High | Growth and Income | Growth-Oriented | Aggressive Growth |

**Figure 5    Recommended allocation strategy.**

Find the row that matches your risk tolerance and apply the amounts for each spending period to the suggested mix. Then add up the dollar amounts dedicated to each investment approach for a final allocation mix. Some examples follow.

*Ron and Cathy*  A retired couple, Ron and Cathy have investment holdings of $800,000. Living expenses that are not covered by social security and pension income are expected to average about $40,000 per year over the next three years and $50,000 per year for the following five years. The two consider their risk tolerance to be low. In this situation, there would be $120,000 in the "less than three years" box, which would be allocated to a money market fund. Another $250,000 of expenses would go in the second box (three to eight years) and would be allocated to an income approach. The remaining $430,000 would be in the third box (eight years or more) and would be allocated to a growth and income approach. When invested in Fidelity mutual funds, this mix of investments should produce a long-term growth rate of about 8 to 9 percent per year. Although dividends alone (the income stream) from this portfolio will probably not be enough to meet living expenses, Ron and Cathy should be comfortable with the idea of selling shares to make up the difference. Over the long term, the portfolio's total return should be high enough to meet living expenses with some growth of capital.

*Tom*   At age 35, Tom considers himself to have medium risk tolerance. His only significant investment is $50,000 in a Fidelity 401(k) retirement plan that his employer offers. Tom figures his salary will cover all of his expenditures until retirement. In this situation, all $50,000 would be in the medium risk box (eight years or more). Tom should pursue a growth-oriented strategy.

*Mike and Lori*   A couple with young children, Mike and Lori have saved $16,000 for their children's college expenses, and they will start needing the money in about 15 years. The couple has an adequate emergency fund but has not saved much for retirement. Both have good jobs that should provide for all expenditures in the next eight years, and the two consider their risk tolerance to be high. In this situation, Mike and Lori could follow the box in the lower right and invest the money in an aggressive growth strategy. The couple should also try to save 10 percent of their combined gross salaries for their retirement.

*Cynthia*   At age 27, Cynthia is saving to purchase a home when her lease expires in about two years. She considers herself to have medium risk tolerance. Cynthia should go with a 100 percent income-oriented approach. Given the short-term need for capital, it doesn't make sense for Cynthia to have much exposure to the stock market.

*Bill and Debbie* As they near retirement with investment savings of $600,000, Bill and Debbie consider themselves to have medium risk tolerance. Bill will quit next year; Debbie has three years left to work. The couple won't need to draw on investments until Debbie retires because Bill's pension is a good one and should provide enough to live on while Debbie works. Upon Debbie's retirement they plan to travel and figure they'll draw an average of $50,000 per year for the following five years. In this situation, $250,000 of expenses are in the medium risk box (three to eight years), where a growth and income strategy is recommended. The remaining $350,000 would go to the eight years or more box and be invested for growth.

Keep in mind that in all of these examples the suggested mix may not be appropriate if the financial situation is complex or if there are unusual circumstances. If you have any doubts, you should meet with a fee-based financial planner to obtain some unbiased personal advice.

## CATEGORIZING YOUR EXISTING HOLDINGS

If you have existing investments, the next step is to group them to see how your existing mix of securities compares to the suggested allocation mix. Here are some grouping guidelines that should provide a reasonable estimate of your current position:

- Any investment with stable principal can be considered a *cash investment*. This includes bank accounts, credit union accounts, CDs, short-term T-bills (less than a year), guaranteed investment contracts, and money market funds.

- The *income-oriented* group includes domestic corporate bonds (except junk bonds), U.S. government bonds, municipal bonds, treasuries maturing in one year or more, and any mutual funds that invest in these types of securities.
- *Growth and income* includes growth and income funds that blend stocks and bonds, junk bonds (and junk bond funds), and foreign bonds (as well as foreign bond funds).
- Diversified stock funds, index funds, foreign stock funds (except emerging-market funds), and any individual blue-chip stocks or dividend stocks belong in the *growth-oriented* category.
- Other stock positions go in the *aggressive growth* group, as do sector funds, emerging market funds, small-cap growth funds, and any other aggressive growth stock funds.

To figure your current mix, divide the total assets in each group by the total value of all your investments. Then compare your current mix to the suggested allocation to see how well you match up.

## WORKING TOWARD YOUR SUGGESTED MIX

The next step is to work toward your suggested allocation mix by purchasing the funds that I recommend (later in this section) in each of the asset groups. Depending on your situation, however, you may not want to move out of your current holdings right away.

Unless you are dealing with assets in a retirement account, selling securities that have increased in value since their purchase could trigger unnecessary capital gains tax on your 1040. If this is the case, you may want to sell selectively and increase your model holdings gradually. For example, if your overall position is more aggressive than the recommended mix, sell the aggressive positions that have appreciated the least and buy conservative funds to obtain a better balance. If possible, you may want to sell losing positions along with profitable ones to offset capital gains. It could even make sense to sell over several years to minimize taxes. For investments that continue to perform well, you may not want to sell at all until you actually need the money.

If you are starting from cash or from a relatively conservative mix of investments, you may want to dollar cost average if you plan to go with a growth-oriented strategy. Dollar cost averaging over two years provides some protection against a market decline and is discussed later in this chapter.

If possible, it may be to your advantage to use retirement accounts to fulfill your growth-oriented or aggressive growth allocation. The benefit of tax-deferred compounding is particularly valuable at higher growth rates (see Chapter 11 for more details).

## ANNUAL REBALANCING

Keep in mind that maintaining your allocation mix is a continuing process, not something you do once and forget. I recommend that investors go through the exercise at least once a year. The reallocation that results from this process has two benefits. First, it takes into account any changes that have occurred in your financial situation and adjusts accordingly. Second, it rebalances the asset classes. Suppose stocks have a strong year, whereas bonds are weak. Selling some of your stock holdings and adding to bond funds may not seem like the right thing to do at the time, but it actually reduces your exposure to a higher-priced group of securities and increases your position in a group that is more attractively valued.

## SELLING TO MEET LIVING EXPENSES

If you are living off your investments, the annual rebalancing of your portfolio is a good time to raise the cash you'll need for the coming year's living expenses. Estimate what you think you'll need over the next 12 months, and then sell assets from the group you are the most overweighted in.

For example, let's say you need $40,000 for the coming year's expenses. Based on earlier steps your target mix is $120,000 income, $200,000 growth and income, and $300,000 growth. Now suppose your actual holdings are $60,000 income, $200,000 growth and income, and $360,000 growth. In this case you would liquidate $60,000 of your growth-oriented holdings, putting $40,000 in a money market fund for living expenses, and $20,000 into additional income investments.

Over the course of the year you can then draw down the balance in the money market fund as you need the cash. If it turns out that the $40,000 gets used up in less than a year, you can always go through another rebalancing cycle at that time.

Here are two additional tips. If you do the rebalancing around tax time, you can sell to raise cash for taxes at the same time you sell to raise money for living expenses. It's more convenient that way, and the capital gains you generate won't show up until the following tax year. Also, when estimating the money needed for living expenses, be sure to reduce it by the appropriate amount if you have other income sources coming in throughout the year—including any bond or money market income that isn't being automatically reinvested.

## FORCED RETIREMENT ACCOUNT DISTRIBUTIONS

Once you reach the age where you are forced to take withdrawals from your retirement account (usually above age 70), you have no choice but to pay taxes on the "income" from the distribution. As such, you should use this money for living expenses before selling other securities. If the distribution exceeds your cash needs, the excess should be invested in a regular taxable account according to the steps described.

## INVESTING IN THE SUGGESTED ALLOCATION

Following is a discussion of the Fidelity funds that are appropriate for each of the five asset groups shown in the allocation chart (Figure 5).

### Money Market Choices

Over the long run, I expect money markets to deliver an average return of around 3 percent, staying ahead of inflation. From a performance standpoint, Fidelity's money market funds are pretty similar, and the taxable group usually offers the best returns for all but the highest-bracket investors. Go with Cash Reserves for low minimums and free services. If you expect to maintain a balance of $50,000 or more, go with Spartan Money Market for slightly higher yields.

### Income-Oriented Fidelity Portfolios

For an income-oriented approach using Fidelity funds, you can follow the Income model published in *Fidelity Monitor,* or you can go with one of the model portfolios shown in Figure 6.

Portfolio A is 50 percent Investment Grade Bond, 25 percent Short-Term Bond, and 25 percent High Income. Over a ten-year period, I estimate that this mix will generate a total return of about 7 to 8 percent annually, with 5 to 6 percent from the regular monthly income and about 2 percent from capital appreciation. This mix of funds could lose 5 percent or more in a bond market sell-off, but the chances of a down year for this portfolio are low. The portfolio includes a variety of corporate and government bonds and a modest stake in conservative stocks and junk bonds (via High-Income fund). This mix tends to provide some stability

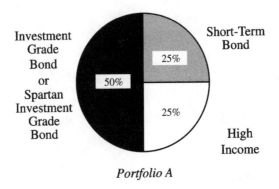

*Portfolio A*

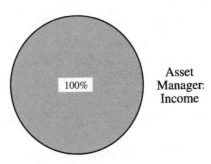

*Portfolio B: Conservative Total Return*

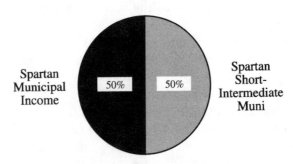

*Portfolio C: Tax-Free Income*

**Figure 6    Income-oriented portfolios.**

because of the differences among the three funds; during most periods in the economic cycle at least two of these three holdings should perform well.

Portfolio B is the single-fund solution—Asset Manager: Income. Backed with a balanced mix of conservative securities, this fund has nearly the same long-term performance potential as Portfolio A, but its income stream is likely to be a bit lower. Risk of loss in a bear market is about the same.

Portfolio C seeks tax-free income with 50 percent in Spartan Municipal Income and 50 percent in Spartan Short-Intermediate Muni. For investors in the top brackets, its long-term after-tax return of 4 to 5 percent per year might be slightly better than for Portfolios A or B. The drawback is greater interest-rate risk; in a bond market sell-off, Portfolio C could lose a little more than Portfolios A or B.

## Growth and Income Fidelity Portfolios

For a Fidelity growth and income approach, you can follow the Growth and Income model published in *Fidelity Monitor*, or you can choose a model portfolio from Figure 7.

Portfolio A is 50 percent Balanced, 25 percent Puritan, and 25 percent Capital & Income. Over a ten-year period, I project a total return averaging 10 percent per year for this mix of funds, with 3 to 4 percent coming from reinvested dividends and 6 to 7 percent from capital appreciation. This portfolio could decline 15 percent or more in a bear market.

Portfolio B is a single fund solution, 100 percent Asset Manager. This approach has the advantage of being simple, but its income stream is a bit lower. Overall characteristics should be similar to those of Portfolio A.

Portfolio C is 40 percent Investment Grade Bond, 30 percent Fidelity Fund, and 30 percent Equity-Income II. This approach uses the classic 60 percent stock and 40 percent bond mix that has proven itself over time. Again, risk and return should be a close match to Portfolio A.

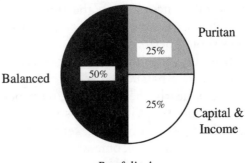

Portfolio A

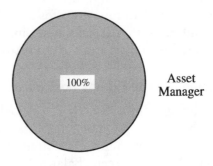

Portfolio B

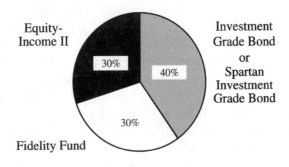

Portfolio C

**Figure 7   Growth and income portfolios.**

## Growth-Oriented Fidelity Portfolios

The Growth model published in *Fidelity Monitor* is my preferred approach for investing in growth-oriented Fidelity funds, but the portfolios in Figure 8 should also perform well.

Portfolio A is 40 percent Spartan Total Market Index, 30 percent Large Cap Stock, and 30 percent Contrafund II. My ten-year total return estimate for this group is 13 percent per year. This mix of funds could decline 25 percent or more in a bear market. Contrafund II tends to be growth-oriented, whereas Large Cap Stock tends to focus on companies that are global leaders. Spartan Total Market Index is a broad-based position in the U.S. stock market (it aims to match the Wilshire 5000 Index). Together these funds cover a broad spectrum of markets, which adds an element of stability to the portfolio.

Portfolio B offers a no-load approach for all accounts (Portfolio A is no-load only for retirement accounts). It holds 40 percent Spartan Total Market Index, 30 percent Large Cap Stock, and 30 percent Growth Company. This approach should provide a growth rate close to that of Portfolio A. Growth Company is substituted for Contrafund II. Bear market risk should be similar to that of Portfolio A.

Portfolio C provides more international exposure. With a mix of 40 percent Spartan Total Market Index, 30 percent Large Cap Stock, and 30 percent Spartan International Index, this portfolio trades off some growth in favor of international diversification. Spartan International Index focuses mainly on European and Japanese stocks. The long-term growth rate of Portfolio C could be slightly less than the other two choices, but it is less likely to suffer as much in a domestic bear market.

## Aggressive Growth Fidelity Portfolios

The Select System model in *Fidelity Monitor* provides a sector-based approach for aggressive growth. In this portfolio I

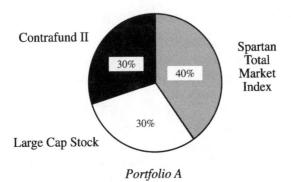

*Portfolio A*

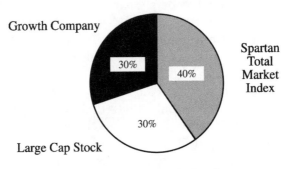

*Portfolio B: No-Load*

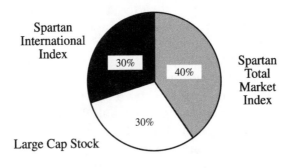

*Portfolio C: Global*

**Figure 8   Growth-oriented portfolios.**

use a relative value model to help identify undervalued sector funds. I've come to prefer a numbers-driven approach for the aggressive side because it takes emotion out of the picture. The fixed portfolios in Figure 9 aren't able to move around to take advantage of new opportunities, but I've tried to choose funds that have a high probability of long-term success.

Portfolio A uses a sector-oriented approach. With 25 percent each in Select Biotechnology, Select Multimedia, Select Technology, and Select Financial Services, this portfolio is capable of a ten-year growth rate of 15 percent per year. In a bear market it could decline 30 percent or more. Following are my thoughts about these choices.

Select Biotechnology is a play on emerging pharmaceutical companies. These firms will be supplying the medical solutions of the future, and there should be many opportunities. Biotech also includes companies that are developing agricultural solutions, which will play a key role in meeting the demands on the world food supply as global growth picks up.

Select Multimedia is in this portfolio because these companies stand to benefit from the growth that the on-line revolution will bring. Also, U.S. companies stand a reasonable chance of dominating the worldwide markets for entertainment and publishing.

An investment in Select Technology takes advantage of a sector with above-average long-term growth potential. Fidelity seems to do a particularly good job of analyzing these firms.

Last but not least, Select Financial Services should do well in a deflationary environment. Many of the banks and financial services companies in this sector are recognized worldwide, and they have the potential for long-term global growth.

Portfolio B uses diversified funds rather than sectors. With 40 percent in Aggressive Growth, 30 percent in Capital

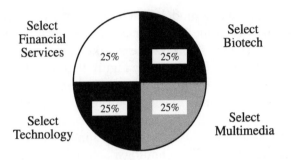

*Portfolio A: Selects Only*

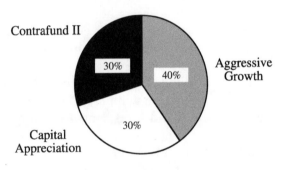

*Portfolio B: Non-Select*

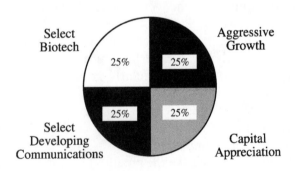

*Portfolio C: All Groups*

**Figure 9    Aggressive growth portfolios.**

Appreciation, and 30 percent in Contrafund II, this portfolio should do almost as well as Portfolio A in terms of total return but may have more downside risk. Fidelity does a pretty good job finding attractive growth stocks, and all three of these funds tend to be growth-oriented in different ways. Aggressive Growth typically focuses on technology stocks. Capital Appreciation tends to look for the most interesting sector plays. Contrafund II can be expected to seek out stocks where the market has overlooked the potential for growth.

Portfolio C includes both sector funds and diversified funds. Each of the four funds accounts for a 25 percent position: Aggressive Growth, Capital Appreciation, Select Developing Communications (a fund that includes elements of both Multimedia and Technology), and Select Biotechnology. Growth potential should be similar to that of Portfolio A, although bear market risk may be slightly higher.

## HOW MANY FUNDS SHOULD YOU OWN?

Depending on where you are in the allocation chart and which portfolios you follow, you can end up having to purchase as few as three or as many as ten different mutual funds for your investment holdings. (Conservative strategies generally involve fewer funds, whereas aggressive strategies involve more.)

Investors who previously owned individual stocks and bonds sometimes feel that this number is too low. If you feel this way, remember that the average fund invests in more than 100 securities, and broadly diversified funds such as Asset Manager often own more than 500 different issues. Owning more than ten funds really isn't necessary to achieve broad diversification, and if you are investing conservatively you don't even need that many.

Along that line of thinking, the number of funds you own does not need to change for a large investment portfolio. Investment bankers rarely put their wealthy clients into more than 500 different securities, a level of diversification that can easily be obtained with just two to three broad-based mutual funds. The mix of funds I've recommended in each set of model portfolios is appropriate whether the amount being invested is $10,000 or $1 million.

In some cases it can make sense to *reduce* the number of funds you hold. Fidelity waives its annual account fee of $12 per fund (currently capped at $24 maximum) if you maintain a balance of $2,500 or more in each fund or a total of $50,000 or more in all of your accounts. Consolidating to eliminate fees may improve your performance by a small amount if you have a number of funds with small balances.

## DOLLAR COST AVERAGING

Dollar cost averaging is an excellent way to move from cash into a growth-oriented or aggressive growth strategy because it disciplines you to buy more shares when prices are lower and to buy fewer when prices are higher. This advantage is significant because most investors will do exactly the opposite when making decisions in an unstructured fashion.

When you dollar cost average, you invest at regular intervals of time (usually monthly or quarterly) with a fixed dollar commitment at each interval. You become a value investor without even trying because your fixed commitment in dollars will automatically buy a larger position after a market decline or a smaller position following a rally. To better understand the benefit, consider the following simple example involving a technology stock. Initially, the stock has a price of $10 per share, and a purchase of $1,000 (100 shares) is made. Three months later the price has plummeted to $5 per share, and another $1,000 is invested (200 shares are purchased). Another quarter later, and the price has rebounded to $7.50 per share. A final purchase is made (133.3 shares).

What are the results? At first glance many investors would say the investor either broke even or lost money. In reality, a gain of 8.3 percent has been realized because of the effects of averaging down. Because more shares were purchased when the price was low, the average cost per share was $6.92 versus an average purchase price of $7.50. The final investment value is $3,250 versus $3,000 paid.

Generally speaking, there are two ways to use dollar cost averaging to your advantage:

- The first and most widely used method is to invest a percentage of your salary into a growth-oriented portfolio during your working years. Often the goal is to build a nest egg for future college expenses or for retirement. Many 401(k) investors are doing this with the added benefits of using pretax money and realizing tax-deferred compounding. Over the long run, this kind of program can be a very powerful tool for building wealth.
- The second approach is useful for reducing the risk of going from cash to a growth-oriented position. The benefit of dollar cost averaging in this situation is that you buy in at a progressively lower price if a market sell-off takes place (as opposed to experiencing the full impact of the decline right after you invest a large sum). When recovery eventually comes, it seldom takes long before your portfolio is worth more than you paid in.

I recommend a buy-in period of two years when dollar cost averaging from a cash position. Take the amount you want to invest, divide by 8, and make purchases once a quarter for eight quarters. Don't wait for a good time to start; it isn't necessary to worry about what the market will do next because dollar cost averaging takes advantage of whatever comes along.

Figure 10 shows the benefit of dollar cost averaging during the worst bear market in modern history. In this

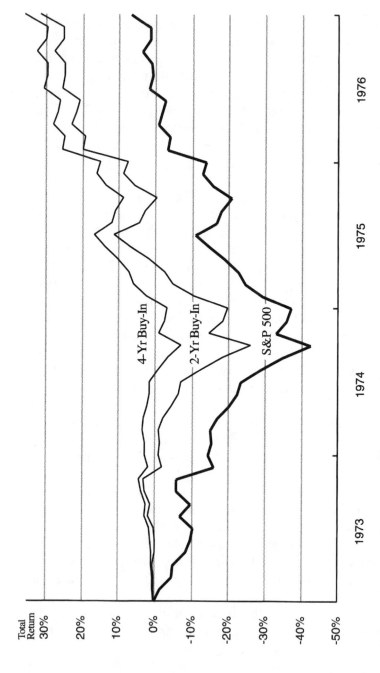

**Figure 10 Impact of dollar cost averaging during worst bear market in modern history.**

example, the initial balance is in a money market fund (represented by short-term T-bills), and quarterly purchases of an S&P 500 index fund are made (both two-year and four-year buy-ins are shown). In both of these examples, the dollar-cost-average portfolios decline less and recover faster than the market as a whole.

Of course, dollar cost averaging won't help you during bullish times. If stocks move up continuously, you'll lag the market because you'll have a heavy cash position while you are joining up with the market. As a practical matter, I favor the two-year buy-in period because it protects reasonably well against a downturn but isn't so long that you sacrifice gains in the more probable scenario of a rising market. Quarterly purchases are the most practical when you consider fund minimums, although a monthly approach could improve performance by a few percentage points during sideways or rising market conditions.

Dollar cost averaging works best with a growth-oriented or aggressive growth strategy. It can be used with the portfolios outlined earlier in this chapter or with the growth-oriented models in *Fidelity Monitor*. In the latter case, each portfolio switch requires that you change the invested portion and any new purchases to reflect the new mix.

The benefit of dollar cost averaging is diminished when investing for growth and income or when pursuing an income-oriented strategy. There simply isn't enough equity risk to reduce; you might as well invest everything in one step. Still, if you prefer a minimum-risk approach, averaging into a growth and income fund over three years is one way to nearly eliminate the risk of loss during the buy-in period.

# 11

# *Taxes and Retirement Accounts*

If a mutual find has a long-term return of 12 percent per year, is that the rate of growth you will achieve in your own account? The answer is yes if your investments are held in a tax-deferred account such as an IRA, Keogh, 401(k) plan, or a 403(b) plan. Such retirement plans do not incur any tax on investment gains (although you do pay tax at full income rates when you make withdrawals in your retirement years).

In a regular account, however, the net rate of return is typically a few percentage points less after you deduct the taxes paid on fund distributions each year. By law, mutual funds must distribute most of the income and capital gains they realize each year. Even if you reinvest a fund's distributions, you still have to pay taxes on the payout unless the fund is held in a retirement account. Your after-tax return, which takes into account the income tax you pay on the reinvested distributions, is the actual rate of return on your holdings.

After-tax return varies depending on your own personal tax bracket, but Figure 11 can give you an idea of the impact. For this chart, I computed the after-tax returns for a number of Fidelity's diversified growth funds for the ten-year period ending December 31, 1998. Two after-tax situations

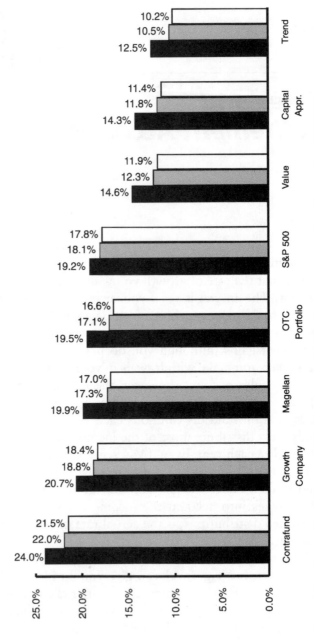

**Figure 11** Annualized return of Fidelity growth funds for ten years ending December 31, 1998.

are shown. The first assumes a 20 percent federal rate for long-term capital gains and a 31 percent rate for dividends and short-term gains. The second scenario also assumes the 20 percent bracket for long-term payouts but uses the top federal rate of 39.6 percent for dividends and short-term gains. In both cases, the chart shows the annualized return that would exist prior to selling the entire fund position and paying tax on the unrealized capital gain.

Not surprisingly, funds that did well on a pretax basis generally performed well after taxes. Some funds outperformed the S&P 500 on an after-tax basis, which counters the argument that an index fund is the only way to go in a taxable account. (Proponents of indexing claim an advantage over regular funds because of their low payouts of capital gains.)

The leader of the pack, Contrafund, did unusually well after taxes because of unique circumstances that are unlikely to be repeated. Because of steady inflows of new money throughout the period, this fund provided its managers plenty of new capital for buying attractive stocks. Accordingly, the fund didn't have to sell much of its portfolio for many years. This made for relatively low payouts of capital gains and relatively high after-tax returns. However, situations like this don't last forever. With assets of more than $35 billion, Contrafund is now relatively mature. Future years are now likely to bring payouts that are similar to those of other growth funds.

## TAX IMPLICATIONS OF EXCHANGES

In a tax-deferred retirement account, you can switch all you want with no tax implications. In a regular account, however, each exchange you make produces a capital gain or capital loss, depending on whether the price at which you sell is higher or lower than the price at which you bought. If the shares you are selling have been held for less than one year, your capital gain is short term. Losses in a period of less than a year are short term to the extent that they are not offset by long-term gains. These rules also apply to municipal funds, which are generally tax-free on dividends but not on capital gains.

The capital gain you incur when selling a fund is usually not the full gain you have obtained in owning the fund. Rather, it is the gain that hasn't already been taxed as a result of the fund's distributions. Prior to selling a fund, the difference between the current share price (NAV) and the purchased price (plus any transaction fees) is called the unrealized capital gain.

## DOES SWITCHING HELP OR HURT LONG-TERM RETURNS?

Some advisors claim an actively managed portfolio will perform worse than a buy and hold portfolio after taxes are figured in. This is often true during a period where stocks post strong gains for many years in a row, as was the case from late 1994 through 1998. In such a situation the tax burden becomes significant because there are few opportunities to offset gains with losses. Buying and holding an index fund (or a fund like Tax Managed Stock) is about the only tax-efficient approach for a straight-up bull market.

However, during normal market conditions, there are usually plenty of opportunities for active investors to keep taxes at a reasonable level. And in bearish times, taking losses and moving on can actually reduce your tax liability. The question of whether to move around freely or remain frozen in one fund has more to do with personal preference than with minimizing taxes.

If you don't mind a pay-as-you-go approach to taxes, you can enjoy the freedom of repositioning your portfolio to fit your changing goals. In this situation it makes sense to liquidate a small part of your portfolio to pay for the capital gains taxes that will come due each year, so that you don't have to curtail your living expenses. When it comes time to live off your portfolio, your tax burden will be relatively light because your unrealized gains will be small.

But, if you want to hold your pre-retirement tax bills to an absolute minimum, or if you are unwilling to liquidate even a small portion of your portfolio to cover annual capital gains, you should probably just buy Tax Managed Stock or Spartan Total Market Index and keep it until you retire and need the money. By building up a large unrealized gain, you delay most of the impact of taxes until you actually start selling shares. The trade-off is that you can't reposition your portfolio when you reach retirement age, or you may end up with a huge tax bill.

## MINIMIZING THE TAX BITE

Following are several techniques you can use to create a tax-advantaged portfolio.

### Retirement Accounts

Keep your growth-oriented and aggressive-growth funds in retirement accounts—especially if you have a Roth IRA. Tax-deferred accounts provide the most benefit at higher long-term growth rates (more on this later in the chapter). You can balance your growth-oriented retirement holdings with conservative holdings in your taxable accounts—where the money will be available without penalty if you need it. I realize this strategy may be the opposite of what many investors practice, but the benefits are significant, especially if you are under age 50 (at this age you still have at least 20 years available before you are required to take money out of your tax-deferred accounts).

### Timely Purchases

Avoid purchasing a stock fund in a taxable account if it is close to making a distribution. Many large payouts of capital gains occur in December, so try to purchase the fund after the payout has occurred.

## Hold Positions

Try to hold profitable positions for at least one year in a taxable account. That way, you'll receive the more favorable 20 percent maximum rate on long-term capital gains. This doesn't mean you should hang on to a fund with deteriorating performance, but other factors being equal, you should strive for a one-year holding period. Likewise, try to take losses short-term if your long-term gains are small. (I use both of these techniques in the *Fidelity Monitor* Growth model.)

## Take Losses with Gains

In a taxable account, it does not pay to hang on to a losing position. Better to sell the fund and realize a tax loss. After all, you can always buy a similar fund or repurchase the same fund 31 days later. The tax loss will help to offset capital gains from distributions and profits on other positions. I realize that in recent years most investors have not had any losing positions, but that's unusual. During normal years there are usually at least a few opportunities to book a loss. Doing so will improve your after-tax return in most cases.

## FILING YOUR INCOME TAXES

Except for retirement account holdings, Fidelity will send you and the IRS a 1099-DIV form after the end of each year. This statement lists all of the mutual fund distributions that must be reported on your federal 1040 form. All taxable dividend income, including the regular monthly income from bond and money market funds, will be listed on this form and must be reported on Schedule B, Interest and Dividend Income. (For IRS purposes, a fund's ordinary dividends include both distribution of income and short-term capital gains.) Long-term capital gains must be reported on Schedule D, Capital Gains and Losses. Note that it does not matter how long you own a fund. A long-term distribution of capital gains must be reported as such even if it was paid out a few days after you bought the fund. Finally, be sure to check Fidelity's state-by-state list of municipal income dividends if you owned a national muni fund. You can avoid state taxes on the percentage of income earned from bonds specific to your state.

If you owned any municipal bond funds or municipal money market funds, Fidelity will send you a statement of tax-exempt income that lists the amount of tax-free dividends you earned and any income subject to Alternative Minimum Tax (AMT).

If you held any limited partnerships (some of Fidelity's funds are structured this way), you'll receive a schedule K-1 listing dividends and capital gains. Like regular funds, these are reported on Schedules B and D, respectively.

Unless you've confined your switching activity to a retirement account or money market fund, all mutual fund redemptions must be reported on Schedule D of your federal 1040 return. Fidelity will send you and the IRS a 1099-B form showing all of the Fidelity transactions you must report. However, it's up to you to do the hard part, figuring out cost basis. (Fidelity sends year-end cost basis information for accounts opened in 1987 or later; it may be a great time-saver if you fit the requirements for using it.)

## Cost Basis

There are four options for determining cost basis, and when you select a method you should state it on your tax form or on an attachment. Once you start using a method for a particular fund, you must get permission from the IRS if you want to change methods before selling all shares owned in that fund. (The only exception is that you are allowed to switch without permission once from either FIFO or specific shares to average cost per share.)

*First In, First Out (FIFO)* This method is relatively simple and easy, and it requires the least record keeping if you are doing your own taxes. It assumes the first shares purchased are the first to be sold. Suppose your first purchase of Magellan was 50 shares at $50 per share and your second was 75 shares at $60 per share. Later you sell 100 shares at $70 per share. Your cost basis for the first 50 shares sold would be $2,500 (50 shares at $50 per share), and your cost basis on the second 50 shares would be $3,000 (50 shares at $60 per share). Together you would have paid $5,500 on the shares you sold. Your gain on the sale would be $1,500, and if both were held for a year or more it would be considered a long-term capital gain.

*Specific Shares* With this approach, you identify specific blocks of shares to sell (usually those that produce the smallest gain or largest loss). Write a letter and let Fidelity know you are selling specific shares, and then identify the specific block of shares by account, quantity, and date purchased. Save a copy of the letter and Fidelity's acknowledgment for your tax records.

*Average Cost per Share, Single Category* With this method, a weighted average of all purchase prices is computed, and the average price is used for the cost basis on all shares you've sold. If the selling activity is spread out over more than one year, the average is updated each year.

If you have not started with a different method, you can use the average cost per share figures Fidelity now provides on accounts opened after 1986. But if you have used a different method in the past, Fidelity's figures will not be valid even if you switch over to this method, because the average cost figure would no longer be accurate after the first sale.

*Average Cost per Share, Double Category* This is similar to the single category method, except that your short-term holdings (positions held less than a year) and long-term holdings are grouped separately, and a weighted average cost per share is computed for each.

## Other Schedule D Considerations

Regardless of which cost basis method you choose, there are some other things to be aware of when filling out your Schedule D (all of which are included in Fidelity's cost basis figures if you are able to use them).

For reinvested dividends and capital gains distributions, each is considered a separate purchase. In the case of a bond fund, for example, you make at least 12 purchases every year, each at a different price. When you sell a long-term position, you may have reinvestment purchases that represent short-term capital gains.

A sale involving a capital loss can be deemed a wash sale (a sale intended solely for creating a tax loss) if the same fund is repurchased within 30 days (or if it is purchased up to 30 days ahead of the sale). Losses are disallowed for wash sales, but the loss can be added to your cost basis on your repurchase of the fund. Wash sale rules can be tripped accidentally, so be sure to consider your situation before you sell at a loss. Also be aware that Fidelity's cost basis statement may not properly detect and adjust for a wash sale if more than one account is involved. (Wash sale rules do not apply to retirement accounts because their transactions are not reported on Schedule D.)

If you sell shares at a loss in a fund you've held for less than six months, you may have to treat part or all of your loss as long-term if you received a distribution of long-term capital gains during the period. For each share sold, the amount that must be treated as a long-term capital loss is equal to the amount of the long-term distribution of capital gains on that share.

## TAX-DEFERRED ACCOUNTS

If you have money in a Roth IRA, a regular IRA, a Keogh, a 401(k) plan, or a 403(b) account, you've got a unique opportunity to grow your portfolio without the burden of taxes to slow you down. Especially in the case of a Roth IRA, you'll want to put the advantage of compounding on your side.

Figure 12 shows how the combination of pretax compounding and a growth-oriented strategy can produce powerful results. You've probably seen this type of graph before, but note that these results are adjusted for inflation (at an assumed rate of 2 percent per year). The results show real increases in purchasing power on an initial $1,000 investment. Although there are no guarantees for the growth rates that are shown, I think the total returns shown are achievable with the model portfolios outlined in Chapter 10.

At lower growth rates, such as those available from money markets, CDs, T-bills, or bond funds, a tax-deferred account offers little advantage over a taxable account (other than the benefit of being able to contribute pretax money). Keeping long-term retirement account assets in cash is like owning a Ferrari and using it only for low-speed trips to the grocery store. A tax-deferred account that's being used for long-term savings can realize its potential only if it includes growth-oriented investments. It should be used for building wealth, not staying even with inflation.

Investors in their working years should use a retirement account only for long-term savings. That's because once you make a contribution you'll pay a 10 percent penalty on any withdrawals you take before age 59½ (unless you become disabled or you annuitize with an IRS-approved method).

If you have the choice, go with a Roth IRA for all new IRA contributions. Chances are, the loss of deductibility on the initial contributions will be a small price to pay for an account that can grow tax-free for as long as you want. That's a big plus when you consider that with a traditional

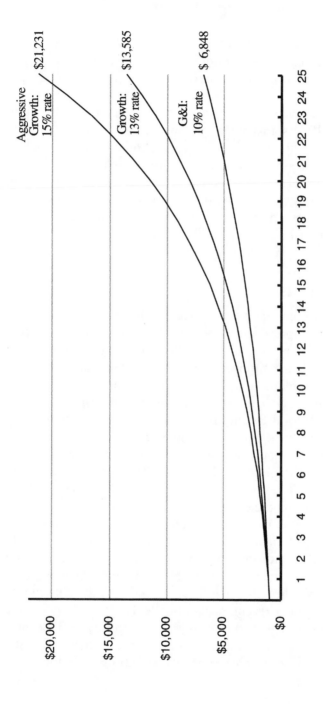

**Figure 12** After-inflation growth of a $1000 investment in a tax-deferred account.

IRA you are subject to forced withdrawals starting around age 70½ (if you don't follow IRS life-expectancy tables, you face a 50 percent excise tax on the amount you should have taken out each year).

Deciding whether to convert from a traditional IRA into a Roth IRA is a tougher call. Such a move is likely to push you into a higher tax bracket, and today's upper brackets are a bit steep when you consider the shrinking role that the federal government is playing in today's economy. If you convert now, you give up the chance to obtain a more favorable tax rate down the road. Unless you will be facing forced distributions that will push you into a higher bracket anyway, it might pay to wait for a lower federal tax rate.

## 401(K) PLANS

Almost insignificant a decade ago, 401(k) plans today are enjoying unprecedented popularity. More than 95 percent of large corporations now offer these unique retirement plans to their employees, and smaller firms are setting up their own plans at a rapid clip. The amount of 401(k) money in Fidelity funds now accounts for perhaps 35 to 40 percent of total Fidelity fund assets, and new contributions from Fidelity 401(k) plans have grown to the point that some funds experience net inflows of capital even during market declines. In the long run, 401(k) money could reshape the entire mutual fund industry and even have a stabilizing effect on the entire domestic stock market.

Companies favor 401(k) plans because they are classified as "defined contribution plans" rather than "defined benefit plans" like traditional pensions. 401(k) programs do not carry the promise of guaranteed retirement benefits, a financial liability that has become increasingly difficult to shoulder with recent accounting changes and increasing government regulations. Many firms want their 401(k) programs to be successful because over the next few decades they would like to phase out their traditional pensions.

Employees also like 401(k) plans because they have control. They decide how much to contribute, and they decide how it should be invested (within the range of choices offered). Unlike a big pension fund, the money is in a designated account and is less likely to be misappropriated if the company gets bought out or falls on hard times. When leaving the company, the money can be transferred tax-free to a rollover IRA account at an institution of the employee's choice.

## Financial Advantages of a 401(k)

What many employees may not realize is that 401(k) programs are an excellent opportunity for accumulating wealth. In addition to tax-deferred compounding, a 401(k) account has several other significant financial advantages.

*Pretax Contributions* The money contributed to your 401(k) account comes out of your paycheck before federal and state taxes are deducted. Suppose your federal tax bracket is 31 percent. To equal the power of a 401(k) plan you would have to save 45 percent more if you were saving on your own. ($145 per month saved on a pretax basis only reduces your take-home pay by about $100, so you can be saving 45 percent more money just by doing it on a pretax basis.)

*Matching Funds* Many employers provide significant matching funds, which give you an immediate large return on your contributions. If your employer makes one for three matching contributions in the preceding example, your 401(k) plan has almost twice the accumulating power of a do-it-yourself approach using after-tax money.

*Dollar Cost Averaging* A 401(k) plan sets aside money from each paycheck and makes predetermined purchases at regular intervals, so dollar cost averaging is working in your favor. In a growth fund, the rate of return you obtain on the invested money can be slightly higher than the fund itself because you'll be purchasing more shares whenever the price is lower.

*Avoiding Load Fees* Mutual fund companies, including Fidelity, generally waive load fees in their 401(k) plans. This allows 100 percent of the money to go to work for you in your chosen fund(s).

## Maximizing 401(k) Contributions

With so many factors working in your favor, it makes strong financial sense to maximize your 401(k) contributions. Consider an example where contributions to a Fidelity growth fund are made for 15 years with an employer match of one for three. With an assumed salary of $30,000 and a 10 percent contribution rate, the balance in the 401(k) account would be at $180,000 at the end of the period (I assumed portfolio growth of 12 percent per year and annual salary growth of 3 percent).

Even if your fund choices are mediocre, you can still do well. One of my relatives was in this situation. His 401(k) choices weren't the best, but he contributed the maximum percentage of his salary for the better part of a decade. Because of pretax savings and matching contributions from his employer, he did well despite the lack of a good fund. Ultimately, he was able to move a portfolio worth $105,000 into a rollover IRA account at Fidelity.

That's one drawback with most 401(k) plans. Companies tend to hold down administrative expenses by providing only three to six investment offerings, and many do not offer good mutual fund choices. Even if you are one of the lucky ones with access to a Fidelity growth fund, it may not be the one you want. More companies should follow the lead of Ford and General Motors, which allow their employees to choose from a large selection of Fidelity funds.

If your company's 401(k) is too restrictive, you may be able to get it changed. Companies add funds to their 401(k) programs all the time; you may be able to convince your company to expand the range of options. Tell your benefits manager that you need more choices to pursue an appropriate investment strategy, and name the funds you would like to see included. Don't expect changes overnight, however; it may take a year or more before program changes can be made.

## Picking Funds in a 401(k) Account

Following are some tips on the best choices for your 401(k) account.

*Retirement Eight or More Years Away*   Go with a growth-oriented fund. Fidelity 401(k) plans usually include at least one of the following good choices: Contrafund, Growth & Income, Growth Company, and Magellan. If your 401(k) doesn't include any Fidelity funds, consider an S & P 500 fund.

*Within Eight Years of Retirement*   Go with a growth and income strategy if you are within eight years of retiring. Choose Asset Manager, Balanced, or Puritan if available, or invest 70 percent in a conservative stock fund such as Growth & Income or Equity-Income and 30 percent in a bond fund such as Intermediate Bond. In a non-Fidelity 401(k), consider 60 percent in an equity-income fund and 40 percent in a bond fund.

*Avoid Guaranteed Investment Contracts (GICs)*   Many GICs are not protected from insolvency the way a mutual fund is, and if the insurer is unable to meet its obligations you could lose some of your principal. Besides, in the long run, a higher level of risk will likely provide a higher rate of return.

*Avoid Taking out a Loan Against Your 401(k) Account*   Taking out a loan against your 401(k) account results in the liquidation of current assets, so you don't see any investment gains until the money is paid back. That may not matter if you are planning to hold cash anyway, but if you liquidate an attractive growth fund you might reduce your long-term returns.

*Changing Employers*  If you leave your employer, take full possession of your 401(k) holdings for maximum flexibility. Arrange for a direct transfer between your company's administrator and the financial institution you choose for the rollover IRA. That way, you don't take the chance of incurring a huge tax bill on your holdings, an event that can occur if you take possession of the money yourself and don't reinvest the full amount (including the 20 percent federal withholding) in 60 days.

# 12

# How and When to Avoid Load Fees

As of early 1999, Fidelity charges a 3 percent front-end load on 8 domestic growth funds, 14 foreign funds, and 39 Selects. This money goes to Fidelity and can be used to pay for advertising, mailings, investor centers, and other sales-related activities. Fidelity seems to charge loads on funds that investors perceive as offering a unique advantage, either in the form of attractive performance or because they provide an investment vehicle that's not available elsewhere (as in the case of the Selects).

When you purchase a Fidelity fund with a 3 percent load, it is reflected in the offering price, which is 3.1 percent higher than the actual net asset value (NAV). The offering price is calculated so that 97 percent of your original investment goes to work in the fund you purchase.

When you pay the load, Fidelity's computers tag your shares with a 3 percent load credit so that those shares won't be charged again on future trades. (I'll go into more detail on Fidelity's load-tracking system later in this chapter.)

## IS A 3 PERCENT FUND WORTH THE PRICE?

When you consider that a Fidelity 3 percent load is paid only once on the money invested, the long-term impact on performance is not significant. Over a ten-year period, the annual impact on performance is less than 0.3 percent annually. Most of Fidelity's domestic stock funds (including the Selects) stand a good chance of outperforming the indexes over the long run, which means there is a reasonably good chance that you'll make up for the load through improved performance.

Still, the decision to pay a front-end load should be based on what the alternatives are. Here are my thoughts for each fund group.

### Growth Funds

Figure 13 compares the performance of load funds and no-load funds over a ten-year period covering through the end of 1998. For each month in this study, I computed separate averages for load funds and no-load funds, based on whether the fund was charging a load during a particular month. Unlike many of the industry-wide studies I've seen, Fidelity load funds did actually have a small advantage over Fidelity no-loads. But this advantage has gone away in recent years as many newer funds have been introduced without loads.

With such a large variety of domestic growth funds to choose from, it probably doesn't make sense to pay a load unless you want access to a specific investment objective.

### International Funds

Fidelity's broadly diversified international funds are no-load, whereas funds that are specific to a particular country or region carry a load. This group can't be compared the way the domestic growth funds can, but based on the fact that Fidelity has been weak in its foreign performance I think investors should give preference to no-loads in this group. Of course, you'll have to make an exception if you want access to a specific country.

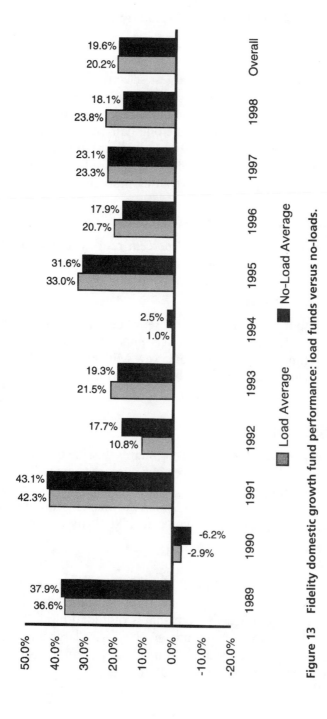

Figure 13   Fidelity domestic growth fund performance: load funds versus no-loads.

### Select Funds

If you want access to the largest selection of sector choices in the industry, the load fee is essentially the price of admission. Nevertheless, it can be justified by the group's attractive long-term record (about one-half of the Selects have outperformed the S&P 500 over the last ten years) and the relatively low cost of exchanges compared to paying commissions and spreads when trading individual stocks.

### WAYS TO AVOID PAYING THE LOAD

If you want to purchase a 3 percent fund, you may be able to avoid paying the load under certain conditions.

### Retirement Accounts

If you purchase the fund in a retirement account, the load may be waived. Retirement accounts currently avoid loads on all funds except Magellan, New Millennium, and the Selects. The 401(k) and 403(b) programs usually avoid loads on all funds in the program.

### Load Credits

If you purchased the fund using shares that have been tagged with a load credit from a previous purchase, you will be able to avoid or reduce the load fee on the fund you want to buy. If you're not sure about whether the shares you own have any load credits on them, you can call Fidelity to find out.

### Gifts

If the load fund is obtained as a gift from someone else, the load is not charged a second time. Suppose your son or daughter could benefit from shares of a load fund that you own. As long as the amount involved isn't large enough to trip the gift tax, the transaction is load-free and tax-free (be sure to check with your tax advisor first).

## Breakpoint Pricing Program

If you have a large portfolio (or if you are managing a combined pool of assets), you may be able to avoid load fees under Fidelity's breakpoint pricing program. Under this system, large purchases can earn permanent load credits that will apply on future trades. This program is available for all funds except Select Money Market (Fidelity excludes Select Money Market so that shareholders won't try to earn permanent load credits without taking on equity risk). Purchases of more than $250,000 but less than $500,000 get a 1 percent load credit, reducing the load paid to 2 percent or less, depending on whether there is a prior load credit on existing shares. Purchases above $500,000 but below $1 million get a 2 percent load credit, which reduces the load fee to 1 percent or less. If you can pull together $1 million or more for a single fund, you'll earn a permanent 3 percent credit without paying any load at all.

Note that your current balance in the fund also factors into the equation. If you have $500,000 in a 3 percent fund and you add another $500,000, you won't pay a load on the second $500,000.

Interestingly enough, this program doesn't carry any switching restrictions. For example, you could put $1million in Contrafund II to earn the load credit. If you then sell and split the money up into other funds a few weeks later, the credit still applies, allowing you to avoid all future loads. Fidelity must figure that investors won't take on equity risk with a large account unless they are serious about buying the fund in the first place.

## USING FIDELITY'S LOAD-TRACKING SYSTEM TO YOUR ADVANTAGE

Although you can't always eliminate Fidelity loads, you can take steps to minimize them. By understanding Fidelity's computerized-load tracking system, you may be able to structure fund switches to your advantage.

All of the money you hold in various Fidelity funds is tagged so that you don't pay a load more than once, provided the money remains in a Fidelity fund. These rules apply also to Fidelity funds held in a Fidelity brokerage account. Depending on which funds your money used to be in, Fidelity's computers may have it tagged for a load credit of 0 percent, 1 percent, 2 percent, or 3 percent. For example, shares of Magellan are tagged with a 3 percent credit. If you bought Equity-Income in a regular account before December 1, 1993, the shares are tagged 2 percent. If you owned International Growth & Income before October 11, 1990, you may have some 1 percent shares. If your money has never been in a load fund, it is tagged 0 percent. The tracking system also knows if you owe any redemption fees on funds purchased before October 12, 1990 (Fidelity charges a 1 percent redemption fee on Selects and a few other funds if they were purchased before that date).

If you are reinvesting capital gains and regular income distributions, the reinvested money will retain the load credit of the shares that generate the payouts. For example, you buy Magellan and pay a 3 percent load. Any reinvested distributions that occur while you are in Magellan will be tagged 3 percent. Then you move to Short-Term Bond. The reinvested income from Short-Term Bond will still be tagged 3 percent, because the load credit of the shares generating the income is 3 percent.

If you buy a fund with a load that's higher than the current status of your shares, you pay the difference and your shares are tagged at the new level. For example, if you purchase Contrafund II with 0 percent money, you pay a 3 percent load. If you purchase Contrafund II with shares loaded at 2 percent, you'll pay a 1 percent load on the transaction.

Once your shares are tagged with a 3 percent credit, you never pay a front-end load again on those shares, provided the money stays in a Fidelity fund. Suppose you sell Contra-fund II and buy Cash Reserves, then you purchase Select Multimedia. There are no charges.

There are only two ways you can lose your load credits:

- From a Fidelity mutual fund account, you lose your load credits if you redeem the shares out of Fidelity. Whether by checkwriting, doing a transfer to a bank, or by having Fidelity send a redemption check, the load credit is lost once the money no longer resides in a Fidelity fund.
- In a Fidelity Brokerage account, load credits are lost when the money is moved into a non-Fidelity fund or any other security such as an individual stock. However, load credits are retained if the money is kept in the core account.

Things start to get more complicated when you combine money with different load credits into a single fund. This is where you need to be careful to avoid paying loads on no-load money when you have loaded shares available. Here's how Fidelity's computers handle the transactions:

- When redeeming shares out of Fidelity, the computer will move the shares with the smallest load credit first. For example, suppose you have $4,000 in Cash Reserves, half of which is no-load money and half of which is tagged with a 3 percent load credit. Then you transfer $2,500 from Cash Reserves to your bank account. The computer will redeem all of the no-load money and $500 of the 3 percent shares when processing the transaction. This algorithm works to your best interest, but there is no warning mechanism to let you know when you are redeeming loaded shares.
- When making an exchange between Fidelity funds, the computer will move the shares that are tagged with the largest load credit first. Suppose you have $10,000 in

Cash Reserves, half of which is tagged 3 percent and half of which is no-load money. You then purchase $5,000 in Contrafund II, and a few days later you move the remaining $5,000 to Short-Term Bond. In this situation, you pay no load fees because the algorithm worked in your best interest.

• Now suppose you had reversed the transactions. Your 3 percent shares would have been "wasted" on Short-Term Bond, and you would have incurred $150 in new load fees when your no-load money was moved into Contrafund II. This time, the computer rules worked against you.

Fortunately, there is a simple way to eliminate the problem of combined load credits in a money market fund. Keep a separate money market fund as a holding place for loaded shares, and use your regular money market account or core account for your no-load money. If all of your loaded shares have a 3 percent load credit, Select Money Market is a good place for loaded money, although it may not always have the best yield.

For non–money market exchanges, there is no easy safeguard. You just have to ask about the load status of your shares and do your trades in the best possible order, waiting a day between each if necessary. The only way to avoid mixing load credits in the first place is to try to always keep your 3 percent money invested in load funds.

One last tip: If you discover after the fact that your 3 percent money was inadvertently sent off to a no-load fund, it is possible to recover if the no-load fund does not carry a redemption fee. Take an equivalent amount of no-load money and double your stake in the fund where your 3 percent money is located. Then wait one day and sell half of the doubled position, and your 3 percent money will come out and go where you want it. This technique is not without some risk. The risk is not large if your 3 percent money is stuck in a bond fund, but if you are doubled up in a stock fund you may lose more than you gain if the market sells off sharply. The other problem is that unless this is done in a retirement account, you can create a taxable transaction costing more than you save if you realize a capital gain on the 3 percent shares. Another issue is that selling the 3 percent shares at a loss can trigger wash sale rules, although in this situation it doesn't cost anything other than the accounting work.

## ANNUAL ACCOUNT FEES

Fidelity investors with total Fidelity assets of less than $30,000 should also pay attention to the annual account fee that is assessed on fund positions of less than $2,500. While the opportunity for saving on fees isn't as great in comparison to front-end loads, it is possible to save up to $24 per year by structuring your accounts differently.

Here's how the current program works. Once a year in the fourth quarter, Fidelity adds up all of the investment dollars held under your social security number. If the total is less than $30,000, each fund position with a balance of less than $2,500 is charged a fee of $12. If you have a total of more than two such fund positions, the total annual fee is capped at $24 (Fidelity brokerage core accounts are not subject to the fee).

There are several ways to reduce these charges. First, Fidelity will waive the $12 fee on any account structured to receive regular additional investments under Account Builder or similar plans. Second, if you don't mind consolidating to a fewer number of funds, you can avoid the charge by maintaining at least $2,500 in all fund positions. Third, you can call Fidelity when the fourth quarter draws near and find out when the valuation date will occur. Then you can temporarily consolidate to beat the fees (zero balance fund positions are not charged), and, if you wish, return to your previous position after the valuation date. (Fidelity allows the latter option, probably figuring most investors won't bother to split apart their portfolio after going to the trouble to consolidate.) Finally, you can transfer some assets from another financial institution to bring the balance of your Fidelity holdings above $30,000.

# 13

# Ten Fidelity Managers to Watch

Choosing a Fidelity fund based solely on a particular manager helps to build confidence, but it can also lead to frustration. There's always the possibility that your favorite manager might move on to something else, and you'll be left wondering what to do.

At Fidelity, manager changes can be relatively frequent. Chairman Ned Johnson has never had any reservations about "shuffling the deck" when the opportunity comes up. There is even some evidence that he prefers to move managers around from time to time. It's not that Johnson or any other Fidelity executives are trying to frustrate shareholders. It's just that Fidelity would like investors to view all of its funds in a favorable light and not worry too much about the person at the helm. To some degree, this is a valid goal. Fidelity has a huge group of analysts, and from the standpoint of basic research all managers are set up for success.

However, there are still performance differences among managers. The company is quick to remove any manager who has significantly lagged for more than two to three years, but among winning funds you can find many successful strategies that have been uniquely shaped by a particular manager. Fidelity's top performing funds often take very different paths to achieve what looks like similar results.

Emphasizing the differences in style, I've listed some of my thoughts and observations on ten managers worth watching. They are listed alphabetically.

## WILLIAM DANOFF

Before joining Fidelity in 1986 as a securities analyst, Will Danoff was a research analyst with Furman Selz in New York, where he followed advertising stocks. He began his career in 1985 as a research analyst with Clabir International in London and Steinhardt Partners in New York. Danoff received a bachelor of arts degree in history from Harvard College in 1982 and an MBA from the Wharton School at the University of Pennsylvania in 1986.

After managing Select Retailing between 1986 and 1989, Danoff assisted at Magellan during Morris Smith's tenure. He became manager of Contrafund, his current assignment, in October 1990. At Contrafund he has returned an impressive 25.3 percent per year through the end of 1998, well ahead of the S&P 500's 21.4 percent return for the same period.

Backed by Fidelity's research team, Danoff achieved his excellent track record with good stockpicking skills and by overweighting the right industry groups throughout his tenure. During most of his years at Contrafund, Danoff has run the fund as a mainstream growth fund. However, at times he has often developed a particular theme, placing as much as 25 percent of holdings into a specific industry or group of stocks (a heavy bet on the energy services group hurt returns in 1997, but emphasizing internet "bandwidth" stocks paid off in 1998). Contrafund is currently closed to new accounts but remains available in many 401(k) plans.

## BETTINA DOULTON

Bettina Doulton joined Fidelity in 1986 as a research associate. She received a bachelor of arts degree in mathematics from Boston College in 1986.

From 1987–90, she served as a research assistant for Magellan. For the next two years, she was an equity analyst following the gaming and lodging industries. In 1991, she began following the auto and tire businesses and became an assistant for Equity-Income. She also managed Select Automotive in 1993, helping to make it one of the better performing Selects that year.

In June 1993 she was assigned to VIP Equity-Income for almost three years. Doulton also ran one of Fidelity's broker-sold funds during the same period, and her good track record led to an additional assignment at Value Fund between March 1995 and March 1996. In addition to running two other broker-sold funds, Doulton manages the equity side of Puritan and the entire portfolio of Equity-Income II as of this writing.

Doulton seems to have an excellent eye for value and seems to favor financial stocks more than other sectors. She leans toward a domestic-only approach, which has helped so far but could hold her back in future years if foreign markets make up for lost time. At any rate, Puritan and Equity-Income II remain excellent choices for growth and income investors.

## KAREN FIRESTONE

Karen Firestone received a bachelor's degree in business in 1977 and completed her MBA in 1983. Both degrees were received from Harvard University.

Firestone currently manages Large Cap Stock, an assignment she has held since April 1998. During her short tenure at this fund she has outperformed the S&P 500 at a time when most funds were struggling to keep up.

Compared with other managers in this chapter, Firestone has relatively little management experience at Fidelity's mainstream funds. Nevertheless, she has logged over 15 "management years" when you add up her combined assignments at Select Biotechnology, Select Health Care, Select

Air Transportation, and Select Leisure. Throughout these assignments Firestone has shown improved performance, and her extensive experience in the biotech and pharmaceutical sectors gives her a key advantage in a group of stocks that should offer many future growth opportunities.

## DAVID GLANCY

David Glancy received a bachelor's degree in business from Tulane University in 1983 and completed his MBA at Emory in 1985.

Glancy is one of Fidelity's most experienced and successful high-yield bond managers. He managed High Income fund between April 1993 and January 1996 and has been at his current post at Capital & Income since January 1996. During both assignments he outperformed the Merrill Lynch High Yield Master Index and beat most of his high-yield competitors in the industry. Fidelity's junk-bond research department has many more analysts than its competitors, so managers like Glancy are definitely set up for success. Nevertheless, Glancy stands out for having consistently outperformed his benchmark for nearly six years.

In recent years it's been hard to get too excited about high-yield bond funds, but this segment of the financial markets is headed for the mainstream. Many companies are now choosing to issue junk bonds as alternatives to IPOs, and an increasing number of investors are considering high-yield bond funds to help reduce risk in today's high-priced stock market (Capital & Income carries about one-half the volatility of the S&P 500). That's a favorable trade-off, considering that junk bond funds may have almost as much total return potential as stock funds in future years.

## STEVEN KAYE

Steven Kaye joined Fidelity in 1985 as an analyst covering the pharmaceuticals, biotechnology, and photography industries. Before joining Fidelity, Kaye spent two years as a research analyst at Strategic Planning Associates in Washington, D.C. He received a bachelor of arts degree in political economics from Johns Hopkins University in 1981 and an MBA in finance from the Wharton School at the University of Pennsylvania in 1985.

Kaye managed Select Energy Services and Select Health Care from the beginning of 1986 until the start of 1990. He also ran Select Biotechnology from the beginning of 1986 until May 1989. His first major fund assignment was Blue Chip Growth. From October 1990 through the end of 1992 he returned 31.4 percent annually versus 21.9 percent for the S&P 500. He then moved to Growth & Income at the beginning of 1993, where he has returned 22.1 percent per year compared to 21.6 percent for the S&P 500 (as of December 31, 1998). During that period Growth & Income's overall risk was about 10 percent lower than that of the S&P 500.

Kaye understands pharmaceuticals and biotech stocks quite well, and he seems to have a good ability to sense when a particular stock or industry is too expensive. Whether in a growth-oriented or value-oriented role, Kaye has shown a proven ability to pick good stocks.

As is the case with Magellan and Contrafund, Growth & Income has become a very large fund. As such, Kaye won't be able to boost returns much by holding small- to medium-size companies. However, if his experience at Blue Chip Growth is any guide, Kaye should still do quite well in the large-cap arena. Growth & Income is currently closed to new accounts but remains available in many 401(k) plans.

## BRADFORD LEWIS

Brad Lewis joined Fidelity as an equity research analyst in 1985. Before that, he was an aviator with the U.S. Navy for six years. He received a bachelor of science degree in operations analysis from the Naval Academy at Annapolis in

1977 and an MBA from the Wharton School at the University of Pennsylvania in 1985.

Lewis is part computer programmer and part fund manager. Whereas other Fidelity managers rely on analysts and researchers to point them in the direction of outperforming stocks, Lewis turns to his computer. He uses quantitative models to identify attractive stocks based on fundamental figures, economic factors, and marketplace pricing trends.

Once an attractive list of stocks is developed, Lewis then uses other programs to develop a portfolio suitable for the fund he is dealing with. Disciplined Equity is structured to maintain similar risk as the S&P 500 and must keep a mix of industries similar to the index. Stock Selector is allowed to be a little more venturesome. It too invests mainly in S&P 500 stocks, but it is allowed to overweight industry groups and take on foreign positions to increase total return. Small Cap Selector is the most aggressive, investing in the Russell 2000 universe of smaller companies. Lewis also helped set up and optimize quantitative models for Diversified International and Fidelity Fifty.

Lewis has had mixed results so far. Disciplined Equity, which has been around since late 1988, has returned 19.5 percent per year versus 19.3 percent for the S&P 500 (at the end of 1998). Stock Selector has gained 21.8 percent annually versus 21.4 percent for the index. Small Cap Selector, on the other hand, has languished. Since June 1993, this fund has returned 11.1 percent annually, versus 16.4 percent for the Russell 2000 index. Lewis also had problems with a foreign model he helped develop for Diversified International, but in recent years it has performed significantly better.

The opportunity with quantitative techniques is significant, but it's a big challenge to evolve computer models fast enough to keep up with the changing attitudes and dynamics of the broad market.

Lewis has amassed considerable expertise during his time at Fidelity, and there has been significant improvement with each major change in his models. At some point in the future Lewis's tactics may rival Fidelity's traditional approach for stock selection.

## ROBERT STANSKY

Bob Stansky joined Fidelity in 1983 as a research analyst. Before that, he was a research assistant in the fixed income department of Kidder, Peabody & Company. He received a bachelor of science degree in 1978 from Nichols College in Dudley, Massachusetts, and an MBA from New York University in 1983. He is also a Certified Public Accountant.

Stansky was a research assistant for Magellan from 1984 to 1987. He managed Select Defense & Aerospace before a long-term assignment at Growth Company. Between March 1987 and May 1996 (a period of just over nine years), he returned 18 percent per year versus 14.6 percent for the S&P 500. He was assigned to Magellan in May 1996.

Stansky is an excellent fit in his current assignment. During his years at Growth Company, he focused mainly on large-cap growth stocks, which is exactly what he has to do at Magellan. He prefers stockpicking to sector bets and tends to move in and out of his positions gradually—ideal for a mammoth fund like Magellan. Finally, he's not the type of manager who will generate a lot of controversy. No doubt Fidelity will appreciate that after seeing the press go after Jeff Vinik with a level of scrutiny formerly reserved only for major political leaders.

Shareholders should be pleased with Stansky. He probably won't exceed the market indexes by as much as he did at Growth Company, but over the long run he should be able to outperform the S&P 500 by at least a few percentage points annually.

## BETH TERRANA

Beth Terrana joined Fidelity in 1983 as a securities analyst in the retail and apparel industries as well as an assistant manager to Equity-Income. Before joining Fidelity, she was assistant vice president of fixed income at Putnam Management Company for three years. Prior to that, she was an assistant manager at Morgan Guaranty Trust Company. Terrana received a bachelor of science degree from the State University of New York, Binghamton, in 1977 and an MBA from Harvard Business School in 1983.

Terrana is one of Fidelity's more experienced growth and income managers. Her first mainstream assignment was Growth & Income at the end of 1985. From March 1986 (when the fund was first available) through October 1990, Terrana returned 12.2 percent per year versus 10.1 percent for the S&P 500. Then she managed Equity-Income until July 1993, gaining an average of 24.6 percent per year compared to 18.8 percent for the S&P 500. Thereafter at Fidelity Fund, Terrana has returned 22.8 percent annually through December 31, 1998, matching the return for the S&P 500 (many funds underperformed during this time because the S&P 500 was unusually strong relative to small-cap, mid-cap, and foreign stocks).

Terrana holds a balanced mix of stocks and industries and usually carries a risk level that's similar to that of the S&P 500. Her investment style at Fidelity Fund is very similar to the approach she used when running Growth & Income. Over time, I suspect she will exceed the S&P 500 while maintaining similar risk.

### JOEL TILLINGHAST

Joel Tillinghast joined Fidelity in 1986 as an analyst covering the tobacco, coal, natural gas, personal care products, and appliance industries. Before then, he spent four years as a financial futures research analyst at Drexel Burnham Lambert in Chicago. He began his investment career in 1980 as an equity analyst with Value Line Investment Survey. Tillinghast received a bachelor of arts degree in economics from Wesleyan University in Connecticut in 1980 and an MBA from the Kellogg School of Management at Northwestern University in 1983.

After putting in some time as assistant manager of Fidelity OTC, Tillinghast became manager of Low-Priced Stock when it was introduced near the end of 1989. From day one this fund has focused on the small-cap value segment of the market, a less-analyzed group of stocks that contains many opportunities if you know where to look. Tillinghast and his team have been able to find them. Through the end of 1998, Low-Priced Stock has returned 18.4 percent annually versus 12.8 percent for the Russell 2000.

The focus on small-cap value and a highly diversified portfolio (around 1,000 stocks) makes for a lower-than-average risk level. In fact, Low-Priced Stock usually has less volatility than many stock-oriented growth and income funds, let alone its growth-oriented cousins. The only problem is that the Russell 2000 universe has a relatively small percentage of stocks that represent the new economy, and Low-Priced Stock may wind up with below-average returns to go with its below-average risk level.

Like other successful managers, Tillinghast has attracted too much capital. Although Low-Priced isn't anywhere near as large as some, keeping this fund invested in attractive small-cap stocks has become more difficult in recent years. Increasingly, Tillinghast and his team are looking outside the domestic market for bargain stocks. As of late 1998, about one-quarter of the fund's stock holdings are outside the United States, with Canadian issues accounting for the lion's share.

Low-Priced Stock may not be the best choice for the new economy, but if Tillinghast ever moves to another fund his stockpicking skills will be worth serious consideration.

## GEORGE VANDERHEIDEN

George Vanderheiden joined Fidelity in 1971 as a research analyst. Prior to that, he was a securities analyst with John

Hancock Insurance Company for three years. He received a bachelor of arts degree in economics from Colby College in 1968 and an MBA from Boston University in 1972.

Vanderheiden was named manager of Destiny I (one of Fidelity's broker-sold funds) around the end of 1980, and 18 years later is still at the helm (although he did take several months off in 1998). He has managed through four bearish periods and six major rallies, returning 20.4 percent annually ($1,000 in Destiny I at the beginning of Vanderheiden's tenure would be worth over $28,000 as of December 31, 1998). During the same period, the S&P 500 returned 16.9 percent per year. Vanderheiden clearly rates as Fidelity's most experienced and most successful stockpicker.

Unfortunately, there isn't any easy way for retail fund investors to take advantage of Vanderheiden's stockpicking abilities. VIP investors can benefit from purchasing VIP Growth Opportunities, although it is not clear if this will be a long-term assignment for Vanderheiden. At this point VIP Growth Opportunities and Destiny I have similar holdings.

# 14

## *The VIP Alternative*

Sold under the name Retirement Reserves, Fidelity's Variable Insurance Products (VIPs) offer an investment alternative that may be appropriate for some investors, although this program is not a panacea for avoiding taxes. Restricted choices and an annual insurance fee of 0.8 percent could reduce your long-term investment performance by one to two percentage points per year compared with a mutual fund approach. In addition, gains are ultimately taxed at full income rates instead of the more favorable 20 percent maximum rate on long-term capital gains. For these reasons, I don't recommend variable annuities except for investors who expect to be in the lowest federal tax bracket during the withdrawal period.

Variable annuities resemble mutual funds in most respects, but they are structured as life insurance to qualify for their favorable tax status. Putting money into the VIP family is like making a nondeductible IRA contribution, except that there is no limit on the amount you may invest and there is no requirement for payroll-based income. Once your money is invested, you must wait until age 59½ to make withdrawals or you'll face an IRS penalty of 10 percent. Compared to an IRA, however, you can keep your money in the VIP family longer before you must make automatic withdrawals. The tax code allows you to keep your money in an annuity account until age 85 (unless the original investment came from a previous qualified retirement plan, in which case the usual age of 70½ still applies).

When you do finally take money out of an annuity account, you are taxed at regular income rates (currently up to 39.6 percent federal) on all investment gains. Under the current tax code, your withdrawals are taxed until you have taken out an amount equal to the investment gains you have realized. After that, the original amount can come out with no additional tax liability (unless the original investment was rolled over from a qualified retirement plan, in which case it also is fully taxed).

An alternative withdrawal approach is to convert your investment to a lifetime income stream. This approach allows you to pull out a portion of the original investment along with the gains, helping to cut down on the tax bite. It can be done without penalty at any age, but once you annuitize you no longer have the flexibility of making withdrawals only when you need them.

### FIDELITY'S VIP LINEUP

When you join Fidelity's Retirement Reserves program, you are allowed to move around within a group of Fidelity and non-Fidelity portfolios. All money in the account is levied with a 0.8 percent annual fee for the insurance features. If you pull your money out within five years (by withdrawal or through a tax-free transfer to another insurance company), there is a redemption fee of up to 5 percent. During the first year, it runs the full 5 percent of assets, but it drops one percentage point per year to reach zero after the fifth year.

Following are the Fidelity choices that are available, listed in increasing order of risk.

## VIP Money Market

VIP Money Market seeks as high a level of current income as is consistent with the preservation of capital and liquidity; it invests in high-quality U.S. dollar-denominated money market instruments. The portfolio's yield will fluctuate.

This portfolio is one of the better-performing money markets in the variable annuity industry. Still, it gets left behind in comparison to regular money market mutual funds, which don't get trimmed by the annual insurance fee. For that reason, this portfolio makes sense only for VIP money that hasn't been put to work in other portfolios or for money earmarked for withdrawal in the near future.

## VIP II Investment Grade Bond

VIP II Investment Grade Bond was started in December 1988 and seeks high current income consistent with preservation of principal. It invests primarily in broad range of investment grade fixed-income securities; the portfolio maintains a weighted average maturity of ten years or less.

This portfolio, like Short-Term Bond, was hurt by the peso decline in late 1994 and early 1995. Today it is run as a regular domestic bond fund with a primary focus on government notes and investment grade corporate debt.

Again, this portfolio makes sense only as a temporary holding place, perhaps for withdrawals that will be made in the next three years or for money being dollar cost averaged into a growth-oriented position. It makes no sense to invest your entire VIP balance in this fund, since your after-tax return could easily be higher in a regular taxable bond fund (or a tax-free muni for high-bracket investors).

## VIP High Income

VIP High Income started in September 1985, and it seeks high current income. It invests primarily in high-yielding lower-rated, fixed-income securities. Growth of capital is also considered in security selection.

Although this portfolio has not performed as well as its mutual fund cousins, it can make a nice addition to a growth and income or income strategy. Over the long term, expect total return to be slightly less than that of the S&P 500, with volatility running about half as much.

### VIP II Asset Manager

VIP II Asset Manager was started in September 1989, and it seeks high total return with reduced risk over the long term by allocating its assets among stocks, bonds, and short-term fixed-income instruments.

This portfolio is a twin of the mutual fund version. The portfolio has a neutral mix of 50 percent stocks, 40 percent bonds, and 10 percent short-term (cash positions and bonds that have a maturity of less than three years are considered "short-term" holdings).

Despite a poor 1994 showing, VIP II Asset Manager is a good long-term choice for a growth and income portfolio. If you want more stock exposure, however, you should probably move up in risk to Asset Manager: Growth.

### VIP III Balanced

VIP III Balanced joined the Retirement Reserves lineup in 1997. It invests in a diversified mix of stocks and bonds, with a neutral mix of 60 percent stock, 40 percent bond.

Although this fund uses an investment strategy similar to its mutual counterpart, its style more closely resembles the approach used by Puritan. As such, I think it should be a core holding for a VIP-oriented growth and income strategy.

### VIP II Asset Manager: Growth

Introduced at the beginning of 1995, this portfolio's objective is maximum total return over the long run by allocation of assets among stocks, bonds, and short-term instruments of U.S. and foreign issuers, including emerging markets.

This portfolio also has the same management approach as its mutual fund twin, and it will typically hold 70 percent stocks, 25 percent bonds, and 5 percent short-term. Along with VIP Growth Opportunities, this portfolio is ideal for a lower-risk approach to long-term growth.

### VIP Equity-Income

VIP Equity-Income was started in October 1986. Its objective is reasonable income by investing at least 65 percent of assets in dividend stocks. The fund seeks a yield that exceeds that of the S&P 500.

Like its mutual fund equivalent, this fund invests mainly in large-cap value stocks, a strategy that has worked over a period of many decades. The only concern is that this portfolios lacks exposure to some of the growth-oriented stocks that are powering the new economy.

### VIP III Growth & Income

This portfolio joined the VIP lineup in early 1997. It invests mainly in stocks that pay dividends and offer potential growth of earnings.

Fidelity has done well with this approach on the mutual fund side, and so far this portfolio is proving to be a good choice for VIP investors as well. Its overall holdings are usually similar to the S&P 500 in risk, but investors could benefit over time from Fidelity's stockpicking abilities.

### VIP III Growth Opportunities

This portfolio also joined the VIP lineup in early 1997. Its objective is long-term capital growth.

The only retail portfolio that is managed by George Vanderheiden, this portfolio should continue to be an attractive "conservative growth" vehicle for as long as Vanderheiden remains at the helm.

### VIP II Index 500

This portfolio started in August 1992, and it seeks investment results that correspond to the total return of the common stocks that compose the S&P 500.

Like Spartan Market Index on the mutual fund side, this portfolio has been quite accurate in mimicking the S&P 500; the only problem is that the management fee and the 0.8 percent annual annuity fee will subtract about 1.1 percentage points from its annual performance.

This portfolio might be a good choice if the alternatives were not as good. Furthermore, the low distribution ratio of an index fund provides no advantage in a tax-deferred account. Over time you're likely to do better with VIP II Contrafund or VIP Growth.

### VIP II Contrafund

Introduced in early 1995, VIP II Contrafund has the objective of capital appreciation from undervalued companies undergoing positive changes and turnarounds. It's a clone of the popular mutual fund by the same name and is also managed by Will Danoff.

Danoff's proven ability as a stockpicker makes this portfolio one of the more attractive offerings in the VIP group. Compared with its mutual fund counterpart, it has the advantage of smaller size but carries the burden of the 0.8 percent annual annuity charge. As long as Danoff remains in place, this portfolio is a solid bet for outperforming the S&P 500 over time.

### VIP Overseas

Introduced in January 1987, VIP Overseas seeks long-term capital appreciation; it invests primarily in foreign securities of issuers whose principal business activities are outside of the United States.

VIP Overseas has concentrated on the major foreign markets in Europe and Japan; the portfolio has not held any significant position in emerging countries.

Manager Rick Mace has a respectable record on Fidelity's mutual fund side; time will tell if he will be able to improve this portfolio's lackluster track record.

## VIP Growth

Introduced in October 1986, VIP Growth seeks long-term capital appreciation; it invests primarily in common stocks. Fidelity has usually selected managers who place a heavy emphasis on growth stocks. Not surprisingly, technology stocks account for a larger share of holdings relative to other sectors.

Although this portfolio is one of the more risky choices in the group, Fidelity's strong research capabilities should make it one of the better long-term performers in the group.

## VIP PORTFOLIOS

The VIP model portfolios published in *Fidelity Monitor* are my preferred approach for investing in Fidelity's VIP family, but the portfolios in Figure 14 should provide similar long-term returns.

Portfolio A is designed for a growth-oriented approach. Holdings are 50 percent VIP II Contrafund, 25 percent VIP III Growth & Income, and 25 percent VIP Growth. My ten-year total return estimate for this split is 12 percent per year after deducting the 0.8 percent annual insurance fee. This mix of funds could decline 25 percent or more in a bear market.

Portfolio B is for conservative growth. It holds 40 percent VIP II Contrafund, 30 percent VIP III Growth Opportunities, and 30 percent VIP II Asset Manager: Growth. This

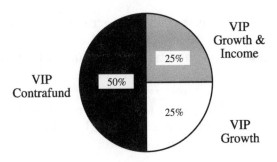

*Portfolio A: Growth*

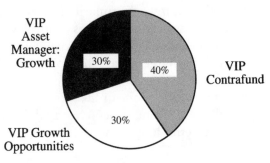

*Portfolio B: Conservative Growth*

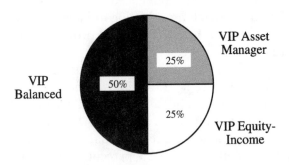

*Portfolio C: Growth and Income*

**Figure 14   VIP portolios.**

approach is a little less risky than that of Portfolio A and will probably grow at a slightly lower rate over the long run. I expect a ten-year return of 11 percent per year after fees, with potential losses of 20 percent or more in a bear market.

Portfolio C is for growth and income. With a mix of 25 percent VIP II Asset Manager, 25 percent VIP Equity-Income, and 50 percent VIP III Balanced, this portfolio should provide a ten-year return in the neighborhood of 10 percent per year after fees. In a bear market, this portfolio could decline 15 percent.

If you are investing for a long-term growth rate of less than 10 percent per year, you'll probably be better off in regular taxable mutual funds. That way, you'll avoid the 0.8 percent annual insurance fee, and you'll have more to choose from.

# 15

# Question-and-Answer Forum

One of my columns in *Fidelity Monitor* features my responses to the questions that subscribers ask. Over the years, I've covered quite a bit of ground with this column, and I've found it useful for addressing topics that don't always fit into the context of the regular columns. This chapter includes some of the more commonly asked questions. Because many *Fidelity Monitor* subscribers will be reading this book, I have included some questions that relate directly to the newsletter service.

**I received a proxy ballot for a fund I own shares in, and it was very confusing. What should I vote for?**

Typical proxy measures include electing the board of directors and okaying the choice of the fund's accounting firm. With Fidelity funds these are routine items that present no concerns.

Sometimes the fund is making fundamental changes to its investment limitations, a procedure that may sound risky but is usually aimed at increasing the manager's flexibility. I usually vote yes on these because I figure that Fidelity can manage risk in a responsible way. If you disagree, you can vote no or move to a fund with tighter restrictions. These types of changes are usually approved.

Finally, the fund may be requesting a change to the management contract. If the management fee will be equal to or lower than the old contract (Fidelity will clearly indicate if this is the case), I vote yes. If the new contract will increase fees, I vote no, assuming that Fidelity will manage the fund to its best ability regardless of the fee structure. Usually these measures pass anyway, in which case you can always cast one final vote by selling your shares. I made such a move in the *Fidelity Monitor* Growth Model after the management fee for Trend nearly doubled in late 1993, but such situations are unusual. Trend's previous management contract from the 1960s was a deal that was too good to last. In the future, I suspect that competition will force Fidelity and other fund companies to make management fees more competitive. One example of this was the small reduction in fees for Puritan and Asset Manager funds in 1996, and there may be more to come. In general, Fidelity expenses are slightly below average in the industry.

**I became nervous and moved my investments to a money market fund. Since then the market has moved up. Should I get back in?**

Unfortunately, your situation is common. It illustrates how market timing seldom works out very well in practice. If you want to get back into growth funds, consider doing it over time. Divide the amount you want to invest by 8, and make quarterly purchases over a two-year period. This approach reduces the risk of loss if the market sells off, and it should reduce your tendency to jump out of the market because you won't be fully exposed to stocks for almost two years.

You may also want to consider lowering your risk level. The very fact that you were nervous indicates that you took on more risk than you were comfortable with. If you were originally invested for aggressive growth, try dollar cost averaging into some regular growth funds. If you were originally in growth funds, try dollar cost averaging into a growth and income fund. Although your long-term potential is lower when you drop down in risk, you'll probably be better off in the long run because you won't be jumping out of the market at the wrong time.

### Does Fidelity limit how much you can put into a fund?

Fidelity has standard trading limits that are different for each fund, based on the fund's total assets. Usually the telephone representative can tell you the limit if you ask; typically it runs about 1 percent of the fund's total assets per day (per hour on the Selects). For most funds, 1 percent of assets is a huge sum, but for some of the smaller Selects you can trip the limit on a $50,000 trade. During market hours, you can usually get permission to exceed the limit. The rep can connect you to the specialty trading group, which will check with fund management for clearance. If you are turned down, you can choose a similar but larger fund or make multiple trades to obtain the desired position.

### How can I get more information on your newsletter service?

For a free trial issue and information, call 800-397-3094 or write *Fidelity Monitor,* P.O. Box 1270, Rocklin, CA 95677. You may also visit our web site (www.fidelity monitor.com).

### Do you offer a managed account service? How does it work?

I am the chief investment strategist (the person who picks the funds and the mix) for Weber Asset Management. Clients with accounts of $100,000 or more can have their portfolio managed for an annual fee of 1.2 percent on diversified fund positions (the fee can be higher for Select holdings). With this approach, exchanges are made for you in a Fidelity brokerage account set up in your name. Your portfolio is kept only in Fidelity mutual funds, and each time a trade is made you get a confirming statement. As of early 1999 we have about $110 million under management.

For an information package on this service, call 800-438-3863 or write to Weber Asset Management, 1983 Marcus Avenue, #221, Lake Success, NY 11042.

**What do you think about using margin to increase your long-term return with growth funds?**

In a brokerage account it is possible to use margin, or borrowed money, to own more shares of a fund than you could buy outright. (This practice is not possible with retirement accounts.) For stock funds the limit is 50 percent, meaning that for a $20,000 purchase you must put up at least $10,000. You pay interest on the extra $10,000 that you borrow.

There's a very simple reason why I don't like margin. In a nutshell, the problem is that margin magnifies losses more than it magnifies gains. As an extreme example, a 50 percent loss will wipe you out. Even under normal market fluctuations, margin can reduce your long-term return. Suppose you are fully margined, having bought $20,000 worth of a market index fund by putting up $10,000. First the market goes up 15 percent, making your shares worth $23,000. Upon reestablishing full margin, you now own $26,000 in shares. Then the market falls 20 percent. After selling to get back to a 50 percent margin position, you own $15,600 in shares. Then the market goes up 15 percent, and you close out your position. Your final balance is $10,140. After deducting the margin interest, you have a net loss. In comparison, you would have realized a 6 percent gain if you had simply bought and held the index fund itself.

Margin would work great if stock funds moved up in a straight line, allowing only gains to be magnified. Unfortunately, that doesn't happen in the real world.

I heard that Fidelity offers a service in which Select funds can be sold short in a Fidelity brokerage account. What do you think of this?

I don't recommend it. Even during a market downturn, it's very difficult to make any money with a strategy of borrowing and selling short Select shares with the idea of buying them back at a lower price. There are three things working against you in this situation:

- You are going against the market. For any random period of time, the odds of being right when betting against the market are only about 33 percent.
- You are betting against the fund manager. In the long run, most Selects outperform market averages, which further reduces your chance of making a profit in a short position.
- Brokerage expenses on the trades and interest paid on the borrowed shares can wipe out the profit even if you do realize an occasional gain.

Granted, there may seem to be times when shorting looks attractive despite these handicaps. When those times occur, however, you probably won't find many shares available for shorting. And the technology Selects, which have the greatest potential for a rapid short-term decline, are not included in the pool of Selects eligible for shorting.

**Is it true that early investors get a better price when a large number of investors are rushing to buy a particular mutual fund?**

You might be thinking about a closed-end fund (which acts like a stock). With regular open-end mutual funds, the price is set by the value of the underlying assets. In order for buying activity to push up the price, it would have to push up the price of all underlying stocks held. That's not likely unless the amount of capital involved is very large and the fund manager is putting it to work as fast as he or she can.

Even then, the effect would be considerably less dramatic than the same amount of money chasing an individual stock.

**I was looking at Magellan, but I decided not to buy it because of the high share price. Will there be a better time to get in?**

A mutual fund's share price is irrelevant. Magellan could be holding cheap stocks, expensive stocks, or even cash, and its share price (NAV) would still be higher than that of other funds because of events that occurred many years ago.

The only thing a high share price means is that the fund went through a period in its history where gains were robust and cash inflows were strong. Under these conditions, a lack of selling activity reduces distributions to very modest amounts. During a situation like this, almost all investment gains become fully reflected in the share price.

Ultimately the fund returns to a normal pattern of payouts, and the price stops moving up. Years later, the share price may remain high relative to other funds (unless Fidelity elects to do a split), but chances are that most of the stock holdings are different. The share price itself says nothing about whether the fund's assets are cheap or expensive.

**I want to sell Equity-Income because I'll need the money for this year's tax bill. However, I don't want to miss out on Equity-Income's year-end distribution. What should I do?**

Unlike a dividend stock, you don't "miss out" by selling a mutual fund before its Ex-date. With stock funds, all stock dividends and capital gains are fully reflected in the share price at all times. For bond funds, any regular income you've earned is always prorated on a daily basis and distributed when you sell.

Waiting until after the payout doesn't benefit you because the share price drops by an amount equal to the distribution. The value of your holdings is not affected by the distribution; you simply own more shares at a lower price.

From a tax standpoint, it usually doesn't matter if you sell before or after the Ex-date if you plan to sell before the end of the year anyway. However, if you have held the fund for more than a year, you may be better off selling before the Ex-date to avoid the chance of an unnecessary distribution of short-term gains and income.

**Why are the Dow and S&P 500 year-to-date figures published in *Fidelity Monitor* higher than the ones I read in the newspaper?**

Our total return figures assume reinvested stock dividends, which typically add around one to three percentage points per year. Many newspapers mislead investors by ignoring the dividends when they report gains or losses for the Dow and the S&P 500. The total return figures we report are consistent with other mutual fund tracking services such as Morningstar and Lipper.

**Why don't you cover Fidelity's Advisor funds?**

The Fidelity Advisor funds are a group of funds designed to be sold with a load by stockbrokers. (Some of these funds include 12(b)-1 fees in their expense ratio.) If you are buying through a stockbroker, these funds are probably a lot better than the alternatives. However, they provide no significant advantage over Fidelity's retail funds, which are sold directly to the public at a maximum 3 percent load.

**I have a large portfolio, and each year I have to sell some of it to pay the taxes on the distributions generated in the previous year. When is the best time to do that?**

Statistically speaking, the best time is right before you have to pay the IRS. Because your investments are growing over the long run, you'll realize an advantage more often than not if you wait as long as possible. If your taxes are due on April 15, you'll also benefit from the stock market's seasonal tendency. Between November and April, stocks usually perform better than during the other half of the year. By selling in early April, you have the best chance for paying the tax bill with the least take on your investment portfolio.

### Is there any advantage to using a Fidelity brokerage account for purchasing Fidelity funds?

The enhanced USA package comes with a wide variety of services, and the core account is able to do almost everything a bank checking account can do. A Fidelity brokerage account is convenient if you have other investments (stocks, bonds, etc.) you want consolidated in a single account, or if you want access to mutual funds from other companies.

If you don't need any of this, you can simply purchase Fidelity funds directly from Fidelity. That way, you'll probably end up with less paperwork to deal with.

### Is it safe to have all my investments with Fidelity?

I do. Each Fidelity mutual fund is actually a separate financial entity that hires Fidelity Management & Research (FMR) to manage the portfolio. Actual fund assets are held with the custodian (usually a bank holding company), where they are protected against insolvency. If Fidelity were to fail, all Fidelity funds would have to hire a new management company, but the assets would still be there. Redemptions might be heavy and performance might deteriorate, but at least you would have access to your money.

### How can I find a complete list of a fund's current holdings?

A complete listing of a fund's portfolio can be found in the annual or semiannual report. If you own shares in the fund, it should be mailed to you automatically. Otherwise, you can request a copy from Fidelity.

Keep in mind that fund managers make trades every day. By the time you get the report, some of the fund's portfolio is likely to have changed. There's really no way to find out exactly what a fund is holding at a given point in time. Fidelity makes it a point not to release a fund's holdings more than a few times a year to prevent other fund companies from profiting from its research efforts.

**Has Fidelity ever blocked investor trades? Will I have any problems if I try to follow your *Fidelity Monitor* newsletter models?**

Fidelity has, on occasion, closed certain funds to new investors when the inflow of cash became difficult to manage. Low-Priced Stock has been closed three times over the years, and in 1987 Growth Company and Contrafund were closed for a few weeks when subscribers to a popular market timing newsletter stampeded into both funds. (A few years later, Fidelity actually sent letters to these investors informing them that future trades with this service would be blocked.)

Since our goal at *Fidelity Monitor* is for our subscribers to follow our models without restrictions, we give Fidelity advance notice to allow the affected fund managers to anticipate the flow of dollars. On the occasion that a Fidelity fund manager has voiced concern, we have changed the timing or amount of the trade to find an acceptable common ground. Because we consider the fund managers, and because all of our trades are within Fidelity's fund group, Fidelity probably won't have reason to restrict our recommended switches.

**Are newsletter subscriptions and managed account fees deductible expenses?**

It depends. Both of these fall into a category called miscellaneous deductions, which includes investment fees, the cost of a safe deposit box, tax advice and preparation fees, subscriptions to professional and investment-related publications, depreciation on computer equipment used for monitoring investments, dues to professional societies, employment-related education, job search expenses, union dues, and a few other things.

Unfortunately, you are allowed to deduct only the portion of these expenses that exceed 2 percent of your adjusted gross income (AGI). Suppose your AGI is $40,000. That means only expenses above and beyond $800 are deductible. Some investors try to bunch their miscellaneous expenses in alternate years, making it easier to exceed the 2 percent threshold. For example, you can take out two-year subscriptions to publications and have your accountant bill you ahead of time on tax preparation every other year.

# GLOSSARY

**Advisor**   The individual or organization who is hired to manage a mutual fund's investments.

**After-Tax Return**   The net return on a mutual fund position after income taxes have been paid on the distributions of dividends and capital gains.

**Aggressive Growth**   An investing style (or fund) that seeks to maximize returns by taking on more risk than the market. The usual approach is to buy stocks in fast-growing, smaller companies.

**Alpha**   A measure of how much a fund exceeds its predicted performance based on its beta and the gain or loss for the S&P 500 over a specified period. Domestic stock funds with high alpha scores usually indicate a talented manager or an overweighted industry group that is performing well.

**AMT**   (Alternative Minimum Tax) A separate income tax system that applies whenever the total tax due under AMT rules is higher than the tax due under the normal rules. Taxpayers usually become subject to AMT when their regular income taxes are significantly reduced by passive losses, excessive deductions for investment expenses, or by various other tax shelters.

**AMT Paper** Municipal bonds (or short-term municipal notes) whose interest is taxable for taxpayers subject to AMT. These debt securities usually provide slightly more income than regular muni bonds because there is less demand for them.

**Annual Report** A yearly document sent to shareholders that provides fund performance figures and lists all of the fund's holdings at the close of the fund's fiscal year.

**Annualized Return (or Average Annual Total Return)** The compound annual rate at which the total return would be realized over a specified period.

**Asset Allocation** The practice of allocating a portfolio between different asset classes (usually stocks, bonds, and cash) based on a desired level of overall risk.

**Average Maturity** See *Weighted Average Maturity.*

**Basis Point** A one-hundredth of one percentage point. For example, 50 basis points is equivalent to one-half of one percentage point.

**Beta** A measure of a fund's volatility relative to the S&P 500. A fund with a beta of 0.5 can be expected to gain or lose 0.5 percent for a 1 percent gain or loss in the S&P 500 index. Beta is useful for estimating the impact of the domestic stock market on a fund. However, beta is not a good indicator of overall risk unless the fund's R-squared is relatively high. For funds with an R-squared of less than 75 percent, relative volatility is generally a better measure of overall risk.

**Blue Chip** Refers to a stock of a large, well-established company. Blue chips generally have large market capitalizations and hold up better in an economic downturn.

**Book Value** The worth of a corporation based on standard accounting rules (assets less liabilities).

**Bond**  A debt security that promises the bondholder a string of specified interest payments and the repayment of principal at maturity.

**Brokerage Account**  An account that can be used for consolidating a wide variety of investments into one holding place. Certain terms and conditions apply depending on the brokerage company that provides the account.

**Brokerage Commission**  The cost of executing a trade when selling or buying a security (also applies to selling or buying a fund from a brokerage account, unless the fee is waived as part of a network program).

**Capital Gain**  The gain (or loss) realized on the price of a security that has been sold. The gain (or loss) is considered short-term if the security was held less than one year, otherwise it is considered long-term. As part of a mutual fund distribution, the capital gain components represent the capital gains the fund has realized in selling securities.

**Carryforward Losses**  A loss on the sale of securities which is carried forward from a previous tax year. In a stock-oriented mutual fund, a large carryforward loss may allow the fund to absorb future capital gains, eliminating the need for a distribution for a few years.

**Cash Position**  The percentage of short-term notes (or repurchase agreements) held by a fund.

**Closed-End Fund**  A mutual fund that can only be bought or sold in the secondary market once the initial offering is completed. This type of fund is listed and traded like an individual stock and usually sells at a premium or discount to its actual net asset value.

**Convertible Security**  Typically a bond (or preferred stock) that can be converted to common stock under certain conditions.

**Cost Basis**    The amount of money paid to accumulate a mutual fund position (or a position in an individual security), including any load fees and transaction costs. Once sold, the selling price less the cost basis is the capital gain (or loss).

**Coupon Rate**    The interest a bond pays on its par value when first issued.

**Credit Rating**    An assessment of a company's ability to repay principal and interest on its bonds. The judgment is made by a credit rating agency such as Standard & Poor's or Moody's. Top-rated corporations are considered AAA or Aaa, and those with excessive credit risk are usually not rated at all (nonrated bonds are often referred to as "junk bonds").

**Credit Risk**    The risk of default by the issuer of a bond. In a mutual fund, credit risk is secondary to interest-rate risk but can still play a key role in junk bond funds (the entire junk bond market can sell off if the market believes credit risk is going up for a large percentage of companies).

**Custodian**    The entity responsible for holding a mutual fund's actual stock certificates, bonds, and other assets for safekeeping. Usually a bank holding company.

**Derivative**    A security with returns that are linked in a specified way to an underlying security or index of securities.

**Disclosure**    The obligation of a mutual fund to clearly state historical performance, risks and potential risks, limitations, fee structure, compensation to the advisor, and any other factors that may affect performance. These items are discussed in a fund's prospectus.

**Distribution**    A payout of income, short-term capital gains, or long-term capital gains from a fund's asset base.

**Diversification**    Investing in many different securities so that a large loss in a single security will not have much impact on the portfolio as a whole. A diversified portfolio does not usually protect against losses from market-related declines. For example, a growth fund with several hundred stocks could still decline 25 to 30 percent in a bear market.

**Dividends** For a stock, the return of a portion of profits to the shareholders. For mutual funds, this is the income portion of a distribution. Most bond and money market funds compute dividends daily and make payouts on a monthly basis.

**Dividend Yield** The annualized rate at which dividends are posted to shareholder accounts. For an individual stock, the percent return of the stock's dividend payouts (over the last 12 months) divided by its share price. The aggregate dividend yield of the S&P 500 has been a closely watched indicator of stock valuations, but is becoming outdated by the increasing popularity of stock buybacks.

**Dollar Cost Averaging** Investing a fixed amount of money at regular intervals. This is considered a low-risk approach to investing in stocks because you end up buying more shares when prices are low and fewer when prices are high. Lacking this kind of disciplined approach, most investors tend to do the opposite.

**Duration** A measure of a bond fund's interest rate sensitivity. For example, a duration of 5 means that, other factors being equal, an across-the-board one percentage point increase in interest rates would cause a 5 percent decline in share price.

**Equity** Stock ownership in a corporation operated for profit. Value is determined by supply and demand in the market, and is affected by earnings, dividends paid, stock buyback programs, assets owned, rate of growth, competition, takeover potential, breakup value, burden of regulation, and other factors.

**Equity-Income**  An investing style (or fund) seeking conservative growth from a strategy of investing in dividend stocks. The risk level of such an approach is slightly less than that of the S&P 500.

**Exchange**  Selling one mutual fund and buying another within the same fund family or network program. Exchanges represent taxable transactions unless they are made within a retirement account.

**Exchange Fee**  A charge for making a switch from one fund to another.

**Excise Distribution**  A special dividend payout on a bond fund that, unlike regular dividends, reduces the fund's share price.

**Ex-date**  The date of record on which a fund distribution reduces the fund's share price by an amount equal to the value of the distribution.

**Expense Cap**  A voluntary limit on a fund's expenses, usually put in place on new bond and money market funds to result in an above average yield and accelerate sales of the fund. Typically the fund's management company absorbs any expenses in excess of the cap. Expense caps can be changed or eliminated without notice to shareholders.

**Expense Ratio**  The cost of running the fund expressed as annual percentage of total fund assets. Does not include the cost of brokerage commissions on securities the fund buys and sells.

**Expense Waiver**  A temporary agreement by a fund's management company to absorb all costs of running the fund. Can be eliminated without notice to shareholders.

**401(k)**  A corporate retirement plan that allows employees to decide (up to IRS limits) how much to contribute and which investment vehicle(s) to use. The employer decides on which choices to make available to employees. Most medium and large corporations offer 401(k) plans, but the range of choices varies widely.

**403(b)**   Similar to a 401(k) plan but designed for nonprofit organizations. Most 403(b) programs allow for more choices than do 401(k)s.

**Front-End Load**   The sales charge that goes to the management company before the remaining dollars go to work in the fund being purchased.

**Fund Network**   A mutual fund purchasing program, usually offered by a brokerage company. Several brokerages waive transaction fees for funds that are part of their program.

**Future**   A contract to buy or sell a security, index, or commodity at a set price at a future date.

**Gain Factor**   A number representing the growth of a fund that, when multiplied by the original investment, will show the final value of the investment.

**Ginnie Mae Fund**   A fund that invests in government bonds backed by mortgages. Compared to Treasuries, the credit risk and yield are usually slightly higher. These funds tend to hold up better than other government bond funds when rates are rising, but because of prepayment risk they don't gain as much when rates are on a decline.

**Growth**   An investing style (or fund) seeking long-term growth from stocks. Usually the risk level of such an approach is slightly higher than that of the S&P 500.

**Growth and Income**   An investing style (or fund) seeking conservative growth from stocks, with a portion of the portfolio allocated to income-producing securities, typically dividend stocks or bonds. Usually the risk level with this approach is less than that of the S&P 500.

**Growth Stock**   An equity security of a company whose revenue and earnings are expected to grow faster than the economy over the long run.

**Hedging**   The practice of buying currency contracts or using other means to reduce or eliminate the effect of exchange-rate fluctuations on a foreign security.

**Index**   An unmanaged collection of securities that can be used to compare the results of an actively managed portfolio. For example, domestic growth funds usually aim to exceed the S&P 500 stock index.

**Inflation**   The average annual rate at which the cost of goods and services increase relative to the nation's currency.

**Interest-Rate Risk**   The risk that a bond will decline in price if interest rates go up (it is not an issue if you plan to hold the bond to maturity). In most bond funds, interest-rate risk is the dominant risk factor, because unlike credit risk it is not reduced through diversification.

**Intermediate-Term**   A period of time (or an average maturity) of more than three but less than ten years.

**Investment Advisor**   See *Advisor.*

**Investment Grade**   Generally refers to corporate bonds that carry ratings above BB (Standard & Poor's) or Bb (Moody's). This represents the mainstream market for corporate debt.

**IRA (Individual Retirement Account)**   An account with special tax status that permits certain types of investments and allows them to compound on a tax-deferred basis. Contributions are deductible under certain conditions, and usually there is a 10 percent penalty that applies if the money is taken out of the account before the owner reaches age 59½.

**Junk Bonds**   Corporate bonds that are not rated or carry a rating of BB and below (Standard & Poor's) or Bb and below (Moody's). Because of their greater credit risk, these bonds generally yield 2 to 5 percentage points more than government bonds with a similar maturity.

**Junk Bond Yield Spread**   The difference in yield between junk bonds and similar maturity government bonds.

**Keogh**   An employer retirement plan similar to a IRA but with unique rules governing contribution amounts.

**Liquidity**   The speed in which a security can be converted to cash without having to reduce the price below market value.

**Load**   See *Front-End Load.*

**Long-Term**   A period of time (or an average maturity) of ten years or more.

**Management Fee**   The money a fund pays to its advisor for managing the fund's investments.

**Manager**   The individual (or team) responsible for a mutual fund's performance. Typically, this person supervises or does the actual buying and selling of securities held in the fund's portfolio.

**Margin**   The practice of borrowing to purchase more shares in a security than could be purchased directly. Margin magnifies both gains and losses, but losses are magnified more than gains.

**Market Capitalization**   The worth of a corporation calculated by multiplying its stock price times total shares outstanding.

**Market Timing**   Attempting to buy stocks or stock funds when the broad market is moving higher, and holding cash when the market is declining. While this approach can reduce the average risk in a portfolio, it seldom improves long-term returns.

**Maturity**   The date when a bond's interest payments terminate and the principal is to be returned to the bondholder.

**Mid-Cap**   A stock with a market capitalization of more than $300 million but less than $3 billion (these limits can be wider under other definitions).

**Momentum**   The tendency for a security to keep moving in the direction it currently is going.

**Moving Average**   An average of a specified number of adjusted NAV data points over fixed intervals of time. For example, some technical traders sell a fund when its current price drops below its 39-week moving average, and buy when it moves back above. Use of moving averages is popular with market timing systems.

**Municipal Bonds**   Debt securities issued at the state or local level to finance public works. Interest earned is exempt from federal income tax, and in the state where the bond is issued interest is typically exempt from state income taxes as well.

**Net Asset Value (NAV)**   The mutual fund equivalent of share price. The mutual fund company's calculation of the total market value of all securities owned by the fund, divided by the total number of shares outstanding. This figure is typically calculated once each day after the market's close, except for Fidelity Selects, which are priced hourly.

**No-Load**   A fund that is sold without a front-end load.

**Objective**   The purpose for which a fund exists; the fund's goal.

**Offering Price (or Asking Price)**   In a no-load fund, the net asset value. In a load fund, the net asset value plus the front-end sales charge.

**Open-End Fund**   Refers to the most common type of mutual fund where shares can be bought or redeemed directly from the fund company (all of the funds discussed in this book are open-end funds).

**Option**   A contract that grants the right to buy or sell a specific security, index, or commodity at a set price up until a specified date.

**Performance**   The return that you realize while owning shares in a fund.

**Price-to-Book Ratio**   The ratio of a corporation's share price divided by its book value per share.

**Price-to-Earnings (P/E) Ratio**   The ratio of a corporation's share price divided by its earnings per share (usually over the last 12 months). This valuation indicator is not defined for companies with zero earnings or with a net loss, and it is not useful for evaluating firms near breakeven. Generally speaking, stocks selling at multiples below the expected rate of earnings growth are considered undervalued. For example, a stock with a P/E of 8 and expected earnings per share growth of 12 percent per year would be considered a good buy.

**Price-to-Sales Ratio**   The ratio of a corporation's share price divided by its revenue per share. Not generally used for evaluating financial stocks and others where sales are not well defined.

**Prospectus**   A legal document that states historical performance, risks and potential risks, limitations, fee structure, compensation of the advisor, and any other factors that may affect performance. Unless you buy through a brokerage account, a fund company is required to ask if you have read the prospectus before they can legally sell you shares in the fund.

**Proxy**   A measure allowing mutual fund shareholders to vote on board members, fee structure, investment limitations, selection of an accounting firm, and other fundamental items that can affect the fund's operation.

**Quantitative Approach**   A method of investing based on mathematical calculations that has been tested against historical data to optimize performance. Some quantitative models are based on neural nets (complex computer programs that "learn" patterns over time).

**R-Squared**   A statistical calculation that indicates how much a fund's performance correlates with a particular index, usually the S&P 500. A figure of 1.00 (or 100 percent) indicates perfect correlation, whereas 0.00 indicates that there is no correlation (although rare, it is possible for a fund to have a negative R-squared if it moves opposite the market).

**Realized Gain**   The capital gain realized from the sale of a security.

**Redemption**   The act of selling mutual fund shares back to the management company for the purpose of switching to another fund or having the money returned to the shareholder.

**Redemption Fee**   A charge against the money being redeemed out of the fund. Some funds charge a redemption fee until the money has been in the fund for a specified length of time; this practice discourages investors from jumping in and out of the fund based on short-term trends.

**Reinvested Distribution**   The automatic purchase of additional shares (of the same fund) when a distribution is paid. Retirement accounts are automatically set up with this structure, and it is a common choice for regular taxable accounts.

**REIT**  A Real Estate Investment Trust. A company that invests in real estate properties and returns income and profits to shareholders.

**Relative Volatility**  A general measure of risk that is computed from a fund's monthly, weekly, or daily gains and losses over a specified interval of time. It is usually computed by taking the standard deviation of the gains and losses (a statistical calculation) and normalizing to the S&P 500. Thus, a fund with price fluctuations equivalent to the index will be 1.00. Relative volatility is similar to beta for funds that are highly correlated to the index.

**Risk**  The probability that an investment could experience a substantial decline in value.

**Risk-Adjusted Return**  An indicator that reduces a fund's total return by the amount of risk it takes on, allowing an apples-to-apples comparison of a wide variety of different securities. Funds with high risk-adjusted returns in the past tend to be above average performers in the future.

**Rollover IRA**  An account that is set up to receive a lump-sum pension, a 401(k) payout, or some other type of qualified retirement distribution. When the transfer is made directly from the previous plan administrator to the financial institution of choice, the taxpayer pays no taxes and gains direct control over how his or her nest egg is invested.

**Roth IRA**  An IRA account that is funded with non-deductible contributions and which allows all investment gains to compound tax-free.

**Russell 2000**  An index that generally includes stocks of smaller-capitalization companies based in the United States.

**S&P 500**  Standard and Poor's composite index of 500 stocks, a capitalization-weighted index that gives the most weight to companies with the greatest total market valuation. The index has existed since 1925 and does not include the reinvestment of stock dividends; as a result the dividends must be figured back in when calculating total return.

**SEC 30-Day Yield**  A method of calculating a bond fund's yield that is specified by the SEC. It is based on yield-to-maturity, with hedging activities excluded from the calculation. It is only an estimate of the actual income you will receive on a monthly basis, and with certain foreign bond funds it can substantially overstate the actual income that is earned. Fund companies are required to calculate bond fund yield using this approach.

**Sector Fund**  A fund that invests in the stocks of a specific industry or group of industries.

**Security**  A financial instrument such as a short-term note, a bond, a share of stock, or a derivative.

**Share Price**  See *Net Asset Value (NAV)*.

**Sharpe Ratio**  A calculation used to determine the relative risk-adjusted returns of various funds or investments. Starting with a population of gains and losses (usually daily, weekly, or monthly), you compute the average gain of a security (or fund) and subtract the average gain of a "riskless" investment (usually 90-day T-bills). The result is then divided by the standard deviation of the gains and losses of the security.

**Short-Term**  A period of time (or an average maturity) of less than three years.

**Soft Dollars**  Money used to pay for goods and services that comes out of the commissions paid for selling or buying securities (or from the price spread between buyer and seller on a purchased security). Soft Dollars are typically "rebated" back to the fund's management company and are used to purchase computer equipment, quote systems, research reports, and other things that would otherwise show up in a fund's expense ratio. The practice is legal, but skirts disclosure rules (it causes a fund's expense ratio to be understated, even though shareholders are still paying the bill). Fund companies may be required to disclose these purchases at some point in the future.

**Stock**  See *Equity.*

**Switch**  See *Exchange.*

**Taxable Equivalent Yield**  Used to compare a municipal bond fund with a taxable bond fund. Figured by dividing the yield of the municipal fund by the quantity of one minus your federal tax bracket in decimal form. For a state-specific fund, divide the yield by [(1 − federal tax bracket) × (1 − state tax bracket)].

**Total Return**  The percentage gain or loss in a fund over a specified interval with distributions reinvested. Unless specified, total return figures usually do not reflect load fees or redemption charges.

**Transfer Agent**  An organization that keeps the records of the fund's shareholders and handles the paperwork for shares that are bought and sold.

**Treasuries**  Bonds or notes issued and backed directly by the U.S. government. Credit risk is considered to be near zero because the U.S. government can always raise taxes, sell more bonds, or print more currency to satisfy an obligation.

**Turnaround**   A company with poor profitability that has taken steps to improve its bottom line.

**Turnover Ratio**   The rate at which securities are bought and sold within a fund's portfolio. A 100 percent turnover is equivalent to replacing every security over a year's time, but it could also mean that a fund kept one-half of its portfolio and replaced the other half twice during the course of a year.

**12b-1 Fee**   An annual fee taken from a fund's asset base and used to pay for sales and marketing expenses.

**Unrealized Gain**   The appreciation of a security, which will become taxable after the security is sold.

**Value**   An investing style (or fund) seeking long-term growth from value stocks. Usually the risk level of such an approach is slightly lower than that of the S&P 500.

**Value Stock**   An equity security of a company whose worth is determined more by dividends and underlying assets than by its potential for growth of earnings

**Variable Annuity**   An investment with special tax treatment (similar to that of a nondeductible IRA) that works somewhat like a mutual fund account; it offers life insurance features and charges an annual fee for them.

**Wash Sale**   When selling at a loss in a regular taxable account, the sale of a security 30 days prior to or after the purchase of a substantially identical asset. In the event of a wash sale you are not allowed to deduct the loss, but you can add it to your cost basis to offset the gain on a future sale.

**Weighted Average Maturity**   The average maturity of a fund's bond holdings in years, weighted in proportion to their dollar value. Generally speaking, the longer the average maturity, the greater the sensitivity to interest rates.

**Wilshire 4500**   The Wilshire 5000 with the S&P 500 companies excluded.

**Wilshire 5000**   An index that includes nearly all stocks traded in the U.S. market.

**Yield**   The annual rate of interest or dividends paid as a percentage of the security's current price (also see *SEC 30-Day Yield* and *Dividend Yield*).

**Yield Curve**   A plot of interest rates versus maturity for Treasury notes and bonds. A steep curve indicates a large spread between short-term and long-term interest rates. A flat curve means rates are similar regardless of the period you invest for, and an inverted curve means short-term rates are higher than long-term interest rates.

**Yield to Maturity**   A method of calculating bond yield that takes into account the fact that bonds selling at a discount or premium to their par value will return to par as they approach their maturity.

# APPENDIX A

### Growth Funds - 1977 Return

| | |
|---|---|
| Magellan | 14.5% |
| Trend | -3.3% |
| S&P 500 | -7.4% |
| Contrafund | -10.9% |

### Growth Funds - 1978 Return

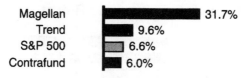

| | |
|---|---|
| Magellan | 31.7% |
| Trend | 9.6% |
| S&P 500 | 6.6% |
| Contrafund | 6.0% |

### Growth Funds - 1979 Return

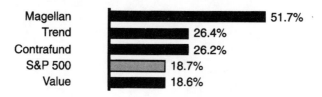

| | |
|---|---|
| Magellan | 51.7% |
| Trend | 26.4% |
| Contrafund | 26.2% |
| S&P 500 | 18.7% |
| Value | 18.6% |

## Growth Funds - 1980 Return

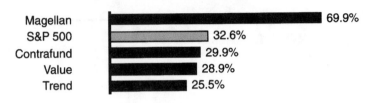

| | |
|---|---|
| Magellan | 69.9% |
| S&P 500 | 32.6% |
| Contrafund | 29.9% |
| Value | 28.9% |
| Trend | 25.5% |

## Growth Funds - 1981 Return

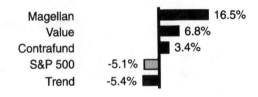

| | |
|---|---|
| Magellan | 16.5% |
| Value | 6.8% |
| Contrafund | 3.4% |
| S&P 500 | -5.1% |
| Trend | -5.4% |

## Growth Funds - 1982 Return

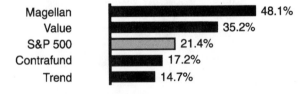

| | |
|---|---|
| Magellan | 48.1% |
| Value | 35.2% |
| S&P 500 | 21.4% |
| Contrafund | 17.2% |
| Trend | 14.7% |

## Growth Funds - 1983 Return

| | |
|---|---|
| Magellan | 38.6% |
| Value | 32.3% |
| Trend | 26.6% |
| Contrafund | 23.3% |
| S&P 500 | 22.4% |

## Growth Funds - 1984 Return

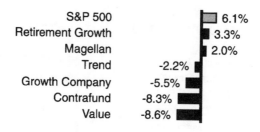

| | |
|---|---|
| S&P 500 | 6.1% |
| Retirement Growth | 3.3% |
| Magellan | 2.0% |
| Trend | -2.2% |
| Growth Company | -5.5% |
| Contrafund | -8.3% |
| Value | -8.6% |

## Growth Funds - 1985 Return

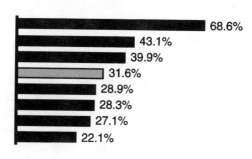

| | |
|---|---|
| OTC Portfolio | 68.6% |
| Magellan | 43.1% |
| Growth Company | 39.9% |
| S&P 500 | 31.6% |
| Retirement Growth | 28.9% |
| Trend | 28.3% |
| Contrafund | 27.1% |
| Value | 22.1% |

## Growth Funds - 1986 Return

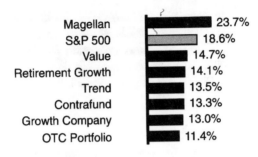

| | |
|---|---|
| Magellan | 23.7% |
| S&P 500 | 18.6% |
| Value | 14.7% |
| Retirement Growth | 14.1% |
| Trend | 13.5% |
| Contrafund | 13.3% |
| Growth Company | 13.0% |
| OTC Portfolio | 11.4% |

## Growth Funds - 1987 Return

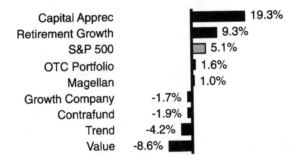

| | |
|---|---|
| Capital Apprec | 19.3% |
| Retirement Growth | 9.3% |
| S&P 500 | 5.1% |
| OTC Portfolio | 1.6% |
| Magellan | 1.0% |
| Growth Company | -1.7% |
| Contrafund | -1.9% |
| Trend | -4.2% |
| Value | -8.6% |

## Growth Funds - 1988 Return

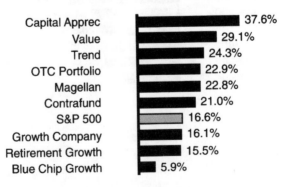

| | |
|---|---|
| Capital Apprec | 37.6% |
| Value | 29.1% |
| Trend | 24.3% |
| OTC Portfolio | 22.9% |
| Magellan | 22.8% |
| Contrafund | 21.0% |
| S&P 500 | 16.6% |
| Growth Company | 16.1% |
| Retirement Growth | 15.5% |
| Blue Chip Growth | 5.9% |

## Growth Funds - 1989 Return

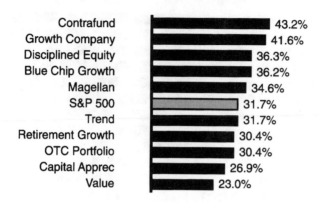

| | |
|---|---|
| Contrafund | 43.2% |
| Growth Company | 41.6% |
| Disciplined Equity | 36.3% |
| Blue Chip Growth | 36.2% |
| Magellan | 34.6% |
| S&P 500 | 31.7% |
| Trend | 31.7% |
| Retirement Growth | 30.4% |
| OTC Portfolio | 30.4% |
| Capital Apprec | 26.9% |
| Value | 23.0% |

## Growth Funds - 1990 Return

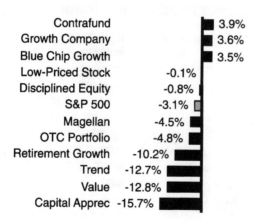

| | |
|---|---|
| Contrafund | 3.9% |
| Growth Company | 3.6% |
| Blue Chip Growth | 3.5% |
| Low-Priced Stock | -0.1% |
| Disciplined Equity | -0.8% |
| S&P 500 | -3.1% |
| Magellan | -4.5% |
| OTC Portfolio | -4.8% |
| Retirement Growth | -10.2% |
| Trend | -12.7% |
| Value | -12.8% |
| Capital Apprec | -15.7% |

## Growth Funds - 1991 Return

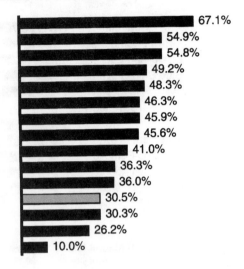

| Fund | Return |
|------|--------|
| Aggressive Growth | 67.1% |
| Contrafund | 54.9% |
| Blue Chip Growth | 54.8% |
| OTC Portfolio | 49.2% |
| Growth Company | 48.3% |
| Low-Priced Stock | 46.3% |
| Stock Selector | 45.9% |
| Retirement Growth | 45.6% |
| Magellan | 41.0% |
| Trend | 36.3% |
| Disciplined Equity | 36.0% |
| S&P 500 | 30.5% |
| Spartan Market Idx | 30.3% |
| Value | 26.2% |
| Capital Apprec | 10.0% |

## Growth Funds - 1992 Return

| Fund | Return |
|------|--------|
| Low-Priced Stock | 29.0% |
| Value | 21.2% |
| Trend | 16.8% |
| Capital Apprec | 16.4% |
| Contrafund | 15.9% |
| Stock Selector | 15.4% |
| OTC Portfolio | 14.9% |
| Disciplined Equity | 13.2% |
| Retirement Growth | 10.6% |
| Aggressive Growth | 8.4% |
| Growth Company | 7.9% |
| S&P 500 | 7.6% |
| Spartan Market Idx | 7.3% |
| Magellan | 7.0% |
| Blue Chip Growth | 6.2% |

## Growth Funds - 1993 Return

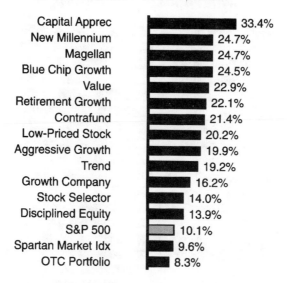

| Fund | Return |
|---|---|
| Capital Apprec | 33.4% |
| New Millennium | 24.7% |
| Magellan | 24.7% |
| Blue Chip Growth | 24.5% |
| Value | 22.9% |
| Retirement Growth | 22.1% |
| Contrafund | 21.4% |
| Low-Priced Stock | 20.2% |
| Aggressive Growth | 19.9% |
| Trend | 19.2% |
| Growth Company | 16.2% |
| Stock Selector | 14.0% |
| Disciplined Equity | 13.9% |
| S&P 500 | 10.1% |
| Spartan Market Idx | 9.6% |
| OTC Portfolio | 8.3% |

## Growth Funds - 1994 Return

| Fund | Return |
|---|---|
| Blue Chip Growth | 9.9% |
| Value | 7.6% |
| Low-Priced Stock | 4.8% |
| Dividend Growth | 4.3% |
| Fidelity Fifty | 4.0% |
| Disciplined Equity | 3.0% |
| Capital Apprec | 2.5% |
| S&P 500 | 1.3% |
| Spartan Market Idx | 1.0% |
| New Millennium | 0.8% |
| Stock Selector | 0.8% |
| Retirement Growth | 0.1% |
| Aggressive Growth | -0.2% |
| Contrafund | -1.1% |
| Magellan | -1.8% |
| Growth Company | -2.2% |
| OTC Portfolio | -2.7% |
| Small Cap Selector | -3.3% |
| Trend | -6.7% |

## Growth Funds - 1995 Return

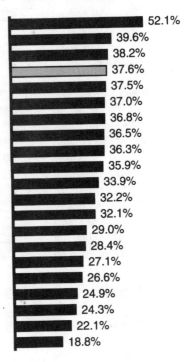

| Fund | Return |
|------|--------|
| New Millennium | 52.1% |
| Growth Company | 39.6% |
| OTC Portfolio | 38.2% |
| S&P 500 | 37.6% |
| Dividend Growth | 37.5% |
| Spartan Market Idx | 37.0% |
| Magellan | 36.8% |
| Stock Selector | 36.5% |
| Contrafund | 36.3% |
| Aggressive Growth | 35.9% |
| Mid-Cap Stock | 33.9% |
| Export | 32.2% |
| Fidelity Fifty | 32.1% |
| Disciplined Equity | 29.0% |
| Blue Chip Growth | 28.4% |
| Value | 27.1% |
| Small Cap Selector | 26.6% |
| Low-Priced Stock | 24.9% |
| Retirement Growth | 24.3% |
| Trend | 22.1% |
| Capital Apprec | 18.8% |

## Growth Funds - 1996 Return

| Fund | Return |
|------|--------|
| Export | 38.6% |
| Dividend Growth | 30.1% |
| Low-Priced Stock | 26.9% |
| OTC Portfolio | 23.7% |
| New Millennium | 23.2% |
| S&P 500 | 23.0% |
| Spartan Market Idx | 22.6% |
| Contrafund | 21.9% |
| Large Cap Stock | 21.6% |
| Mid-Cap Stock | 18.1% |
| Stock Selector | 17.1% |
| Trend | 17.0% |
| Value | 16.9% |
| Growth Company | 16.8% |
| Fidelity Fifty | 15.9% |
| Aggressive Growth | 15.8% |
| Blue Chip Growth | 15.4% |
| Capital Apprec | 15.1% |
| Disciplined Equity | 15.1% |
| Small Cap Selector | 13.6% |
| Magellan | 11.7% |
| Retirement Growth | 8.3% |

## Growth Funds - 1997 Return

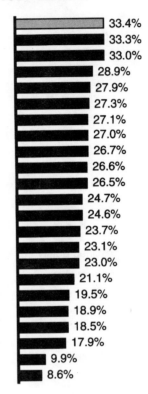

| Fund | Return |
|------|--------|
| S&P 500 | 33.4% |
| Disciplined Equity | 33.3% |
| Spartan Market Idx | 33.0% |
| Stock Selector | 28.9% |
| Dividend Growth | 27.9% |
| Small Cap Selector | 27.3% |
| Mid-Cap Stock | 27.1% |
| Blue Chip Growth | 27.0% |
| Low-Priced Stock | 26.7% |
| Magellan | 26.6% |
| Capital Apprec | 26.5% |
| Large Cap Stock | 24.7% |
| New Millennium | 24.6% |
| Export | 23.7% |
| Fidelity Fifty | 23.1% |
| Contrafund | 23.0% |
| Value | 21.1% |
| Aggressive Growth | 19.5% |
| Growth Company | 18.9% |
| Retirement Growth | 18.5% |
| TechnoQuant Growth | 17.9% |
| OTC Portfolio | 9.9% |
| Trend | 8.6% |

## Growth Funds - 1998 Return

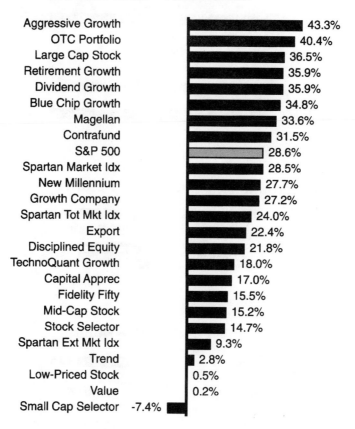

| Fund | Return |
|------|--------|
| Aggressive Growth | 43.3% |
| OTC Portfolio | 40.4% |
| Large Cap Stock | 36.5% |
| Retirement Growth | 35.9% |
| Dividend Growth | 35.9% |
| Blue Chip Growth | 34.8% |
| Magellan | 33.6% |
| Contrafund | 31.5% |
| S&P 500 | 28.6% |
| Spartan Market Idx | 28.5% |
| New Millennium | 27.7% |
| Growth Company | 27.2% |
| Spartan Tot Mkt Idx | 24.0% |
| Export | 22.4% |
| Disciplined Equity | 21.8% |
| TechnoQuant Growth | 18.0% |
| Capital Apprec | 17.0% |
| Fidelity Fifty | 15.5% |
| Mid-Cap Stock | 15.2% |
| Stock Selector | 14.7% |
| Spartan Ext Mkt Idx | 9.3% |
| Trend | 2.8% |
| Low-Priced Stock | 0.5% |
| Value | 0.2% |
| Small Cap Selector | -7.4% |

### International Funds - 1985 Return

Overseas  78.7%

### International Funds - 1986 Return

Overseas  69.3%

### International Funds - 1987 Return

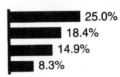

| | |
|---|---|
| Pacific Basin | 25.0% |
| Overseas | 18.4% |
| Europe | 14.9% |
| Int'l Growth & Inc | 8.3% |

### International Funds - 1988 Return

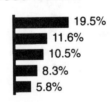

| | |
|---|---|
| Canada | 19.5% |
| Int'l Growth & Inc | 11.6% |
| Pacific Basin | 10.5% |
| Overseas | 8.3% |
| Europe | 5.8% |

### International Funds - 1989 Return

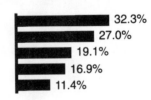

| | |
|---|---|
| Europe | 32.3% |
| Canada | 27.0% |
| Int'l Growth & Inc | 19.1% |
| Overseas | 16.9% |
| Pacific Basin | 11.4% |

## International Funds - 1990 Return

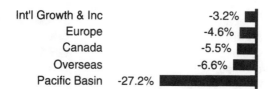

| | |
|---|---|
| Int'l Growth & Inc | -3.2% |
| Europe | -4.6% |
| Canada | -5.5% |
| Overseas | -6.6% |
| Pacific Basin | -27.2% |

## International Funds - 1991 Return

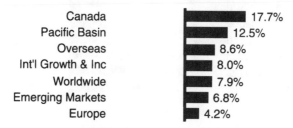

| | |
|---|---|
| Canada | 17.7% |
| Pacific Basin | 12.5% |
| Overseas | 8.6% |
| Int'l Growth & Inc | 8.0% |
| Worldwide | 7.9% |
| Emerging Markets | 6.8% |
| Europe | 4.2% |

## International Funds - 1992 Return

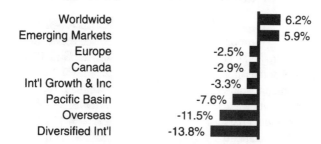

| | |
|---|---|
| Worldwide | 6.2% |
| Emerging Markets | 5.9% |
| Europe | -2.5% |
| Canada | -2.9% |
| Int'l Growth & Inc | -3.3% |
| Pacific Basin | -7.6% |
| Overseas | -11.5% |
| Diversified Int'l | -13.8% |

## International Funds - 1993 Return

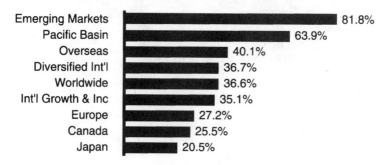

| | |
|---|---|
| Emerging Markets | 81.8% |
| Pacific Basin | 63.9% |
| Overseas | 40.1% |
| Diversified Int'l | 36.7% |
| Worldwide | 36.6% |
| Int'l Growth & Inc | 35.1% |
| Europe | 27.2% |
| Canada | 25.5% |
| Japan | 20.5% |

## International Funds - 1994 Return

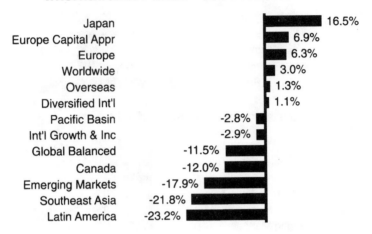

| | |
|---|---|
| Japan | 16.5% |
| Europe Capital Appr | 6.9% |
| Europe | 6.3% |
| Worldwide | 3.0% |
| Overseas | 1.3% |
| Diversified Int'l | 1.1% |
| Pacific Basin | -2.8% |
| Int'l Growth & Inc | -2.9% |
| Global Balanced | -11.5% |
| Canada | -12.0% |
| Emerging Markets | -17.9% |
| Southeast Asia | -21.8% |
| Latin America | -23.2% |

## International Funds - 1995 Return

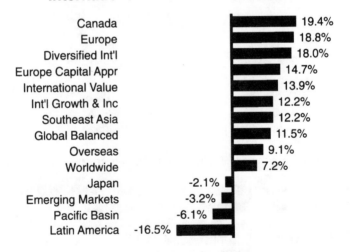

| | |
|---|---|
| Canada | 19.4% |
| Europe | 18.8% |
| Diversified Int'l | 18.0% |
| Europe Capital Appr | 14.7% |
| International Value | 13.9% |
| Int'l Growth & Inc | 12.2% |
| Southeast Asia | 12.2% |
| Global Balanced | 11.5% |
| Overseas | 9.1% |
| Worldwide | 7.2% |
| Japan | -2.1% |
| Emerging Markets | -3.2% |
| Pacific Basin | -6.1% |
| Latin America | -16.5% |

## International Funds - 1996 Return

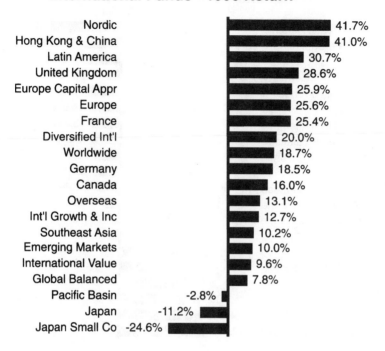

| Fund | Return |
|------|--------|
| Nordic | 41.7% |
| Hong Kong & China | 41.0% |
| Latin America | 30.7% |
| United Kingdom | 28.6% |
| Europe Capital Appr | 25.9% |
| Europe | 25.6% |
| France | 25.4% |
| Diversified Int'l | 20.0% |
| Worldwide | 18.7% |
| Germany | 18.5% |
| Canada | 16.0% |
| Overseas | 13.1% |
| Int'l Growth & Inc | 12.7% |
| Southeast Asia | 10.2% |
| Emerging Markets | 10.0% |
| International Value | 9.6% |
| Global Balanced | 7.8% |
| Pacific Basin | -2.8% |
| Japan | -11.2% |
| Japan Small Co | -24.6% |

## International Funds - 1997 Return

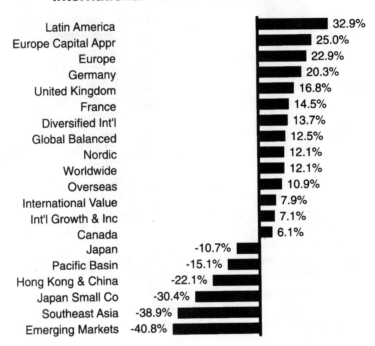

| Fund | Return |
|------|-------:|
| Latin America | 32.9% |
| Europe Capital Appr | 25.0% |
| Europe | 22.9% |
| Germany | 20.3% |
| United Kingdom | 16.8% |
| France | 14.5% |
| Diversified Int'l | 13.7% |
| Global Balanced | 12.5% |
| Nordic | 12.1% |
| Worldwide | 12.1% |
| Overseas | 10.9% |
| International Value | 7.9% |
| Int'l Growth & Inc | 7.1% |
| Canada | 6.1% |
| Japan | -10.7% |
| Pacific Basin | -15.1% |
| Hong Kong & China | -22.1% |
| Japan Small Co | -30.4% |
| Southeast Asia | -38.9% |
| Emerging Markets | -40.8% |

# International Funds - 1998 Return

| | |
|---|---|
| Japan Small Co | 31.2% |
| Nordic | 29.5% |
| France | 28.9% |
| Germany | 23.3% |
| Europe Capital Appr | 21.7% |
| Europe | 20.8% |
| Global Balanced | 17.8% |
| Diversified Int'l | 14.4% |
| Japan | 13.1% |
| Overseas | 12.8% |
| International Value | 11.7% |
| United Kingdom | 10.3% |
| Int'l Growth & Inc | 10.0% |
| Pacific Basin | 8.3% |
| Worldwide | 7.2% |
| Hong Kong & China | -5.3% |
| Southeast Asia | -5.8% |
| Canada | -14.9% |
| Emerging Markets | -26.6% |
| Latin America | -38.3% |

## Growth & Income - 1977 Return

| | |
|---|---|
| Equity-Income | 5.0% |
| Puritan | 0.8% |
| Fidelity | -3.3% |
| S&P 500 | -7.4% |

## Growth & Income - 1978 Return

| | |
|---|---|
| Equity-Income | 11.4% |
| Fidelity | 9.4% |
| S&P 500 | 6.6% |
| Puritan | 4.5% |

## Growth & Income - 1979 Return

| | |
|---|---|
| Equity-Income | 30.8% |
| Fidelity | 18.7% |
| S&P 500 | 18.7% |
| Puritan | 14.8% |

## Growth & Income - 1980 Return

| | |
|---|---|
| Fidelity | 33.9% |
| S&P 500 | 32.6% |
| Equity-Income | 32.3% |
| Puritan | 20.3% |

## Growth & Income - 1981 Return

| | |
|---|---|
| Puritan | 10.8% |
| Equity-Income | 9.5% |
| Fidelity | -3.3% |
| S&P 500 | -5.1% |

## Growth & Income - 1982 Return

| | |
|---|---|
| Equity-Income | 34.6% |
| Fidelity | 34.5% |
| Puritan | 29.1% |
| S&P 500 | 21.4% |

## Growth & Income - 1983 Return

| | |
|---|---|
| Equity-Income | 29.2% |
| Puritan | 25.9% |
| Fidelity | 22.4% |
| S&P 500 | 22.4% |

## Growth & Income - 1984 Return

| | |
|---|---|
| Puritan | 10.6% |
| Equity-Income | 10.5% |
| S&P 500 | 6.1% |
| Fidelity | 1.5% |

## Growth & Income - 1985 Return

| | |
|---|---|
| S&P 500 | 31.6% |
| Puritan | 28.7% |
| Fidelity | 27.7% |
| Equity-Income | 25.1% |

## Growth & Income - 1986 Return

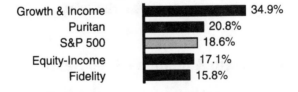

| | |
|---|---|
| Growth & Income | 34.9% |
| Puritan | 20.8% |
| S&P 500 | 18.6% |
| Equity-Income | 17.1% |
| Fidelity | 15.8% |

## Growth & Income - 1987 Return

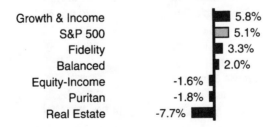

| | |
|---|---|
| Growth & Income | 5.8% |
| S&P 500 | 5.1% |
| Fidelity | 3.3% |
| Balanced | 2.0% |
| Equity-Income | -1.6% |
| Puritan | -1.8% |
| Real Estate | -7.7% |

## Growth & Income - 1988 Return

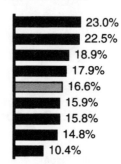

| | |
|---|---|
| Growth & Income | 23.0% |
| Equity-Income | 22.5% |
| Puritan | 18.9% |
| Fidelity | 17.9% |
| S&P 500 | 16.6% |
| Convertible Sec | 15.9% |
| Balanced | 15.8% |
| Utilities | 14.8% |
| Real Estate | 10.4% |

## Growth & Income - 1989 Return

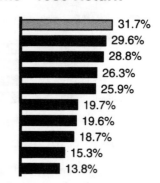

| | |
|---|---|
| S&P 500 | 31.7% |
| Growth & Income | 29.6% |
| Fidelity | 28.8% |
| Convertible Sec | 26.3% |
| Utilities | 25.9% |
| Balanced | 19.7% |
| Puritan | 19.6% |
| Equity-Income | 18.7% |
| Asset Mgr | 15.3% |
| Real Estate | 13.8% |

## Growth & Income - 1990 Return

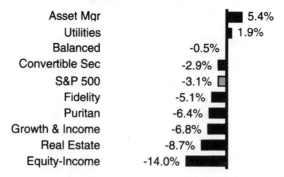

| | |
|---|---|
| Asset Mgr | 5.4% |
| Utilities | 1.9% |
| Balanced | -0.5% |
| Convertible Sec | -2.9% |
| S&P 500 | -3.1% |
| Fidelity | -5.1% |
| Puritan | -6.4% |
| Growth & Income | -6.8% |
| Real Estate | -8.7% |
| Equity-Income | -14.0% |

## Growth & Income - 1988 Return

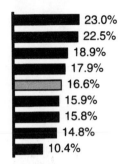

| | |
|---|---|
| Growth & Income | 23.0% |
| Equity-Income | 22.5% |
| Puritan | 18.9% |
| Fidelity | 17.9% |
| S&P 500 | 16.6% |
| Convertible Sec | 15.9% |
| Balanced | 15.8% |
| Utilities | 14.8% |
| Real Estate | 10.4% |

## Growth & Income - 1989 Return

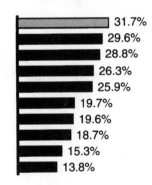

| | |
|---|---|
| S&P 500 | 31.7% |
| Growth & Income | 29.6% |
| Fidelity | 28.8% |
| Convertible Sec | 26.3% |
| Utilities | 25.9% |
| Balanced | 19.7% |
| Puritan | 19.6% |
| Equity-Income | 18.7% |
| Asset Mgr | 15.3% |
| Real Estate | 13.8% |

## Growth & Income - 1990 Return

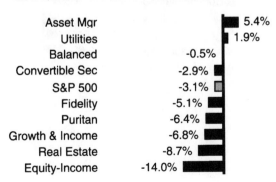

| | |
|---|---|
| Asset Mgr | 5.4% |
| Utilities | 1.9% |
| Balanced | -0.5% |
| Convertible Sec | -2.9% |
| S&P 500 | -3.1% |
| Fidelity | -5.1% |
| Puritan | -6.4% |
| Growth & Income | -6.8% |
| Real Estate | -8.7% |
| Equity-Income | -14.0% |

## Growth & Income - 1993 Return

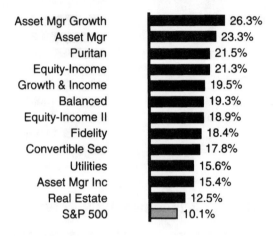

| | |
|---|---|
| Asset Mgr Growth | 26.3% |
| Asset Mgr | 23.3% |
| Puritan | 21.5% |
| Equity-Income | 21.3% |
| Growth & Income | 19.5% |
| Balanced | 19.3% |
| Equity-Income II | 18.9% |
| Fidelity | 18.4% |
| Convertible Sec | 17.8% |
| Utilities | 15.6% |
| Asset Mgr Inc | 15.4% |
| Real Estate | 12.5% |
| S&P 500 | 10.1% |

## Growth & Income - 1994 Return

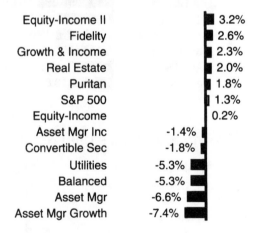

| | |
|---|---|
| Equity-Income II | 3.2% |
| Fidelity | 2.6% |
| Growth & Income | 2.3% |
| Real Estate | 2.0% |
| Puritan | 1.8% |
| S&P 500 | 1.3% |
| Equity-Income | 0.2% |
| Asset Mgr Inc | -1.4% |
| Convertible Sec | -1.8% |
| Utilities | -5.3% |
| Balanced | -5.3% |
| Asset Mgr | -6.6% |
| Asset Mgr Growth | -7.4% |

## Growth & Income - 1995 Return

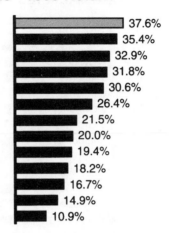

| | |
|---|---|
| S&P 500 | 37.6% |
| Growth & Income | 35.4% |
| Fidelity | 32.9% |
| Equity-Income | 31.8% |
| Utilities | 30.6% |
| Equity-Income II | 26.4% |
| Puritan | 21.5% |
| Asset Mgr Growth | 20.0% |
| Convertible Sec | 19.4% |
| Asset Mgr | 18.2% |
| Asset Mgr Inc | 16.7% |
| Balanced | 14.9% |
| Real Estate | 10.9% |

## Growth & Income - 1996 Return

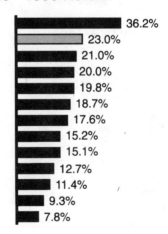

| | |
|---|---|
| Real Estate | 36.2% |
| S&P 500 | 23.0% |
| Equity-Income | 21.0% |
| Growth & Income | 20.0% |
| Fidelity | 19.8% |
| Equity-Income II | 18.7% |
| Asset Mgr Growth | 17.6% |
| Puritan | 15.2% |
| Convertible Sec | 15.1% |
| Asset Mgr | 12.7% |
| Utilities | 11.4% |
| Balanced | 9.3% |
| Asset Mgr Inc | 7.8% |

## Growth & Income - 1997 Return

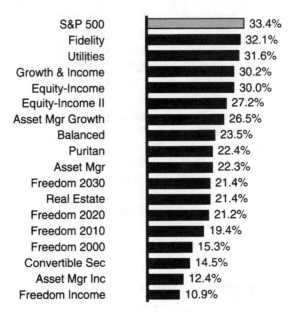

| | |
|---|---|
| S&P 500 | 33.4% |
| Fidelity | 32.1% |
| Utilities | 31.6% |
| Growth & Income | 30.2% |
| Equity-Income | 30.0% |
| Equity-Income II | 27.2% |
| Asset Mgr Growth | 26.5% |
| Balanced | 23.5% |
| Puritan | 22.4% |
| Asset Mgr | 22.3% |
| Freedom 2030 | 21.4% |
| Real Estate | 21.4% |
| Freedom 2020 | 21.2% |
| Freedom 2010 | 19.4% |
| Freedom 2000 | 15.3% |
| Convertible Sec | 14.5% |
| Asset Mgr Inc | 12.4% |
| Freedom Income | 10.9% |

## Growth & Income - 1998 Return

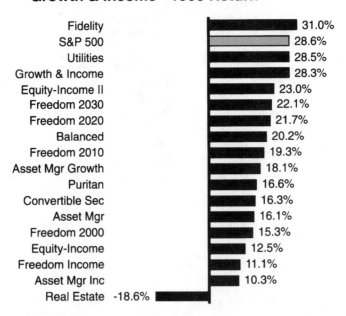

| | |
|---|---|
| Fidelity | 31.0% |
| S&P 500 | 28.6% |
| Utilities | 28.5% |
| Growth & Income | 28.3% |
| Equity-Income II | 23.0% |
| Freedom 2030 | 22.1% |
| Freedom 2020 | 21.7% |
| Balanced | 20.2% |
| Freedom 2010 | 19.3% |
| Asset Mgr Growth | 18.1% |
| Puritan | 16.6% |
| Convertible Sec | 16.3% |
| Asset Mgr | 16.1% |
| Freedom 2000 | 15.3% |
| Equity-Income | 12.5% |
| Freedom Income | 11.1% |
| Asset Mgr Inc | 10.3% |
| Real Estate | -18.6% |

### Bond Funds - 1977 Return

Invest Grade Bond      15.8%
Intermediate Bond      3.1%

### Bond Funds - 1978 Return

Capital & Income      4.0%
Intermediate Bond      3.1%
Invest Grade Bond      1.4%

### Bond Funds - 1979 Return

Intermediate Bond      7.2%
Capital & Income      4.7%
Invest Grade Bond      1.2%

### Bond Funds - 1980 Return

Intermediate Bond      10.5%
Gov't Income      6.7%
Capital & Income      4.4%
Invest Grade Bond      2.3%

### Bond Funds - 1981 Return

Intermediate Bond      12.4%
Gov't Income      10.5%
Capital & Income      6.9%
Invest Grade Bond      3.9%

### Bond Funds - 1982 Return

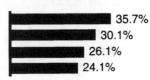

Capital & Income      35.7%
Invest Grade Bond      30.1%
Gov't Income      26.1%
Intermediate Bond      24.1%

# Bond Funds - 1983 Return

Capital & Income
Intermediate Bond
Invest Grade Bond
Gov't Income

18.5%
9.4%
6.6%
6.1%

# Bond Funds - 1984 Return

Intermediate Bond
Invest Grade Bond
Gov't Income
Capital & Income

13.6%
11.8%
11.3%
10.5%

# Bond Funds - 1985 Return

Capital & Income
Invest Grade Bond
Intermediate Bond
Gov't Income

25.5%
21.1%
20.6%
17.7%

# Bond Funds - 1986 Return

Capital & Income
Gov't Income
Invest Grade Bond
Intermediate Bond
GNMA Portfolio

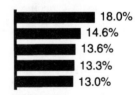

18.0%
14.6%
13.6%
13.3%
13.0%

# Bond Funds - 1987 Return

Int'l Bond
Short-Term Bond
Intermediate Bond
Capital & Income
GNMA Portfolio
Gov't Income
Invest Grade Bond

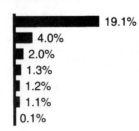

19.1%
4.0%
2.0%
1.3%
1.2%
1.1%
0.1%

## Bond Funds - 1988 Return

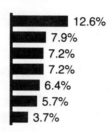

| | |
|---|---|
| Capital & Income | 12.6% |
| Invest Grade Bond | 7.9% |
| Intermediate Bond | 7.2% |
| GNMA Portfolio | 7.2% |
| Gov't Income | 6.4% |
| Short-Term Bond | 5.7% |
| Int'l Bond | 3.7% |

## Bond Funds - 1989 Return

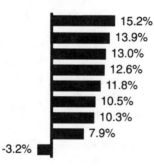

| | |
|---|---|
| Spartan Gov't Inc | 15.2% |
| GNMA Portfolio | 13.9% |
| Invest Grade Bond | 13.0% |
| Gov't Income | 12.6% |
| Intermediate Bond | 11.8% |
| Short-Term Bond | 10.5% |
| Int Gov't Income | 10.3% |
| Int'l Bond | 7.9% |
| Capital & Income | -3.2% |

## Bond Funds - 1990 Return

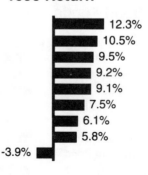

| | |
|---|---|
| Int'l Bond | 12.3% |
| GNMA Portfolio | 10.5% |
| Gov't Income | 9.5% |
| Spartan Gov't Inc | 9.2% |
| Int Gov't Income | 9.1% |
| Intermediate Bond | 7.5% |
| Invest Grade Bond | 6.1% |
| Short-Term Bond | 5.8% |
| Capital & Income | -3.9% |

## Bond Funds - 1991 Return

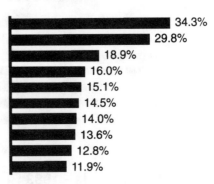

| | |
|---|---|
| High Income | 34.3% |
| Capital & Income | 29.8% |
| Invest Grade Bond | 18.9% |
| Gov't Income | 16.0% |
| Spartan Gov't Inc | 15.1% |
| Intermediate Bond | 14.5% |
| Short-Term Bond | 14.0% |
| GNMA Portfolio | 13.6% |
| Int'l Bond | 12.8% |
| Int Gov't Income | 11.9% |

## Bond Funds - 1992 Return

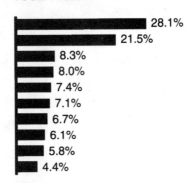

| | |
|---|---|
| Capital & Income | 28.1% |
| High Income | 21.5% |
| Invest Grade Bond | 8.3% |
| Gov't Income | 8.0% |
| Short-Term Bond | 7.4% |
| Spartan Gov't Inc | 7.1% |
| GNMA Portfolio | 6.7% |
| Intermediate Bond | 6.1% |
| Int Gov't Income | 5.8% |
| Int'l Bond | 4.4% |

## Bond Funds - 1993 Return

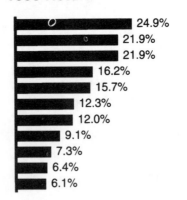

| | |
|---|---|
| Capital & Income | 24.9% |
| Int'l Bond | 21.9% |
| High Income | 21.9% |
| Invest Grade Bond | 16.2% |
| Spartan Inv Grade | 15.7% |
| Gov't Income | 12.3% |
| Intermediate Bond | 12.0% |
| Short-Term Bond | 9.1% |
| Spartan Gov't Inc | 7.3% |
| Int Gov't Income | 6.4% |
| GNMA Portfolio | 6.1% |

## Bond Funds - 1994 Return

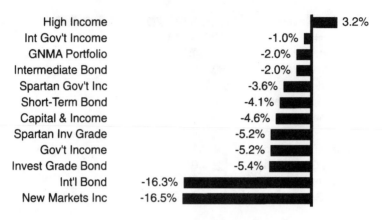

| | |
|---|---|
| High Income | 3.2% |
| Int Gov't Income | -1.0% |
| GNMA Portfolio | -2.0% |
| Intermediate Bond | -2.0% |
| Spartan Gov't Inc | -3.6% |
| Short-Term Bond | -4.1% |
| Capital & Income | -4.6% |
| Spartan Inv Grade | -5.2% |
| Gov't Income | -5.2% |
| Invest Grade Bond | -5.4% |
| Int'l Bond | -16.3% |
| New Markets Inc | -16.5% |

## Bond Funds - 1995 Return

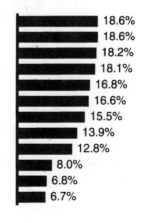

| | |
|---|---|
| High Income | 18.6% |
| Spartan Inv Grade | 18.6% |
| Spartan Gov't Inc | 18.2% |
| Gov't Income | 18.1% |
| Capital & Income | 16.8% |
| GNMA Portfolio | 16.6% |
| Invest Grade Bond | 15.5% |
| Int Gov't Income | 13.9% |
| Intermediate Bond | 12.8% |
| New Markets Inc | 8.0% |
| Short-Term Bond | 6.8% |
| Int'l Bond | 6.7% |

## Bond Funds - 1996 Return

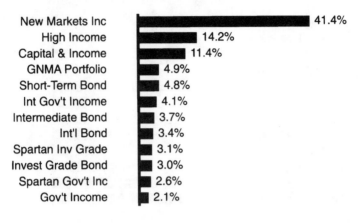

| | |
|---|---|
| New Markets Inc | 41.4% |
| High Income | 14.2% |
| Capital & Income | 11.4% |
| GNMA Portfolio | 4.9% |
| Short-Term Bond | 4.8% |
| Int Gov't Income | 4.1% |
| Intermediate Bond | 3.7% |
| Int'l Bond | 3.4% |
| Spartan Inv Grade | 3.1% |
| Invest Grade Bond | 3.0% |
| Spartan Gov't Inc | 2.6% |
| Gov't Income | 2.1% |

## Bond Funds - 1997 Return

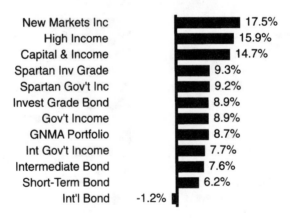

| | |
|---|---|
| New Markets Inc | 17.5% |
| High Income | 15.9% |
| Capital & Income | 14.7% |
| Spartan Inv Grade | 9.3% |
| Spartan Gov't Inc | 9.2% |
| Invest Grade Bond | 8.9% |
| Gov't Income | 8.9% |
| GNMA Portfolio | 8.7% |
| Int Gov't Income | 7.7% |
| Intermediate Bond | 7.6% |
| Short-Term Bond | 6.2% |
| Int'l Bond | -1.2% |

## Bond Funds - 1998 Return

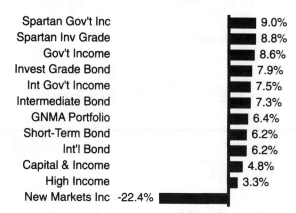

| Fund | Return |
|------|--------|
| Spartan Gov't Inc | 9.0% |
| Spartan Inv Grade | 8.8% |
| Gov't Income | 8.6% |
| Invest Grade Bond | 7.9% |
| Int Gov't Income | 7.5% |
| Intermediate Bond | 7.3% |
| GNMA Portfolio | 6.4% |
| Short-Term Bond | 6.2% |
| Int'l Bond | 6.2% |
| Capital & Income | 4.8% |
| High Income | 3.3% |
| New Markets Inc | -22.4% |

## Muni Bond Funds - 1977 Return

Municipal Income              -0.1%

## Muni Bond Funds - 1978 Return

Spartan Muni Inc              -0.1%
Spartan Int Muni              -3.6%

## Muni Bond Funds - 1979 Return

Spartan Muni Inc              1.3%
Spartan Int Muni              0.5%

## Muni Bond Funds - 1980 Return

Spartan Int Muni              -6.5%
Spartan Muni Inc              -12.6%

## Muni Bond Funds - 1981 Return

Spartan Int Muni              -2.9%
Spartan Muni Inc              -6.0%

## Muni Bond Funds - 1982 Return

Spartan Muni Inc        36.0%
Spartan Int Muni                            25.9%

## Muni Bond Funds - 1983 Return

Spartan Muni Inc
Spartan Int Muni Inc

12.7%
9.9%

## Muni Bond Funds - 1984 Return

Spartan Muni Inc
Spartan Int Muni Inc
Spartan MA Muni Inc

9.9%
9.9%
8.5%

## Muni Bond Funds - 1985 Return

Spartan Muni Inc
Spartan NY Muni Inc
Spartan MA Muni Inc
Spartan Int Muni Inc
Spartan CA Muni Inc

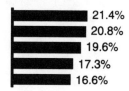

21.4%
20.8%
19.6%
17.3%
16.6%

## Muni Bond Funds - 1986 Return

Spartan MI Muni Inc
Spartan Muni Inc
Spartan CA Muni Inc
Spartan MN Muni Inc
Spartan MA Muni Inc
Spartan NY Muni Inc
Spartan OH Muni Inc
Spartan Int Muni Inc

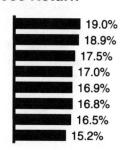

19.0%
18.9%
17.5%
17.0%
16.9%
16.8%
16.5%
15.2%

## Muni Bond Funds - 1987 Return

| Fund | Return |
|------|-------:|
| Spartan Int Muni Inc | 1.1% |
| Spartan S-Int Muni | 0.3% |
| Spartan MA Muni Inc | -1.3% |
| Spartan OH Muni Inc | -2.4% |
| Spartan NY Muni Inc | -2.4% |
| Spartan MI Muni Inc | -2.8% |
| Spartan Muni Inc | -2.8% |
| Spartan CA Muni Inc | -3.7% |
| Spartan MN Muni Inc | -3.8% |
| Spartan PA Muni Inc | -5.7% |

## Muni Bond Funds - 1988 Return

| Fund | Return |
|------|-------:|
| Spartan PA Muni Inc | 14.2% |
| Spartan MI Muni Inc | 13.0% |
| Spartan OH Muni Inc | 12.9% |
| Spartan MN Muni Inc | 12.6% |
| Spartan Muni Inc | 12.2% |
| Spartan NY Muni Inc | 11.9% |
| Spartan CA Muni Inc | 11.8% |
| Spartan MA Muni Inc | 10.7% |
| Spartan CT High Yld | 10.1% |
| Spartan Int Muni Inc | 8.2% |
| Spartan S-Int Muni | 4.9% |

## Muni Bond Funds - 1989 Return

| Fund | Return |
|------|-------:|
| Spartan Muni Inc | 11.4% |
| Spartan CT High Yld | 10.4% |
| Spartan NJ Muni Inc | 10.3% |
| Spartan MI Muni Inc | 10.2% |
| Spartan OH Muni Inc | 10.0% |
| Spartan PA Muni Inc | 9.8% |
| Spartan CA Muni Inc | 9.7% |
| Spartan NY Muni Inc | 9.3% |
| Spartan MA Muni Inc | 9.3% |
| Spartan MN Muni Inc | 9.2% |
| Spartan Int Muni Inc | 7.8% |
| Spartan S-Int Muni | 6.3% |

## Muni Bond Funds - 1990 Return

| | |
|---|---|
| Spartan Muni Inc | 8.5% |
| Spartan OH Muni Inc | 7.5% |
| Spartan MA Muni Inc | 7.4% |
| Spartan MN Muni Inc | 7.2% |
| Spartan PA Muni Inc | 7.2% |
| Spartan NJ Muni Inc | 7.1% |
| Spartan Int Muni Inc | 7.0% |
| Spartan CA Muni Inc | 7.0% |
| Spartan CT High Yld | 6.7% |
| Spartan S-Int Muni | 6.4% |
| Spartan MI Muni Inc | 5.2% |
| Spartan NY Muni Inc | 5.1% |

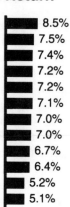

## Muni Bond Funds - 1991 Return

| | |
|---|---|
| Spartan NY Muni Inc | 13.4% |
| Spartan PA Muni Inc | 12.5% |
| Spartan NJ Muni Inc | 12.3% |
| Spartan MI Muni Inc | 12.0% |
| Spartan Int Muni Inc | 11.9% |
| Spartan OH Muni Inc | 11.5% |
| Spartan MA Muni Inc | 11.3% |
| Spartan CT High Yld | 10.6% |
| Spartan Muni Inc | 10.2% |
| Spartan CA Muni Inc | 10.2% |
| Spartan S-Int Muni | 8.8% |
| Spartan MN Muni Inc | 8.5% |

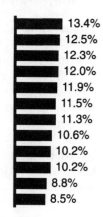

## Muni Bond Funds - 1992 Return

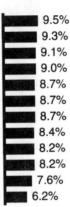

| | |
|---|---|
| Spartan MI Muni Inc | 9.5% |
| Spartan MA Muni Inc | 9.3% |
| Spartan PA Muni Inc | 9.1% |
| Spartan NY Muni Inc | 9.0% |
| Spartan CA Muni Inc | 8.7% |
| Spartan NJ Muni Inc | 8.7% |
| Spartan OH Muni Inc | 8.7% |
| Spartan Muni Inc | 8.4% |
| Spartan CT High Yld | 8.2% |
| Spartan Int Muni Inc | 8.2% |
| Spartan MN Muni Inc | 7.6% |
| Spartan S-Int Muni | 6.2% |

## Muni Bond Funds - 1993 Return

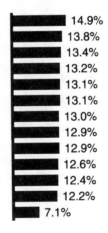

| | |
|---|---|
| Spartan FL Muni Inc | 14.9% |
| Spartan MI Muni Inc | 13.8% |
| Spartan CA Muni Inc | 13.4% |
| Spartan PA Muni Inc | 13.2% |
| Spartan Muni Inc | 13.1% |
| Spartan NJ Muni Inc | 13.1% |
| Spartan CT High Yld | 13.0% |
| Spartan MA Muni Inc | 12.9% |
| Spartan NY Muni Inc | 12.9% |
| Spartan OH Muni Inc | 12.6% |
| Spartan MN Muni Inc | 12.4% |
| Spartan Int Muni Inc | 12.2% |
| Spartan S-Int Muni | 7.1% |

## Muni Bond Funds - 1994 Return

| | |
|---|---|
| Spartan S-Int Muni | -0.1% |
| Spartan Int Muni Inc | -4.8% |
| Spartan PA Muni Inc | -5.0% |
| Spartan OH Muni Inc | -5.5% |
| Spartan NJ Muni Inc | -5.8% |
| Spartan MN Muni Inc | -5.9% |
| Spartan MA Muni Inc | -6.1% |
| Spartan FL Muni Inc | -6.8% |
| Spartan CT High Yld | -7.0% |
| Spartan Muni Inc | -7.5% |
| Spartan MI Muni Inc | -7.5% |
| Spartan MD Muni Inc | -7.5% |
| Spartan NY Muni Inc | -8.0% |
| Spartan CA Muni Inc | -8.8% |

## Muni Bond Funds - 1995 Return

| | |
|---|---|
| Spartan NY Muni Inc | 19.6% |
| Spartan CA Muni Inc | 19.2% |
| Spartan FL Muni Inc | 18.6% |
| Spartan AZ Muni Inc | 18.5% |
| Spartan MA Muni Inc | 18.1% |
| Spartan MD Muni Inc | 17.8% |
| Spartan PA Muni Inc | 17.4% |
| Spartan CT High Yld | 17.1% |
| Spartan OH Muni Inc | 16.4% |
| Spartan Muni Inc | 16.2% |
| Spartan MN Muni Inc | 16.0% |
| Spartan NJ Muni Inc | 15.4% |
| Spartan MI Muni Inc | 15.4% |
| Spartan Int Muni Inc | 14.8% |
| Spartan S-Int Muni | 8.5% |

## Muni Bond Funds - 1996 Return

| Fund | Return |
|------|--------|
| Spartan Muni Inc | 4.9% |
| Spartan CA Muni Inc | 4.8% |
| Spartan Int Muni Inc | 4.4% |
| Spartan CT High Yld | 4.2% |
| Spartan NJ Muni Inc | 4.1% |
| Spartan FL Muni Inc | 4.0% |
| Spartan PA Muni Inc | 4.0% |
| Spartan OH Muni Inc | 4.0% |
| Spartan MD Muni Inc | 3.9% |
| Spartan S-Int Muni | 3.9% |
| Spartan NY Muni Inc | 3.8% |
| Spartan MN Muni Inc | 3.8% |
| Spartan MA Muni Inc | 3.6% |
| Spartan AZ Muni Inc | 3.5% |
| Spartan MI Muni Inc | 3.4% |

## Muni Bond Funds - 1997 Return

| Fund | Return |
|------|--------|
| Spartan CA Muni Inc | 9.8% |
| Spartan NY Muni Inc | 9.7% |
| Spartan MA Muni Inc | 9.3% |
| Spartan Muni Inc | 9.2% |
| Spartan CT High Yld | 9.1% |
| Spartan MI Muni Inc | 9.0% |
| Spartan MN Muni Inc | 8.9% |
| Spartan FL Muni Inc | 8.8% |
| Spartan MD Muni Inc | 8.8% |
| Spartan OH Muni Inc | 8.7% |
| Spartan NJ Muni Inc | 8.4% |
| Spartan PA Muni Inc | 8.3% |
| Spartan Int Muni Inc | 8.2% |
| Spartan AZ Muni Inc | 8.0% |
| Spartan S-Int Muni | 5.5% |

## Muni Bond Funds - 1998 Return

| Fund | Return |
|------|-------:|
| Spartan CA Muni Inc | 6.6% |
| Spartan NY Muni Inc | 6.3% |
| Spartan FL Muni Inc | 6.3% |
| Spartan Muni Inc | 6.0% |
| Spartan MD Muni Inc | 6.0% |
| Spartan Int Muni Inc | 5.9% |
| Spartan CT High Yld | 5.8% |
| Spartan OH Muni Inc | 5.8% |
| Spartan NJ Muni Inc | 5.8% |
| Spartan PA Muni Inc | 5.8% |
| Spartan MI Muni Inc | 5.7% |
| Spartan MA Muni Inc | 5.6% |
| Spartan MN Muni Inc | 5.5% |
| Spartan AZ Muni Inc | 5.3% |
| Spartan S-Int Muni | 4.7% |

## Money Markets - 1979 Return

FDIT                                            11.9%

## Money Markets - 1980 Return

Cash Reserves                                   12.9%
FDIT                                            12.8%

## Money Markets - 1981 Return

Cash Reserves                                   17.2%
FDIT                                            17.0%

## Money Markets - 1982 Return

Cash Reserves                                   13.0%
FDIT                                            12.8%
U.S. Gov't Reser                                11.5%

## Money Markets - 1983 Return

FDIT                                            8.9%
Cash Reserves                                   8.8%
U.S. Gov't Reser                                8.6%

## Money Markets - 1984 Return

Cash Reserves                                   10.2%
FDIT                                            10.1%
U.S. Gov't Reser                                9.8%

## Money Markets - 1985 Return

FDIT                                            7.9%
Cash Reserves                                   7.9%
U.S. Gov't Reser                                7.8%

## Money Markets - 1986 Return

| | |
|---|---|
| Select MM | 6.6% |
| Cash Reserves | 6.5% |
| FDIT | 6.5% |
| U.S. Gov't Reser | 6.4% |

## Money Markets - 1987 Return

| | |
|---|---|
| Cash Reserves | 6.4% |
| FDIT | 6.1% |
| U.S. Gov't Reser | 6.0% |
| Select MM | 6.0% |

## Money Markets - 1988 Return

| | |
|---|---|
| Cash Reserves | 7.3% |
| FDIT | 7.2% |
| Select MM | 7.1% |
| U.S. Gov't Reser | 7.0% |

## Money Markets - 1989 Return

| | |
|---|---|
| Select MM | 9.0% |
| FDIT | 9.0% |
| Cash Reserves | 9.0% |
| U.S. Gov't Reser | 8.8% |
| Spart U.S. Treas | 8.3% |

## Money Markets - 1990 Return

| | |
|---|---|
| Spart MM | 8.4% |
| Spart U.S. Treas | 7.9% |
| FDIT | 7.8% |
| Cash Reserves | 7.8% |
| Select MM | 7.8% |
| U.S. Gov't Reser | 7.7% |

## Money Markets - 1991 Return

| | |
|---|---|
| Spart MM | 6.2% |
| Spart U.S. Treas | 6.1% |
| Spart U.S. Gov't | 6.1% |
| Cash Reserves | 6.0% |
| FDIT | 5.8% |
| Select MM | 5.8% |
| U.S. Gov't Reser | 5.7% |

## Money Markets - 1992 Return

| | |
|---|---|
| Spart MM | 4.0% |
| Spart U.S. Gov't | 3.8% |
| Cash Reserves | 3.8% |
| Spart U.S. Treas | 3.7% |
| FDIT | 3.6% |
| Select MM | 3.5% |
| U.S. Gov't Reser | 3.4% |

## Money Markets - 1993 Return

| | |
|---|---|
| Spart MM | 3.1% |
| Cash Reserves | 2.9% |
| Spart U.S. Gov't | 2.8% |
| FDIT | 2.8% |
| Spart U.S. Treas | 2.7% |
| Select MM | 2.7% |
| U.S. Gov't Reser | 2.6% |

## Money Markets - 1994 Return

| | |
|---|---|
| Spart MM | 4.1% |
| Cash Reserves | 4.0% |
| Spart U.S. Gov't | 3.9% |
| FDIT | 3.9% |
| U.S. Gov't Reser | 3.9% |
| Select MM | 3.7% |
| Spartan US Treas | 3.7% |

## Money Markets - 1995 Return

| | |
|---|---|
| Spartan MM | 5.8% |
| Spartan U.S. Gov't | 5.7% |
| Cash Reserves | 5.7% |
| Select MM | 5.7% |
| FDIT | 5.7% |
| U.S. Gov't Reserves | 5.6% |
| Spartan U.S. Treas | 5.4% |

## Money Markets - 1996 Return

| | |
|---|---|
| Spartan MM | 5.2% |
| Spartan U.S. Gov't | 5.2% |
| Cash Reserves | 5.2% |
| FDIT | 5.1% |
| U.S. Gov't Reserves | 5.1% |
| Select MM | 5.1% |
| Spartan U.S. Treas | 4.9% |

## Money Markets - 1997 Return

| | |
|---|---|
| Spartan MM | 5.4% |
| Cash Reserves | 5.3% |
| Spartan U.S. Gov't | 5.3% |
| U.S. Gov't Reserves | 5.3% |
| FDIT | 5.3% |
| Select MM | 5.2% |
| Spartan U.S. Treas | 5.0% |

## Money Markets - 1998 Return

| | |
|---|---|
| Spartan MM | 5.3% |
| Select MM | 5.3% |
| Cash Reserves | 5.3% |
| U.S. Gov't Reserves | 5.2% |
| Spartan U.S. Gov't | 5.2% |
| FDIT | 5.2% |
| Spartan U.S. Treas | 4.9% |

## Muni MM Funds - 1981 Return

Municipal MM       7.0%

## Muni MM Funds - 1982 Return

Municipal MM       7.1%

## Muni MM Funds - 1983 Return

Municipal MM       5.0%

## Muni MM Funds - 1984 Return

Municipal MM       5.8%
MA Muni MM       5.2%

## Muni MM Funds - 1985 Return

Municipal MM       5.2%
CA Muni MM       5.0%
NY Muni MM       4.9%
MA Muni MM       4.7%

## Muni MM Funds - 1986 Return

Municipal MM       4.5%
CA Muni MM       4.5%
MA Muni MM       4.2%
NY Muni MM       4.2%

## Muni MM Funds - 1987 Return

Municipal MM       4.3%
Spart PA MM       4.3%
CA Muni MM       4.1%
MA Muni MM       4.0%
NY Muni MM       3.8%

## Muni MM Funds - 1988 Return

| | |
|---|---|
| Spart PA MM | 5.0% |
| Municipal MM | 4.9% |
| CA Muni MM | 4.8% |
| MA Muni MM | 4.6% |
| NY Muni MM | 4.5% |

## Muni MM Funds - 1989 Return

| | |
|---|---|
| NJ Muni MM | 6.4% |
| Spart PA MM | 6.3% |
| Municipal MM | 6.0% |
| MA Muni MM | 5.9% |
| CA Muni MM | 5.8% |
| NY Muni MM | 5.5% |

## Muni MM Funds - 1990 Return

| | |
|---|---|
| Spart PA MM | 6.0% |
| OH Muni MM | 5.9% |
| Spart CA MM | 5.9% |
| CT Muni MM | 5.7% |
| NJ Muni MM | 5.7% |
| Municipal MM | 5.6% |
| MA Muni MM | 5.3% |
| CA Muni MM | 5.2% |
| NY Muni MM | 5.1% |

## Muni MM Funds - 1991 Return

| | |
|---|---|
| Spart CA MM | 4.6% |
| Spart NJ MM | 4.6% |
| Spart PA MM | 4.6% |
| OH Muni MM | 4.5% |
| MI Muni MM | 4.5% |
| Municipal MM | 4.4% |
| CT Muni MM | 4.4% |
| Spart NY MM | 4.3% |
| NJ Muni MM | 4.1% |
| MA Muni MM | 4.0% |
| CA Muni MM | 4.0% |
| NY Muni MM | 3.9% |

## Muni MM Funds - 1992 Return

| | |
|---|---|
| Spart Muni MM | 3.3% |
| Spart CA MM | 3.0% |
| Spart CT MM | 3.0% |
| Spart NJ MM | 2.9% |
| Spart PA MM | 2.9% |
| Municipal MM | 2.9% |
| OH Muni MM | 2.8% |
| Spart MA MM | 2.7% |
| NJ Muni MM | 2.7% |
| Spart NY MM | 2.7% |
| MI Muni MM | 2.7% |
| CA Muni MM | 2.6% |
| CT Muni MM | 2.6% |
| NY Muni MM | 2.5% |
| MA Muni MM | 2.2% |

## Muni MM Funds - 1993 Return

| | |
|---|---|
| Spart Muni MM | 2.5% |
| Spart FL MM | 2.5% |
| Spart CA MM | 2.4% |
| Spart PA MM | 2.2% |
| Municipal MM | 2.2% |
| Spart CT MM | 2.1% |
| OH Muni MM | 2.1% |
| Spart NJ MM | 2.1% |
| Spart NY MM | 2.0% |
| CA Muni MM | 2.0% |
| MI Muni MM | 2.0% |
| Spart MA MM | 2.0% |
| NJ Muni MM | 1.9% |
| CT Muni MM | 1.9% |
| NY Muni MM | 1.9% |
| MA Muni MM | 1.7% |

## Muni MM Funds - 1994 Return

| | |
|---|---|
| Spart CA MM | 2.8% |
| Spart Muni MM | 2.8% |
| Spart NJ MM | 2.7% |
| Spart PA MM | 2.6% |
| Spart FL MM | 2.6% |
| Municipal MM | 2.5% |
| OH Muni MM | 2.5% |
| MI Muni MM | 2.4% |
| Spart NY MM | 2.4% |
| Spart CT MM | 2.4% |
| CA Muni MM | 2.4% |
| CT Muni MM | 2.3% |
| NJ Muni MM | 2.3% |
| NY Muni MM | 2.3% |
| Spart MA MM | 2.3% |
| MA Muni MM | 2.2% |

## Muni MM Funds - 1995 Return

| | |
|---|---|
| Spart AZ MM | 3.9% |
| Spart Muni MM | 3.7% |
| Spart CA MM | 3.7% |
| Spart NJ MM | 3.7% |
| Spart PA MM | 3.6% |
| Spart FL MM | 3.6% |
| Municipal MM | 3.5% |
| OH Muni MM | 3.5% |
| Spart NY MM | 3.5% |
| Spart CT MM | 3.4% |
| MI Muni MM | 3.4% |
| NY Muni MM | 3.3% |
| NJ Muni MM | 3.3% |
| Spart MA MM | 3.3% |
| CA Muni MM | 3.3% |
| CT Muni MM | 3.3% |
| MA Muni MM | 3.2% |

## Muni MM Funds - 1996 Return

| | |
|---|---|
| Spartan AZ MM | 3.4% |
| Spartan Municipal | 3.3% |
| Spartan PA MM | 3.2% |
| Spartan CA MM | 3.2% |
| Spartan NJ MM | 3.2% |
| Spartan FL MM | 3.1% |
| Tax Exempt MM | 3.1% |
| OH Muni MM | 3.1% |
| Spartan NY MM | 3.1% |
| Spartan CT MM | 3.0% |
| MI Free MM | 3.0% |
| Spartan MA MM | 3.0% |
| NY Free MM | 2.9% |
| CT Muni MM | 2.9% |
| NJ Free MM | 2.9% |
| CA Free MM | 2.9% |
| MA Free MM | 2.9% |

## Muni MM Funds - 1997 Return

| | |
|---|---|
| Spartan AZ MM | 3.5% |
| Spartan Municipal | 3.5% |
| Spartan PA MM | 3.4% |
| Tax Exempt MM | 3.3% |
| Spartan FL MM | 3.3% |
| OH Muni MM | 3.3% |
| Spartan CA MM | 3.3% |
| Spartan NY MM | 3.2% |
| Spartan NJ MM | 3.2% |
| MI Free MM | 3.2% |
| Spartan MA MM | 3.2% |
| Spartan CT MM | 3.1% |
| NY Free MM | 3.1% |
| MA Free MM | 3.1% |
| CT Muni MM | 3.1% |
| CA Free MM | 3.1% |
| NJ Free MM | 3.0% |

## Muni MM Funds - 1998 Return

| | |
|---|---|
| Spart Muni | 3.3% |
| Spart AZ MM | 3.2% |
| Spart PA MM | 3.2% |
| Tax Exempt MM | 3.1% |
| Spart FL MM | 3.1% |
| OH Muni MM | 3.1% |
| Spart NY MM | 3.1% |
| Spart MA MM | 3.0% |
| Spart NJ MM | 3.0% |
| Spart CT MM | 3.0% |
| MI Free MM | 3.0% |
| Spart CA MM | 2.9% |
| NY Free MM | 2.9% |
| MA Free MM | 2.9% |
| CT Muni MM | 2.9% |
| NJ Free MM | 2.9% |
| CA Free MM | 2.8% |

### Select Funds - 1982 Return

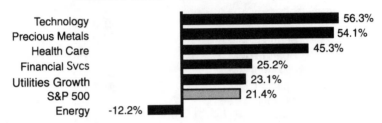

| | |
|---|---|
| Technology | 56.3% |
| Precious Metals | 54.1% |
| Health Care | 45.3% |
| Financial Svcs | 25.2% |
| Utilities Growth | 23.1% |
| S&P 500 | 21.4% |
| Energy | -12.2% |

### Select Funds - 1983 Return

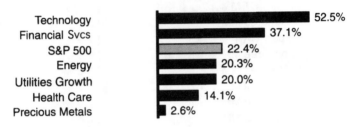

| | |
|---|---|
| Technology | 52.5% |
| Financial Svcs | 37.1% |
| S&P 500 | 22.4% |
| Energy | 20.3% |
| Utilities Growth | 20.0% |
| Health Care | 14.1% |
| Precious Metals | 2.6% |

### Select Funds - 1984 Return

| | |
|---|---|
| Utilities Growth | 20.9% |
| Financial Svcs | 18.0% |
| S&P 500 | 6.1% |
| Energy | 2.4% |
| Health Care | -1.1% |
| Technology | -16.9% |
| Precious Metals | -26.1% |

### Select Funds - 1985 Return

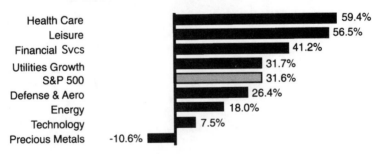

| | |
|---|---|
| Health Care | 59.4% |
| Leisure | 56.5% |
| Financial Svcs | 41.2% |
| Utilities Growth | 31.7% |
| S&P 500 | 31.6% |
| Defense & Aero | 26.4% |
| Energy | 18.0% |
| Technology | 7.5% |
| Precious Metals | -10.6% |

## Select Funds - 1986 Return

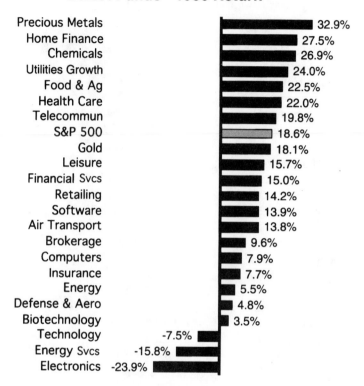

| Fund | Return |
|------|--------|
| Precious Metals | 32.9% |
| Home Finance | 27.5% |
| Chemicals | 26.9% |
| Utilities Growth | 24.0% |
| Food & Ag | 22.5% |
| Health Care | 22.0% |
| Telecommun | 19.8% |
| S&P 500 | 18.6% |
| Gold | 18.1% |
| Leisure | 15.7% |
| Financial Svcs | 15.0% |
| Retailing | 14.2% |
| Software | 13.9% |
| Air Transport | 13.8% |
| Brokerage | 9.6% |
| Computers | 7.9% |
| Insurance | 7.7% |
| Energy | 5.5% |
| Defense & Aero | 4.8% |
| Biotechnology | 3.5% |
| Technology | -7.5% |
| Energy Svcs | -15.8% |
| Electronics | -23.9% |

## Select Funds - 1987 Return

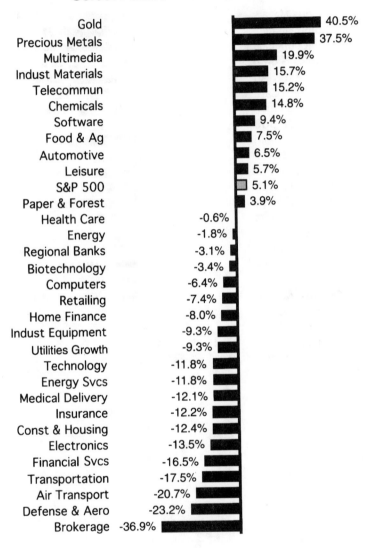

| | |
|---|---|
| Gold | 40.5% |
| Precious Metals | 37.5% |
| Multimedia | 19.9% |
| Indust Materials | 15.7% |
| Telecommun | 15.2% |
| Chemicals | 14.8% |
| Software | 9.4% |
| Food & Ag | 7.5% |
| Automotive | 6.5% |
| Leisure | 5.7% |
| S&P 500 | 5.1% |
| Paper & Forest | 3.9% |
| Health Care | -0.6% |
| Energy | -1.8% |
| Regional Banks | -3.1% |
| Biotechnology | -3.4% |
| Computers | -6.4% |
| Retailing | -7.4% |
| Home Finance | -8.0% |
| Indust Equipment | -9.3% |
| Utilities Growth | -9.3% |
| Technology | -11.8% |
| Energy Svcs | -11.8% |
| Medical Delivery | -12.1% |
| Insurance | -12.2% |
| Const & Housing | -12.4% |
| Electronics | -13.5% |
| Financial Svcs | -16.5% |
| Transportation | -17.5% |
| Air Transport | -20.7% |
| Defense & Aero | -23.2% |
| Brokerage | -36.9% |

## Select Funds - 1988 Return

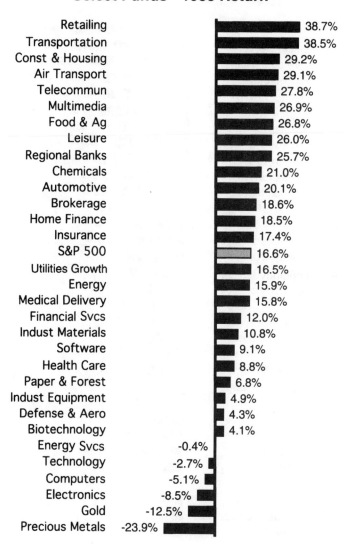

| | |
|---|---|
| Retailing | 38.7% |
| Transportation | 38.5% |
| Const & Housing | 29.2% |
| Air Transport | 29.1% |
| Telecommun | 27.8% |
| Multimedia | 26.9% |
| Food & Ag | 26.8% |
| Leisure | 26.0% |
| Regional Banks | 25.7% |
| Chemicals | 21.0% |
| Automotive | 20.1% |
| Brokerage | 18.6% |
| Home Finance | 18.5% |
| Insurance | 17.4% |
| S&P 500 | 16.6% |
| Utilities Growth | 16.5% |
| Energy | 15.9% |
| Medical Delivery | 15.8% |
| Financial Svcs | 12.0% |
| Indust Materials | 10.8% |
| Software | 9.1% |
| Health Care | 8.8% |
| Paper & Forest | 6.8% |
| Indust Equipment | 4.9% |
| Defense & Aero | 4.3% |
| Biotechnology | 4.1% |
| Energy Svcs | -0.4% |
| Technology | -2.7% |
| Computers | -5.1% |
| Electronics | -8.5% |
| Gold | -12.5% |
| Precious Metals | -23.9% |

## Select Funds - 1989 Return

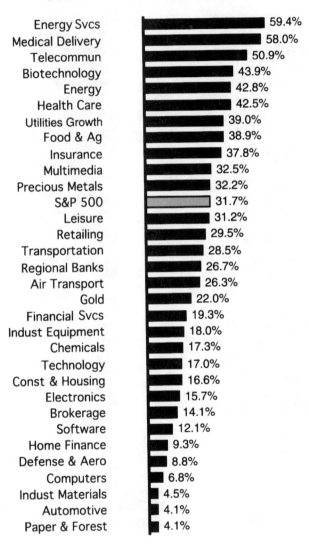

| Fund | Return |
|------|--------|
| Energy Svcs | 59.4% |
| Medical Delivery | 58.0% |
| Telecommun | 50.9% |
| Biotechnology | 43.9% |
| Energy | 42.8% |
| Health Care | 42.5% |
| Utilities Growth | 39.0% |
| Food & Ag | 38.9% |
| Insurance | 37.8% |
| Multimedia | 32.5% |
| Precious Metals | 32.2% |
| S&P 500 | 31.7% |
| Leisure | 31.2% |
| Retailing | 29.5% |
| Transportation | 28.5% |
| Regional Banks | 26.7% |
| Air Transport | 26.3% |
| Gold | 22.0% |
| Financial Svcs | 19.3% |
| Indust Equipment | 18.0% |
| Chemicals | 17.3% |
| Technology | 17.0% |
| Const & Housing | 16.6% |
| Electronics | 15.7% |
| Brokerage | 14.1% |
| Software | 12.1% |
| Home Finance | 9.3% |
| Defense & Aero | 8.8% |
| Computers | 6.8% |
| Indust Materials | 4.5% |
| Automotive | 4.1% |
| Paper & Forest | 4.1% |

## Select Funds - 1990 Return

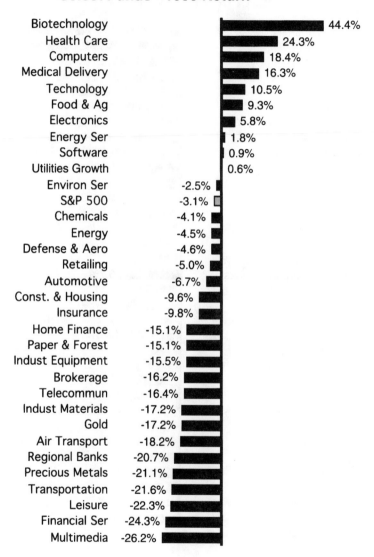

| | |
|---|---|
| Biotechnology | 44.4% |
| Health Care | 24.3% |
| Computers | 18.4% |
| Medical Delivery | 16.3% |
| Technology | 10.5% |
| Food & Ag | 9.3% |
| Electronics | 5.8% |
| Energy Ser | 1.8% |
| Software | 0.9% |
| Utilities Growth | 0.6% |
| Environ Ser | -2.5% |
| S&P 500 | -3.1% |
| Chemicals | -4.1% |
| Energy | -4.5% |
| Defense & Aero | -4.6% |
| Retailing | -5.0% |
| Automotive | -6.7% |
| Const. & Housing | -9.6% |
| Insurance | -9.8% |
| Home Finance | -15.1% |
| Paper & Forest | -15.1% |
| Indust Equipment | -15.5% |
| Brokerage | -16.2% |
| Telecommun | -16.4% |
| Indust Materials | -17.2% |
| Gold | -17.2% |
| Air Transport | -18.2% |
| Regional Banks | -20.7% |
| Precious Metals | -21.1% |
| Transportation | -21.6% |
| Leisure | -22.3% |
| Financial Ser | -24.3% |
| Multimedia | -26.2% |

## Select Funds - 1991 Return

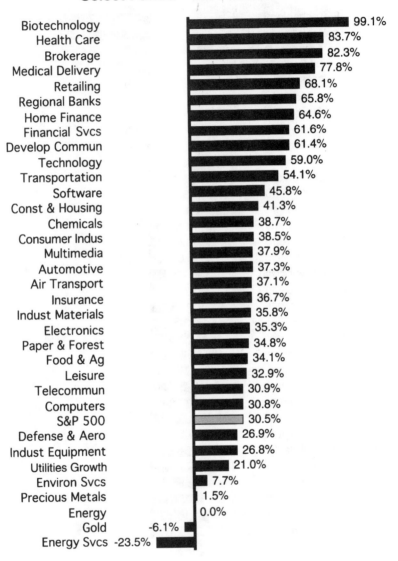

| Fund | Return |
|------|--------|
| Biotechnology | 99.1% |
| Health Care | 83.7% |
| Brokerage | 82.3% |
| Medical Delivery | 77.8% |
| Retailing | 68.1% |
| Regional Banks | 65.8% |
| Home Finance | 64.6% |
| Financial Svcs | 61.6% |
| Develop Commun | 61.4% |
| Technology | 59.0% |
| Transportation | 54.1% |
| Software | 45.8% |
| Const & Housing | 41.3% |
| Chemicals | 38.7% |
| Consumer Indus | 38.5% |
| Multimedia | 37.9% |
| Automotive | 37.3% |
| Air Transport | 37.1% |
| Insurance | 36.7% |
| Indust Materials | 35.8% |
| Electronics | 35.3% |
| Paper & Forest | 34.8% |
| Food & Ag | 34.1% |
| Leisure | 32.9% |
| Telecommun | 30.9% |
| Computers | 30.8% |
| S&P 500 | 30.5% |
| Defense & Aero | 26.9% |
| Indust Equipment | 26.8% |
| Utilities Growth | 21.0% |
| Environ Svcs | 7.7% |
| Precious Metals | 1.5% |
| Energy | 0.0% |
| Gold | -6.1% |
| Energy Svcs | -23.5% |

## Select Funds - 1992 Return

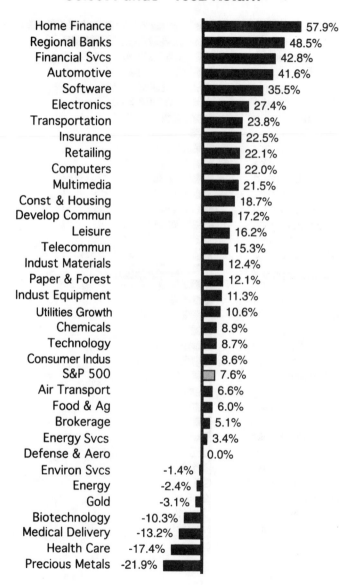

| Fund | Return |
|---|---|
| Home Finance | 57.9% |
| Regional Banks | 48.5% |
| Financial Svcs | 42.8% |
| Automotive | 41.6% |
| Software | 35.5% |
| Electronics | 27.4% |
| Transportation | 23.8% |
| Insurance | 22.5% |
| Retailing | 22.1% |
| Computers | 22.0% |
| Multimedia | 21.5% |
| Const & Housing | 18.7% |
| Develop Commun | 17.2% |
| Leisure | 16.2% |
| Telecommun | 15.3% |
| Indust Materials | 12.4% |
| Paper & Forest | 12.1% |
| Indust Equipment | 11.3% |
| Utilities Growth | 10.6% |
| Chemicals | 8.9% |
| Technology | 8.7% |
| Consumer Indus | 8.6% |
| S&P 500 | 7.6% |
| Air Transport | 6.6% |
| Food & Ag | 6.0% |
| Brokerage | 5.1% |
| Energy Svcs | 3.4% |
| Defense & Aero | 0.0% |
| Environ Svcs | -1.4% |
| Energy | -2.4% |
| Gold | -3.1% |
| Biotechnology | -10.3% |
| Medical Delivery | -13.2% |
| Health Care | -17.4% |
| Precious Metals | -21.9% |

## Select Funds - 1993 Return

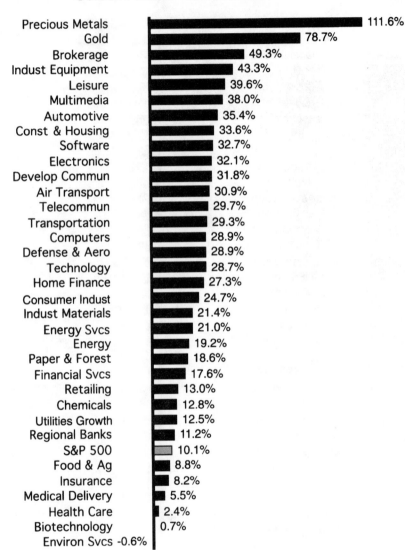

| Fund | Return |
|------|--------|
| Precious Metals | 111.6% |
| Gold | 78.7% |
| Brokerage | 49.3% |
| Indust Equipment | 43.3% |
| Leisure | 39.6% |
| Multimedia | 38.0% |
| Automotive | 35.4% |
| Const & Housing | 33.6% |
| Software | 32.7% |
| Electronics | 32.1% |
| Develop Commun | 31.8% |
| Air Transport | 30.9% |
| Telecommun | 29.7% |
| Transportation | 29.3% |
| Computers | 28.9% |
| Defense & Aero | 28.9% |
| Technology | 28.7% |
| Home Finance | 27.3% |
| Consumer Indust | 24.7% |
| Indust Materials | 21.4% |
| Energy Svcs | 21.0% |
| Energy | 19.2% |
| Paper & Forest | 18.6% |
| Financial Svcs | 17.6% |
| Retailing | 13.0% |
| Chemicals | 12.8% |
| Utilities Growth | 12.5% |
| Regional Banks | 11.2% |
| S&P 500 | 10.1% |
| Food & Ag | 8.8% |
| Insurance | 8.2% |
| Medical Delivery | 5.5% |
| Health Care | 2.4% |
| Biotechnology | 0.7% |
| Environ Svcs | -0.6% |

## Select Funds - 1994 Return

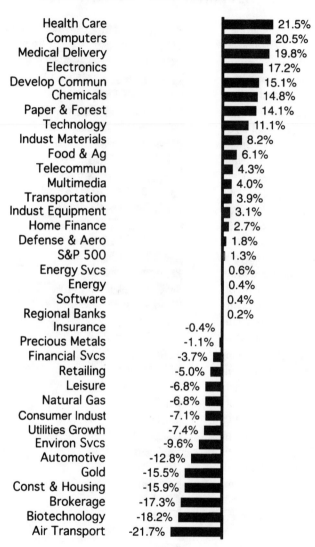

| | |
|---|---|
| Health Care | 21.5% |
| Computers | 20.5% |
| Medical Delivery | 19.8% |
| Electronics | 17.2% |
| Develop Commun | 15.1% |
| Chemicals | 14.8% |
| Paper & Forest | 14.1% |
| Technology | 11.1% |
| Indust Materials | 8.2% |
| Food & Ag | 6.1% |
| Telecommun | 4.3% |
| Multimedia | 4.0% |
| Transportation | 3.9% |
| Indust Equipment | 3.1% |
| Home Finance | 2.7% |
| Defense & Aero | 1.8% |
| S&P 500 | 1.3% |
| Energy Svcs | 0.6% |
| Energy | 0.4% |
| Software | 0.4% |
| Regional Banks | 0.2% |
| Insurance | -0.4% |
| Precious Metals | -1.1% |
| Financial Svcs | -3.7% |
| Retailing | -5.0% |
| Leisure | -6.8% |
| Natural Gas | -6.8% |
| Consumer Indust | -7.1% |
| Utilities Growth | -7.4% |
| Environ Svcs | -9.6% |
| Automotive | -12.8% |
| Gold | -15.5% |
| Const & Housing | -15.9% |
| Brokerage | -17.3% |
| Biotechnology | -18.2% |
| Air Transport | -21.7% |

## Select Funds - 1995 Return

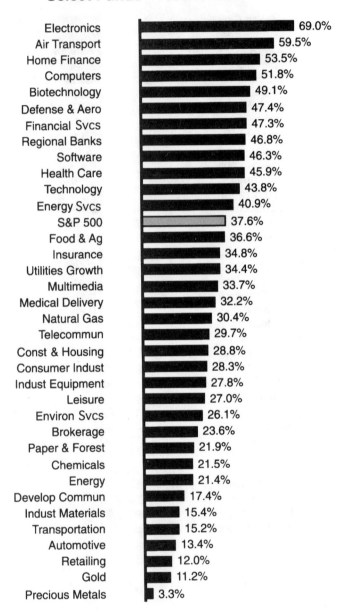

| | |
|---|---|
| Electronics | 69.0% |
| Air Transport | 59.5% |
| Home Finance | 53.5% |
| Computers | 51.8% |
| Biotechnology | 49.1% |
| Defense & Aero | 47.4% |
| Financial Svcs | 47.3% |
| Regional Banks | 46.8% |
| Software | 46.3% |
| Health Care | 45.9% |
| Technology | 43.8% |
| Energy Svcs | 40.9% |
| S&P 500 | 37.6% |
| Food & Ag | 36.6% |
| Insurance | 34.8% |
| Utilities Growth | 34.4% |
| Multimedia | 33.7% |
| Medical Delivery | 32.2% |
| Natural Gas | 30.4% |
| Telecommun | 29.7% |
| Const & Housing | 28.8% |
| Consumer Indust | 28.3% |
| Indust Equipment | 27.8% |
| Leisure | 27.0% |
| Environ Svcs | 26.1% |
| Brokerage | 23.6% |
| Paper & Forest | 21.9% |
| Chemicals | 21.5% |
| Energy | 21.4% |
| Develop Commun | 17.4% |
| Indust Materials | 15.4% |
| Transportation | 15.2% |
| Automotive | 13.4% |
| Retailing | 12.0% |
| Gold | 11.2% |
| Precious Metals | 3.3% |

## Select Funds - 1996 Return

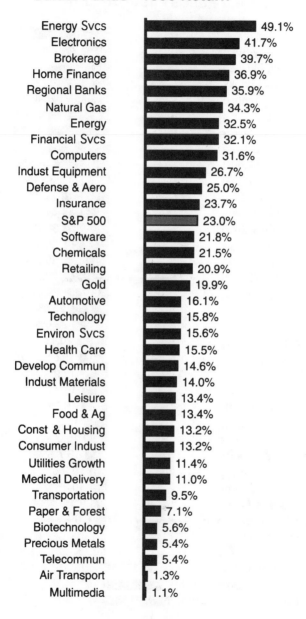

| | |
|---|---|
| Energy Svcs | 49.1% |
| Electronics | 41.7% |
| Brokerage | 39.7% |
| Home Finance | 36.9% |
| Regional Banks | 35.9% |
| Natural Gas | 34.3% |
| Energy | 32.5% |
| Financial Svcs | 32.1% |
| Computers | 31.6% |
| Indust Equipment | 26.7% |
| Defense & Aero | 25.0% |
| Insurance | 23.7% |
| S&P 500 | 23.0% |
| Software | 21.8% |
| Chemicals | 21.5% |
| Retailing | 20.9% |
| Gold | 19.9% |
| Automotive | 16.1% |
| Technology | 15.8% |
| Environ Svcs | 15.6% |
| Health Care | 15.5% |
| Develop Commun | 14.6% |
| Indust Materials | 14.0% |
| Leisure | 13.4% |
| Food & Ag | 13.4% |
| Const & Housing | 13.2% |
| Consumer Indust | 13.2% |
| Utilities Growth | 11.4% |
| Medical Delivery | 11.0% |
| Transportation | 9.5% |
| Paper & Forest | 7.1% |
| Biotechnology | 5.6% |
| Precious Metals | 5.4% |
| Telecommun | 5.4% |
| Air Transport | 1.3% |
| Multimedia | 1.1% |

## Select Funds - 1997 Return

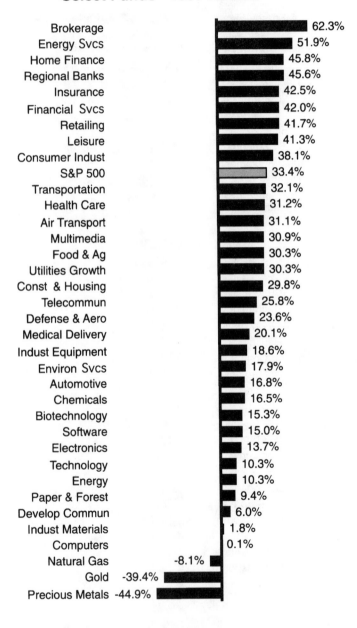

| | |
|---|---|
| Brokerage | 62.3% |
| Energy Svcs | 51.9% |
| Home Finance | 45.8% |
| Regional Banks | 45.6% |
| Insurance | 42.5% |
| Financial Svcs | 42.0% |
| Retailing | 41.7% |
| Leisure | 41.3% |
| Consumer Indust | 38.1% |
| S&P 500 | 33.4% |
| Transportation | 32.1% |
| Health Care | 31.2% |
| Air Transport | 31.1% |
| Multimedia | 30.9% |
| Food & Ag | 30.3% |
| Utilities Growth | 30.3% |
| Const & Housing | 29.8% |
| Telecommun | 25.8% |
| Defense & Aero | 23.6% |
| Medical Delivery | 20.1% |
| Indust Equipment | 18.6% |
| Environ Svcs | 17.9% |
| Automotive | 16.8% |
| Chemicals | 16.5% |
| Biotechnology | 15.3% |
| Software | 15.0% |
| Electronics | 13.7% |
| Technology | 10.3% |
| Energy | 10.3% |
| Paper & Forest | 9.4% |
| Develop Commun | 6.0% |
| Indust Materials | 1.8% |
| Computers | 0.1% |
| Natural Gas | -8.1% |
| Gold | -39.4% |
| Precious Metals | -44.9% |

## Select Funds - 1998 Return

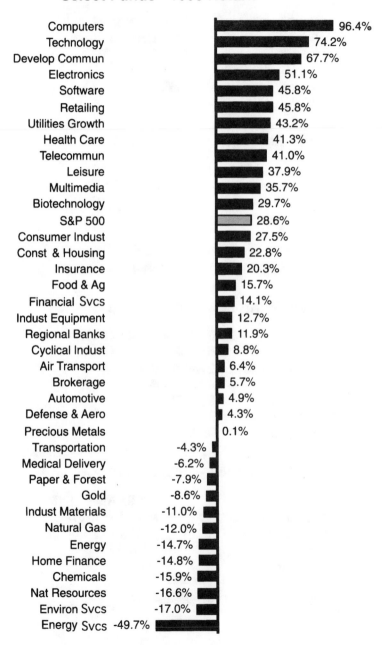

| Fund | Return |
|------|-------:|
| Computers | 96.4% |
| Technology | 74.2% |
| Develop Commun | 67.7% |
| Electronics | 51.1% |
| Software | 45.8% |
| Retailing | 45.8% |
| Utilities Growth | 43.2% |
| Health Care | 41.3% |
| Telecommun | 41.0% |
| Leisure | 37.9% |
| Multimedia | 35.7% |
| Biotechnology | 29.7% |
| S&P 500 | 28.6% |
| Consumer Indust | 27.5% |
| Const & Housing | 22.8% |
| Insurance | 20.3% |
| Food & Ag | 15.7% |
| Financial Svcs | 14.1% |
| Indust Equipment | 12.7% |
| Regional Banks | 11.9% |
| Cyclical Indust | 8.8% |
| Air Transport | 6.4% |
| Brokerage | 5.7% |
| Automotive | 4.9% |
| Defense & Aero | 4.3% |
| Precious Metals | 0.1% |
| Transportation | -4.3% |
| Medical Delivery | -6.2% |
| Paper & Forest | -7.9% |
| Gold | -8.6% |
| Indust Materials | -11.0% |
| Natural Gas | -12.0% |
| Energy | -14.7% |
| Home Finance | -14.8% |
| Chemicals | -15.9% |
| Nat Resources | -16.6% |
| Environ Svcs | -17.0% |
| Energy Svcs | -49.7% |

## VIP Portfolios - 1989 Return

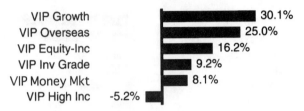

| | |
|---|---|
| VIP Growth | 30.1% |
| VIP Overseas | 25.0% |
| VIP Equity-Inc | 16.2% |
| VIP Inv Grade | 9.2% |
| VIP Money Mkt | 8.1% |
| VIP High Inc | -5.2% |

## VIP Portfolios - 1990 Return

| | |
|---|---|
| VIP Money Mkt | 7.0% |
| VIP Asset Mgr | 5.8% |
| VIP Inv Grade | 5.0% |
| VIP Overseas | -2.7% |
| VIP High Inc | -3.4% |
| VIP Growth | -12.6% |
| VIP Equity-Inc | -16.1% |

## VIP Portfolios - 1991 Return

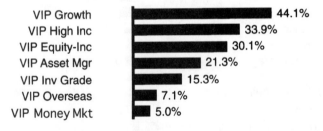

| | |
|---|---|
| VIP Growth | 44.1% |
| VIP High Inc | 33.9% |
| VIP Equity-Inc | 30.1% |
| VIP Asset Mgr | 21.3% |
| VIP Inv Grade | 15.3% |
| VIP Overseas | 7.1% |
| VIP Money Mkt | 5.0% |

## VIP Portfolios - 1992 Return

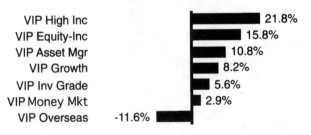

| | |
|---|---|
| VIP High Inc | 21.8% |
| VIP Equity-Inc | 15.8% |
| VIP Asset Mgr | 10.8% |
| VIP Growth | 8.2% |
| VIP Inv Grade | 5.6% |
| VIP Money Mkt | 2.9% |
| VIP Overseas | -11.6% |

## VIP Portfolios - 1993 Return

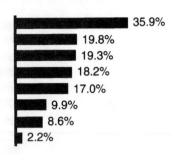

| | |
|---|---|
| VIP Overseas | 35.9% |
| VIP Asset Mgr | 19.8% |
| VIP High Inc | 19.3% |
| VIP Growth | 18.2% |
| VIP Equity-Inc | 17.0% |
| VIP Inv Grade | 9.9% |
| VIP Index 500 | 8.6% |
| VIP Money Mkt | 2.2% |

## VIP Portfolios - 1994 Return

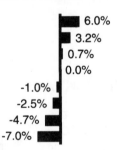

| | |
|---|---|
| VIP Equity-Inc | 6.0% |
| VIP Money Mkt | 3.2% |
| VIP Overseas | 0.7% |
| VIP Index 500 | 0.0% |
| VIP Growth | -1.0% |
| VIP High Inc | -2.5% |
| VIP Inv Grade | -4.7% |
| VIP Asset Mgr | -7.0% |

## VIP Portfolios - 1995 Return

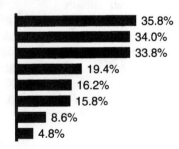

| | |
|---|---|
| VIP Index 500 | 35.8% |
| VIP Growth | 34.0% |
| VIP Equity-Income | 33.8% |
| VIP High Income | 19.4% |
| VIP Inv Grade Bond | 16.2% |
| VIP Asset Manager | 15.8% |
| VIP Overseas | 8.6% |
| VIP Money Mkt | 4.8% |

## VIP Portfolios - 1996 Return

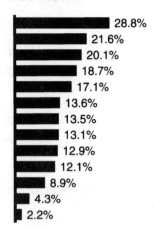

| | |
|---|---|
| VIP Growth & Inc | 28.8% |
| VIP Index 500 | 21.6% |
| VIP Contrafund | 20.1% |
| VIP Asset Mgr Gro | 18.7% |
| VIP Growth Opp | 17.1% |
| VIP Growth | 13.6% |
| VIP Asset Manager | 13.5% |
| VIP Equity-Income | 13.1% |
| VIP High Income | 12.9% |
| VIP Overseas | 12.1% |
| VIP Balanced | 8.9% |
| VIP Money Market | 4.3% |
| VIP Inv Grade Bond | 2.2% |

## VIP Portfolios - 1997 Return

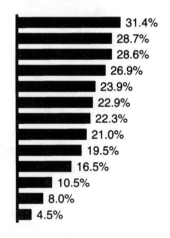

| | |
|---|---|
| VIP Index 500 | 31.4% |
| VIP Growth Opp | 28.7% |
| VIP Growth & Inc | 28.6% |
| VIP Equity-Income | 26.9% |
| VIP Asset Mgr Gro | 23.9% |
| VIP Contrafund | 22.9% |
| VIP Growth | 22.3% |
| VIP Balanced | 21.0% |
| VIP Asset Manager | 19.5% |
| VIP High Income | 16.5% |
| VIP Overseas | 10.5% |
| VIP Inv Grade Bond | 8.0% |
| VIP Money Market | 4.5% |

## VIP Portfolios - 1998 Return

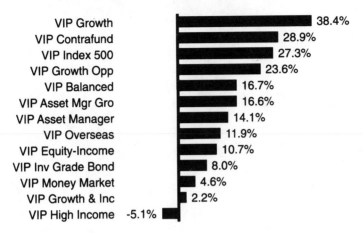

| | |
|---|---|
| VIP Growth | 38.4% |
| VIP Contrafund | 28.9% |
| VIP Index 500 | 27.3% |
| VIP Growth Opp | 23.6% |
| VIP Balanced | 16.7% |
| VIP Asset Mgr Gro | 16.6% |
| VIP Asset Manager | 14.1% |
| VIP Overseas | 11.9% |
| VIP Equity-Income | 10.7% |
| VIP Inv Grade Bond | 8.0% |
| VIP Money Market | 4.6% |
| VIP Growth & Inc | 2.2% |
| VIP High Income | -5.1% |

# APPENDIX B

The numbers listed below are those most commonly used by Fidelity customers. In case you prefer to conduct business in person, I've also listed the locations of Fidelity's network of investor centers.

## PHONE NUMBERS
*(available 24 hours unless otherwise indicated)*

| | |
|---|---|
| 800-FIDELITY | Mutual fund sales |
| 800-544-8888 | Mutual fund information |
| 800-544-6666 | Mutual fund service |
| 800-544-7777 | Mutual fund exchanges and redemptions |
| 800-544-5555 | Mutual fund price quotes, account balances, and transactions (automated access) |
| 800-544-1877 | Tax information line |
| 800-544-4774 | IRA assistance |
| 800-544-3455 | Portfolio Advisory Services (9 A.M. to 6 P.M. EST weekdays) |
| 800-544-0118 | TDD hearing-impaired service (9 A.M. to 9 P.M. EST weekdays) |
| 800-544-8666 | Fidelity Brokerage/USA service |
| 800-544-7272 | Fidelity Brokerage product information |
| 800-544-3939 | Fidelity Brokerage trades |

| | |
|---|---|
| 800-872-7212 | Chinese-speaking representatives (EST business hours) |
| 800-544-5670 | Spanish-speaking representatives (EST business hours) |
| 800-544-9697 | FundsNetwork |
| 801-534-1910 | International Service (collect calls accepted) |
| 800-544-4702 | Annuity specialists (EST business hours) |
| 800-634-9361 | Annuity Service Center |
| 800-258-5759 | Charitable services (EST business hours) |
| 800-544-9797 | To reach investor center near you (EST business hours) |

## INVESTOR CENTER LOCATIONS

### Arizona

*Scottsdale*
7373 North Scottsdale Road, Suite 182A

### California

*Brea*
815 East Birch St.

*Campbell/San Jose*
851 East Hamilton Ave., Suite 100

*Glendale*
527 North Brand Blvd.

*Irvine*
The Atrium
19100 Von Karman Ave.

*Los Angeles—Century City*
10100 Santa Monica Blvd.

*Palo Alto*
251 University Ave.

*Sacramento*
1760 Challenge Way

*San Diego*
Hazard Center Office Tower
7676 Hazard Center Drive, Suite 210

*San Francisco*
8 Montgomery St.

*San Rafael*
950 Northgate Drive, Suite 101

*Walnut Creek*
1400 Civic Drive

*Woodland Hills*
6300 Canoga Ave.,
  Suite 1001

## Colorado

*Denver*
Dekalb Energy Tower
1625 Broadway, Suite 110

## Connecticut

*Greenwich*
48 West Putnam Ave.

*West Hartford*
Town Center
29 South Main St.

*New Haven*
One Century Tower
265 Church St.

*Stamford*
300 Atlantic St.

## Delaware

*Wilmington*
222 Delaware Ave., Suite 5

## Florida

*Boca Raton*
Tower Shops at the Sanctuary
4400 North Federal Hwy.

*Coral Gables*
90 Alhambra St.

*Ft. Lauderdale*
4090 North Ocean Blvd.
  (Route A1A)

*Naples*
8880 Tamiami Trail North

*Orlando/Longwood*
The Longwood Village
  Shoppes
1907 West State Road 434

*Palm Beach Gardens*
The Harbour Shops
2401 PGA Blvd., Suite 186

*Sarasota*
8065 Beneva Road South,
  Suite 2

*Tampa*
1502 North Westshore Blvd.

## Georgia

*Atlanta—Buckhead*
3445 Peachtree Road NE
2 Live Oak Center

*Atlanta—Dunwoody*
Northpark Town Center
1000 Abernathy Road,
Building 400

## Hawaii

*Honolulu*
AMFAC Center
700 Bishop St., Ground
  Floor

## Illinois

*Chicago—Loop*
1 North Franklin,
    Gound Floor

*Wilmette*
3232 Lake Ave., Suite 155

*Oak Brook*
Oak Brook Regency Towers
1415 West 22nd St.

*Schaumburg*
Santa Fe Building
1700 East Golf Road,
    Suite 150

## Indiana

*Indianapolis*
Clearwater Village
4729 East 82nd St.

## Maine

*Portland*
3 Canal Plaza

## Maryland

*Towson*
Towson Commons
1 West Pennsylvania Ave.

## Massachusetts

*Boston—Back Bay*
470 Boylston St.

*Boston—Financial District*
155 Congress St.

*Braintree*
Plaza Executive Center
300 Granite St., Suite 102

*Burlington*
44 Burlington Mall Road,
    Suite 100

*Worcester*
416 Belmont Ave.

## Michigan

*Birmingham*
280 North Woodward Blvd.

*Southfield*
Franklin Plaza
29155 Northwestern
    Hwy.

## Minnesota

*Minneapolis—Edina*
7600 France Ave. South,
    Suite 110

## Missouri

*Kansas City*
The Plaza Steppes
700 West 47th St., Suite 120

*Ladue*
8885 Ladue Road, Suite 1

## New Jersey

*Morristown*
56 South St.

*Paramus*
501 Route 17 South

*Milburn*
150 Essex St.

## New York

*Garden City*
1050 Franklin Ave., Suite 100

*Melville*
999 Walt Whitman Road

*New York—Financial
District*
71 Broadway, Main Level

*New York—Park Avenue*
350 Park Ave.

*New York*
1271 Avenue of the Americas

*White Plains*
10 Bank St., Suite 100

## North Carolina

*Charlotte*
2 Coltsgate
4611 Sharon Road,
   Suite 125

*Durham*
Erwin Square
2200 West Main St.

## Ohio

*Woodmere Village*
Eton Collection
28699 Chagrin Blvd.

*Cincinnati*
600 Vine St., Suite 108

*Cleveland—Downtown*
1903 East Ninth St.

## Oregon

*Portland*
Bridgeport Retail Center
SW 72nd Avenue and
   SW Durham Road

## Pennsylvania

*Philadelphia*
Mellon Bank Center
1735 Market St.

*Pittsburgh*
Union Trust Building
439 Fifth Ave., Suite 157

## Tennessee

*Memphis*
Regalia Center
6150 Poplar Road, Suite 110

## Texas

*Austin*
The Arboretum
10000 Research Blvd.,
   Suite 214

*Dallas*
The Plaza at Preston Center
4017 Northwest Pkwy

*Houston—North*
19740 1H
45 North Spring

*Houston—Galleria*
2701 Drexel Drive

*Houston—West*
1155 Dairy Ashford,
   Suite 104

*Las Colinas*
400 East Las Colinas Blvd.,
   Suite 120

*San Antonio*
14100 San Pedro, Suite 110

## Utah
*Salt Lake City*
215 South State St.,
   Suite 130

## Vermont
*Burlington*
Courthouse Plaza,
199 Main St.

## Virginia
*Tysons Corner*
Greensboro Park
8180 Greensboro Drive

## Washington
*Bellevue*
1 Bellevue Center
411 108th Ave. NE

*Seattle*
511 Pine St.

## Washington, D.C.
1900 K St. NW,
   Suite 110

## Wisconsin
*Milwaukee—Brookfield*
595 North Barker Road

# INDEX